The Making
of Telephone
Unionism
1920–1947

JOHN N. SCHACHT

RUTGERS UNIVERSITY PRESS

New Brunswick, New Jersey

Library of Congress Cataloging in Publication Data

Schacht, John N., 1943–
  The making of telephone unionism, 1920–1947.

  Bibliography: p.
  Includes index.
  1. Communication Workers of America—History.
2. Trade-unions—Communication and traffic—United States—
History. 3. Trade-unions—Telephone workers—United States—
History. I. Title.
HD6515.T33S33   1985   331.88′113846′0973   84–27632
ISBN 0–8135–1136–4

To Liz

CONTENTS

ACKNOWLEDGMENTS

I HAVE INCURRED many debts during this study's long gestation. During the early stages, from 1968 to 1972, the University of Iowa Center for Labor and Management employed me as interviewer and research assistant with the Communications Workers of America–University of Iowa Oral History Project, and the center's personnel, particularly Viola Kuebler, Sarah Spencer, Jude West, and Anthony Sinicropi, were helpful during all stages of research. The CWA generously opened its archives to me, helped me locate interviewees, and offered me every courtesy while I was working at CWA headquarters and other places across the country. Several officers and members were especially helpful: Joseph A. Beirne, Mr. and Mrs. John Clevenger, John Crull, William Dunn, George Gill, D. L. McCowen, June McDonald, George Miller, Glenn Watts, and J. W. Webb. The recollections and insights offered by the project's interviewees were indispensable, as were the personal files that several interviewees allowed me to examine. Helpful too were people in the labor movement who did not participate in the project but imparted their knowledge through correspondence or interviews: Mary Gannon, Patricia Harris, Albert Kanagy, Henry Mayer, Jeannette Reedy, and Joe Selly.

I also owe thanks to Lewis Gum, of AT&T's information office, who permitted me to examine some materials in AT&T's archives; to the seven management officials who spoke or corresponded with me (but not for attribution); and particularly to Jack G. Bradbury, retired operating vice-president of Southern Bell, who allowed me to examine papers in his possession and who, in the course of a tape-recorded interview, responded to my questions with candor and in detail.

I wish to thank the editors of *Labor History* for allowing me to reprint Portions of chapters two and three of this volume. They were originally published as "Toward Industrial Unionism: Bell Telephone Workers and Company Unions, 1919–1937," in *Labor History* 16 (Winter 1975): 5–36.

For their many thoughful services I am indebted to my colleagues Frank Allen, David Gregory, Rebecca Johnson, Robert McCown, Mary McInroy, Keith Rageth, and Wayne Rawley of the University of Iowa Libraries; Ken Kekke, Richard M. Runge, and Donna Sandrock of Iowa City; Tom Cullen of Atlanta; Dallas Chrislock, of the Archives/Manuscripts Division of the Minnesota Historical Society; and James Hansen of the State Historical Society of Wisconsin. I have benefited from the suggestions of Robert H. Zieger, professor at Wayne State University. I owe special thanks to Ellis Hawley, professor at the University of Iowa, who devoted much effort to guiding this study; he was consistently inspiring, exacting, and patient.

During 1976–1977, when the study was nearing completion in its dissertation form, I needed help of all kinds from my parents, Sylvia N. and the late John H. Schacht, and they never failed me. My daughters Emily and Angela have afforded me patience beyond their years. My greatest debt is to my wife Elizabeth. Without her understanding and sacrifices, the study could never have been completed.

THE MAKING OF TELEPHONE UNIONISM

1920–1947

INTRODUCTION

IN 1937 the telephone industry seemed an unlikely field for the growth of a vigorous union movement. A dispersed and largely white-collar work force had long shown little interest in joining unions. A sophisticated management, unified through the pervasive ownership of the Bell System, controlled a strike-resistant technology and an elaborate personnel program aimed at promoting employee loyalty. AFL and CIO unions shunned telephone organizing. Virtually the only labor organizations in the industry were the isolated and timid company union successors, newly reconstituted by Bell to escape the Wagner Act's ban on outright company unionism.

Yet during the next decade these separate unions, representing workers in the various segments of the far-flung Bell System, reorganized themselves, gained skill and mettle in bargaining, and developed a militancy reflected in several wartime strikes. In 1946 they wrested gains that rivaled those in steel and automobiles, and in 1947 they waged a long, nationwide strike. The culmination was the June 1947 formation of the Communications Workers of America, an industrially structured national union and a force to be reckoned with in the telephone industry. During the following decades the stature of the CWA was to increase. In 1949 it joined the CIO as its fourth largest affiliate; by 1960 it had won Bell's grudging acceptance as a permanent force; and by 1980 it had passed the half-million mark in membership—which by then included communications workers outside the telephone field, as well as Bell and non-Bell telephone workers.

This study confines itself to the period ending in 1947.[1] Its first aim is to show how a vigorous union movement rose from the unpromising beginnings described, and in doing so it recognizes the diligence that telephone workers brought to the day-to-day tasks of building a union movement. But it also argues that union building in this case followed an unusual path, diverging from conventional lines and adapting itself to the unusual circumstances and obstacles. Lacking guidance from AFL or CIO unions, aspiring telephone unionists at first relied heavily on their experience they had drawn from the company union period — 1920 to 1937 in the case of most Bell groups. And this experience proved valuable. It had taught workers skills that could be turned to genuine trade union activity, had helped to overcome geographical and departmental divisions within Bell companies (which had been barriers to labor unity), and had provided information that led many workers to see a need for systemwide labor organization. In the absence of support from the AFL or CIO, telephone workers used the labor organizations at hand, namely, the 180 "independent" unions that Bell had fostered in the wake of the Wagner Act. These company-union successor organizations — unlike those fostered by nontelephone employers during the same period — eventually evolved into a legitimate, industrially structured, national union.

Significant in this process was the 1939 formation of the National Federation of Telephone Workers, a strange but useful amalgam that was unlike the organizational forms that evolved into national unions in other industries. Workers had recognized the need for linking their individual unions together; in forming the NFTW they departed from Bell's blueprint for atomized telephone labor organization. Yet regional and departmental separatism died hard, as was reflected in constitutional guarantees that the NFTW's affiliates would retain absolute autonomy in their bargaining and internal affairs. Militancy and the vigor to challenge Bell finally came in the wartime 1940s. But the search for effective bargaining tools continued on a vacillating and sometimes errant course.

The second aim of this study is to show how and why centralization took place within the telephone union movement—why it was, in other words, that the small core of unionists who early saw a need for a single national union eventually succeeded in bringing one into being. Part of the explanation here, it will be argued, was the steady expansion of this core of national unionists to include more of the union leadership and membership; and this expansion, it will be further argued, was a product of experience—of frustrations accruing from failure as well as the pleasanter lessons drawn from success. Gradually it became evident that "success" or "failure" in achieving workers' goals depended on the ability of their organizations to deal with surrounding and related institutions, most notably the Bell System, but also the U.S. government. The key characteristic of the government agencies and Bell was their centralization, and dealing with them in any effective way required telephone unionists to develop some kind of comparable structure.

Indeed, a main contention of this study is that the centralized character of the Bell System was the primary cause of a centralized union structure. As the following chapters show, it was the telephone unionists' experience with the Bell System that led them to recognize the need for centralization, and this recognition was the strongest force in the transformation of the NFTW into the CWA. Forces that pushed other unions toward centralization had little or no impact among telephone workers. In their industry there was not the emergence of national product markets that John R. Commons and his associates used to explain nationalization in a number of craft unions.[2] On the contrary, the market for the product remained local, in that telephone service could be practically supplied to a community only by a plant located in or near that community. Nor was the industry characterized by the type of national labor market that Lloyd Ulman used to explain nationalization in a variety of other unions. The development of such a market was thwarted by the Bell System's restrictions on the movement of workers from one Bell company to another.[3] Centralization, moreover, was not implicit in the method by which telephone workers were initially unionized. They were not unionized "from the top down," as many steelworkers were by the Steel Workers Organizing Committee.[4] Nor was centralization spurred by the kind of government pressures that, according to Nelson Lichtenstein and others, pushed several CIO unions toward tight control over those locals that permitted wartime shop floor militancy and strikes.[5] Far from feeding on the suppression of militancy, telephone union centralization hinged on its growth, in that leaders and activists refused to entertain seriously the question of how best to array their structure for confrontations with Bell management until they had a *desire* for such confrontations.

Also lacking were the patterns identified by scholars working in the tradition of Robert Michels, patterns whereby decision-making power gradually accrues to national leaders as they exercise their control over expertise, pertinent information, channels of communication, and other facets of bureaucratic organization.[6] (Such patterns appeared mainly after the CWA was formed, not before.) Again, it would seem that the important factor in the formation of a national telephone union was the rational, grass-roots adjustment of once-segmented groups to the centralized character of surrounding institutions, notably that of the Bell System.

The interpretation here advanced is not new. It is a truism among journalists, sociologists, union officers, and specialists in industrial relations that the structure of unions "follows the structure of the industry whose workers they represent."[7] Of the telephone industry, Jack Barbash wrote in 1956: "The integrated character of the Bell System has been the most important influence in pushing the CWA in the direction of industrial unionism."[8] But his earlier *Unions and Telephones: The Story of the Communications Workers of America* did not develop this theme, nor has such a theme ever been comprehensively explored and documented with respect to the telephone industry, or any other American industry.

This study makes such an exploration. It draws not only on the usual sources for labor union history but also on sixty-six tape-recorded interviews, conducted over a period of three years, with union members and others who played active roles in union organization and centralization. It reconstructs the flow of events in telephone unionization, identifying main currents in a stream of developments that were highly visible since they occurred at a relatively leisurely pace, over a long period, and in ways generally unmuddled by massive organizing campaigns or strikes—at least until the spring of 1947. The industry's clashes between union and management tended to be direct ones, insulated from such outside forces as the AFL, the CIO, and leftist labor groups (though the influence of government observation and participation is not to be discounted). In this respect, they followed a rare pattern that seemed to emerge from the industrial structure itself rather than from the outside initiatives so important in many other industries. Yet the impulses at work may well have had their counterparts elsewhere. Consequently, it is hoped that by casting light on the experience of telephone unionists, this study will shed indirect light on similar impulses among unionists in other industries, impulses perhaps thwarted or masked by early AFL or CIO affiliation that enforced shortcuts toward the kind of organization arrived at by telephone unionists gradually, and on their own.

Chapter 1

PROLOGUE:

THE FAILURE OF OUTSIDE UNIONISM,

1878–1920

BETWEEN THE SUMMERS of 1935 and 1937, more than 180 labor organizations were formed in the traditionally antiunion telephone industry. While most fell outside the Wagner Act's definition of an illegal, company-dominated union, most deserved the title "independent" only in the most formal sense of the term. In reality they were formed in cooperation with, and at the instigation of, the management of the American Telephone and Telegraph Company's Bell System. Without exception they were directly descended from the network of Bell company unions that had constituted labor representation in the industry since 1920—a network put in place by the company in the summer of 1919 with the purpose of thwarting union growth. In short, they appeared to be just one more phase in Bell management's long and generally successful campaign to keep genuine unions out of the industry.

The forming of such quasi-independent labor organizations was not unusual in the middle and late 1930s. Along with Bell (whose average work force of 289,000 had by then made it the nation's largest corporate employer), a number of other large corporations encouraged workers to reconstitute their company unions in ways that would enable them to escape the Wagner Act's ban yet would also discourage the entry of truly independent unions.[1] The subsequent development of the Bell groups, however, was highly unusual. While similar organizations in other industries were destroyed by the entry of legitimate AFL or CIO unions (as in the steel, automobile, rubber, and electrical products industries) or else remained anemic and fragmented (as in the oil-

6

refining and chemical industries), the Bell organizations evolved, through a series of stages, into a vigorous national union.

Why were the Bell organizations not swept away by the organizing campaigns of established AFL or CIO unions? What enabled them not only to survive but to grow and coalesce, by 1947, into a legitimate, unified labor organization, industrial in structure and nationwide in scope? Much of the answer can be found only by examining the events of 1935–1947, but part can be gained through an examination of the industry, its work force, and its company unions during the 1920–1935 period. And if one is to do the latter, the period from 1878 to 1920 also merits brief examination, for in a sense later developments hinged upon it. If "outside" unionism had not failed in the degree that it did during this early period, the making of telephone unionism in the following decades might have been vastly different.

DURING THE FIRST FORTY-TWO YEARS of the telephone industry, labor-management relations were characteristically in one of two modes: quietly cooperative or sharply adversarial. Each condition in its own way illustrated the dominance of management, represented increasingly as time went on by the Bell System.

From its beginnings in 1878 until the middle 1890s, the industry was virtually free of union activity. The only union to take any marked notice of telephone workers was the International Brotherhood of Electrical Workers, founded in 1891, and the IBEW's interest was prompted less by organizing ambitions than by its members drifting into such telephone "craft" jobs as lineman and cable splicer. The first contract in the industry was signed in 1898 between an IBEW telephone craftsmen's local and a non-Bell company in Indianapolis. The first strike occurred in the same year, involving four hundred craftsmen in St. Louis.[2]

During the next decade there were perhaps two dozen organizing ventures and strikes, most of them local in origin and scope, some of them bitter and even violent. In 1899 craftsmen struck in Cleveland, and in 1900–1901 they struck in Chicago, Detroit, Akron, Terre Haute, Los Angeles, San Antonio, and several towns in New Jersey.

The San Antonio walkout was the first instance in which craftsmen were joined by striking telephone operators, who in this case were fellow IBEW members. Craftsmen struck in Los Angeles and San Francisco in 1903 and in Salt Lake City in 1904. In 1906 they struck jointly for sixteen weeks in Atlanta, Birmingham, Mobile, Jacksonville, and other places in the Southern Bell territory. The next year craftsmen waged a bitter strike in Wheeling, West Virginia; craftsmen and telephone operators walked out together in Helena and Great Falls, Montana; and an AFL federal local union of operators struck in the San Francisco Bay area.[3] By that time Bell officials were receiving reports from detective agencies employing spies among telephone workers. And the IBEW was accusing Bell of deploying professional "plug uglies" during strikes and engaging in systematic discrimination toward its members.[4]

The frequency of strikes in these early years was by no means a sign of union strength. On the contrary, it appears that the formation of a local union ordinarily met with swift and hostile action by the company —refusal to bargain, enforced signing of loyalty pledges, dismissal of union activists. Such tactics often led to strikes on the part of the freshly formed local unions, strikes that management was usually ready to face. As an early IBEW activist put it, a premature strike "is the weapon of the employer rather than of the worker, and so it usually proved in the telephone industry." Outside of Montana, none of the early strikes seems to have gained a contract for the strikers, and by 1910 telephone locals endured only in Montana, Chicago, and several cities in California.[5]

If anything, the industry was becoming yet more hostile to unionism, by virtue of the expansion of the staunchly antiunion Bell System relative to other, weaker telephone companies. In 1907 Bell employed 96,000 workers while other companies employed 36,000. By 1917 Bell's employment had shot up to 199,000 while the other companies' had only expanded to 46,000. Bell's increasing control of the industry alarmed the IBEW national office, but telephone craftsmen's locals secured a few more footholds in the years before 1917, particularly in the Bell companies in New England and the Pacific Northwest.[6] Strikes continued to occur—in Chicago in 1911, in Granite City, Illinois, in 1913, and in Brownsville, Texas, in 1916.[7]

Two developments in this period warrant special mention. One was the onset of IBEW efforts to claim for its electricians certain kinds of telephone *work*, as distinct from its attempts to organize telephone *workers*. While the union continued to support organizing efforts among telephone company employees, it was undoubtedly somewhat discouraged by the results, and in 1913 it began to support IBEW electricians who were employed by building contractors and who were trying to wrest from nonunion telephone company employees the work of installing telephone cables and wires on construction projects. In the ensuing years, this policy of gaining "electrical work for electrical workers" met with some success, due in part to the support of fellow AFL building tradesmen who, when called on by the IBEW, would sometimes refuse to work on the same site with nonunion telephone company employees.[8]

The second development was an upsurge of union membership among telephone operators, beginning in 1912 and centered in the Bell company in Boston. Here operators complained of long hours (nine-hour workdays six days a week, plus compulsory overtime), low pay (an average of $7.61 per week), lack of extra pay for "split tricks" (shifts in which operators had to divide their nine work hours to cover both morning and evening), the nerve-wracking quality of the work, heavy-handed supervision and observation, and the absence of any avenue of appeal from decisions made by low-level management, particularly regarding disciplinary action and the scheduling of individuals' work shifts. Before 1912 IBEW organizers had expended almost no effort in unionizing operators, and the union at times had even refused organizing aid when groups of operators had requested it. But in 1912 the IBEW relented and sent an organizer to assist the Boston group, which also got help from the Women's Trade Union League. (Nearly all operators by this time were women, a situation that would persist into the mid-1970s.) Calling itself the Boston Operators Union–IBEW, the organization increased its membership from fifty in April 1912 to sixteen hundred in September.[9]

In March 1913, following a union strike threat, the company made major concessions, including an eight-hour day for most operators, a seven-hour day for those working split tricks, and the establishment of a Joint Adjustment Board, which offered quick adjudication of all grievances brought before it by operators. This victory brought most of the remaining Boston operators into the union, swelling its membership to three thousand. It now outnumbered all other telephone workers in the IBEW put together, and it was soon receiving requests from groups of operators in other cities that information and organizers be sent to them. By April 1917, on the eve of American entry into World War I, operators had formed locals in nineteen outlying New England cities, in four cities in the Pacific Northwest, and in Denison, Texas. In addition, the already existing operators' locals in Montana had begun to cooperate with the others. It appears, however, that the only operators' locals strong enough to force concessions from management were those in Boston and Montana.[10]

In the tumultuous years following the nation's entry into war, unionism among telephone workers followed a course common in many industries: rapid gains in membership and bargaining strength, followed by precipitous decline. The parallelism bears qualification, however, in that the ascent of unionism in the telephone industry, if rapid, was never more than modest. The descent, on the other hand, if less dramatic than that in the steel mills and stockyards and other scenes of massive postwar labor strife, could hardly have brought telephone unionism lower.

The war at first strengthened telephone unionism by creating a labor shortage and by placing a premium on uninterrupted service. New locals sprang up, and for the first time outside Montana, a full-fledged strike wrung concessions from Bell management. On the West Coast a November 1917 walkout of some thirty-two hundred craftsmen and nine thousand operators brought wage gains and adoption of a grievance procedure, though unionists soon charged the company with using loopholes in the procedure to harass union activists.[11]

On August 1, 1918, the federal government took over the telephone industry, with the aim of insuring uninterrupted service and secrecy of war communications. Under the terms of the takeover, the companies were to regain control in one year; company managers were left in charge of day-to-day operations; and the companies were generously compensated. (It was during the federal administration, for example, that companies were first allowed to charge customers for installation of their telephones.) But telephone unionists soon found cause for resentment. As director of the industry, Postmaster General Albert S. Burleson suspended wage hikes and union recognition pending the findings of a commission of inquiry that was given resources too slim to do its job and that, in any case, was heavily weighted against the unions. The commission reached no decisions, and the IBEW failed in its appeals for action by other government agencies. Under the circumstances, telephone companies told workers they could not grant wage increases on their own authority; some companies, so the unionists charged, took further advantage by stepping up discriminatory practices against union members.[12]

This policy (or lack of policy) angered telephone unionists—and, incidentally, left among them the lasting impression that government ownership or control of their industry was no answer to their problems.[13] Strikes in Minneapolis–St. Paul, Jacksonville, and Witchita—the latter two conducted after the November 1918 armistice in Europe—were defeated, partly through dismissals and threats of dismissal. Finally the unionists forced a change. On April 15, 1919, the Boston local led some nine thousand New England operators out on strike, halting telephone service in the five New England states served by the New England Bell company. (Connecticut was served by a separate Bell company and was not affected.) IBEW craftsmen joined the strike in its third day, bringing the total number of strikers to about twelve thousand. The strike ended five days later when an emissary from Burleson signed a union-management agreement giving wage increases to both operators and craftsmen, retroactive to January 1.[14]

Heartened by this breakthrough, the IBEW on June 2 demanded that Burleson give all telephone union members guarantees against discrimination and that he permit labor organizations to bargain with the companies over wages and other matters. The IBEW then called upon all its telephone locals to launch a strike on June 16 if Burleson did not meet the demands; in response Burleson on June 14 directed that workers have "the right to bargain as individuals or collectively through committees of their representatives," that companies must bargain with such individuals or committees, and that "no employees shall be discharged, demoted, or otherwise discriminated against because of membership in any labor organization." Issued as it was less than seven weeks before Burleson's administrative rule was to end, the directive was no telephone Magna Carta. But it did meet the letter of the IBEW's demands, and the national office called off the projected strike.[15]

Still, major problems were left unresolved. Except in New England, telephone locals had yet to win wage hikes and union recognition from the companies. Further, militancy had been inflamed by the year-long stalemate, the New England operators' victory, and the setting of the national strike date. Against the express wishes of the IBEW national office, telephone locals in the South, the Midwest, and California began to walk out, in some cases before June 16 and in a few cases without even informing the national office. Union leaders lacked the means of preventing the strike wave from spilling forward. There was no telephone strike fund, the withholding of which might cause locals to reconsider. And many of those who struck were not even union members.[16]

In this strike summer of 1919, the IBEW's telephone membership peaked at a figure perhaps as high as 25,000, or 9 percent of the industry's 278,000 employees.[17] From that time on, events caused membership to plummet. In the South, strikes in Atlanta, Norfolk, Columbia, and several other cities were defeated, in large part because many workers stayed on the job, some of them no doubt influenced by threats of dismissal for strike activity. The defeated strikers were eventually allowed to return to work, but with forfeiture of all seniority rights, whereupon some of the strongest unionists left telephone employment, and union activity became weaker than ever. In the Midwest the outcome of strikes in Cleveland, Youngstown, and St. Louis seemed at first something of a standoff. The locals there won wage increases though not official recognition, and strikers were allowed to return to work without penalty. But subsequently management pressed workers to drop their union membership. In Cleveland, for example, low-level managers interviewed union operators, hinting that their continued membership put their jobs in jeopardy. They then gave the operators stationery and stamps to mail in their union resignations.[18]

In California a six-week strike that initially involved more than nine thousand workers and crippled service in most cities eventually proved nearly as disastrous as the southern strikes. In its third week, locals in Oregon and Washington joined the strike. But up and down the coast, service was gradually restored as the company hired strikebreakers and the strikers heeded injunctions barring picketing. A leader of the operators characterized the strike as "unsupported by organization, discipline, and experience." Eventually the defeated strikers accepted terms that included elimination of the grievance procedure, a nonretroactive wage increase, and disturbingly cloudy statements that strikers could return to work without discrimination.[19]

As soon as the strike was over, the union began receiving complaints that strikers were being given their seniority rights only in return for forfeiture of union membership, that some of those who did not cooperate were being given only half-day shifts, and that workers were being forced into Bell's new company unions by threats of assignment to undesirable hours and loss of chances for promotion or seniority rights. Most locals collapsed; those that remained were virtually destroyed in the course of a much smaller strike in February 1920, launched against what the union interpreted as an ultimatum that all workers had to become members of company unions.[20]

Aided by lost strikes and company pressure on IBEW members, Bell company unions enjoyed considerable growth from 1919 onward. As we shall see in the next chapter, company unions would eventually contribute to the building of a new, genuine telephone union movement, becoming vivid illustrations of William A. Leiserson's dictum that "human organizations, once they are created, have a way of evolving . . . in quite unforeseen directions."[21] Having sown the wind, Bell in due time would reap the whirlwind. But in their first years, company unions undoubtedly furthered the antiunion aims that Bell had intended.

Writing in June 1922, the Bell System's chief officer, AT&T's President Henry B. Thayer, summarized the history of Bell labor relations in a letter to a major stockholder: The years before World War I had been marked by "very good relations between the management and the other employees of the Bell System, with, however, a slow increase in unionism in spots." Unionism had "somewhat accelerated during the early part of the war," and the year of federal control had resulted in "a good deal of unrest." While management wished to allay the unrest and had no desire to deny the worker "the right of representation by someone in whom he felt confidence," it nonetheless

felt that at least in their operation and probably in their principles, the trades unions were utterly wrong from the fact that the union does not work for the laborer but for the union and from the fact that the union only thrives on the discontent of its members.

In our business we have not the problem of the mill-owner or the steel manufacturer. We have an exceptionally intelligent lot of people with more education than the average of working people. Among the men we have a large proportion with a considerable term of service and among the supervisory women [sic].

The plan we evolved, therefore, was to encourage friendly organizations of the employees and systematically to inform the whole body of employees as to the purposes and policies of the business.[22]

These "friendly" organizations were, of course, the company unions. Although Thayer wrote of "encouraging" employees to join such organizations, and an AT&T vice-president, E. K. Hall, explained that participation was "invited,"[23] workers of that period and later saw company aims and tactics somewhat differently. D. L. McCowen, in the 1920s a Southwestern Bell plant craftsman and later an important figure in telephone unionism, recalls: "Everybody belonged. It was considered more or less a requirement. There was no choice; you just belonged. And my recollection is they even deducted the quarter [for monthly dues] from your paycheck." A Seattle man recounts, "After reporting on the job, I was approached later on in the day by one of the supervisors, who handed me a [membership] card and asked me to sign." "If you didn't," a former operator reports of the procedure in Dallas, "you not only had to go to the district man, but on up to the division superintendent, and explain why you didn't want to join. They were still on a witchhunt for union-minded people."[24]

Thus many workers who were loyal IBEW members and saw no attraction in company union membership nonetheless found themselves driven out of the IBEW and into company unions during the 1919–1920 strike aftermath. Their signing of company union cards under these circumstances tended to formalize and confirm their break with genuine unionism. As Julia O'Connor, a leader of the IBEW operators, put it, "The psychological effect upon the operators occasioned by signing something was duly appreciated by the Company."[25] In addition, among the huge majority of telephone workers who had never been union members, the company unions probably reduced to some degree the potential appeal of the IBEW. Certainly the organizations were an important medium for management's ongoing theme that the company was fair and deserved the workers' loyalty. And at little or no cost in dues to the workers, the company unions did fulfill some of the functions that might otherwise have been handled by the IBEW.[26]

At any rate the results, according to President Thayer,

have more than met our expectations. Friendly organizations have taken the place of such unions as existed practically everywhere except in New England and to an encouraging extent in New England.

. . . It is our hope that . . . before very long, the employees of the Bell System throughout the country will have no affiliation with any outside labor organizations and will cooperate thoroughly for the good of the business.[27]

Vice-President Hall, while denying that the objective of the Bell personnel policy was to eliminate trade unionism, agreed that trade unionism might ultimately prove unnecessary. He indicated that Bell would be able to face that prospect with equanimity.[28]

Indeed, conditions by the end of 1920 had already come close to meeting Thayer's and Hall's hopes. Telephone unionism, never an industry-wide force and only sporadically effective during its peak 1917–1919 strength, by 1921 had been virtually wiped out in all but three areas of the country. And the largest by far of these union groups—the New England operators to whom Thayer referred— clearly faced perils ahead.

In the first place, the New England operators were weakened by their tenuous relations with the IBEW national office. Though operators had been welcome in the IBEW after first joining in large numbers in 1912, leaders representing the union's core of electricians feared the day when operators at IBEW conventions, "casting their votes as a block," would shape decisions affecting electricians' livelihood. The union leaders opposed any voting method "which requires men handling the sting of electricity to submit forever to the rule of telephone operators."[29] The result was a series of arrangements designed to keep operators in the union but safely away from the levers of union power. In 1912 operators were disfranchised through confinement in semi-independent "sublocals." In 1913 they were segregated in "regular" locals—locals that in most respects were equal to other IBEW locals but that charged half the normal per capita dues and held half the normal per capita voting rights at conventions. And from 1918 on, these locals were grouped entirely outside the mainstream of IBEW governance, in a nearly autonomous Telephone Operators' Department. The post-1913 arrangements, while acceptable to the operators themselves, left the New England operators' organization with financial reserves inadequate to meet a serious test. And when that test came, the operators could not count on—and in fact did not receive—strong support from the IBEW national office, which at the time was absorbed in problems besetting its core membership.[30]

In the second place, the operators lost important allies. In March 1920 the IBEW craftsmen's locals in New England petitioned the national office for semiautonomous departmental status, similar to that of the Telephone Operators' Department. When this request was refused, the leaders of most of the locals formed a new organization called the International Brotherhood of Telephone Workers (IBTW), and used it to draw their membership out of the IBEW. Their campaign was successful, owing in part to steps taken by the New England company. The company ended all relations with the IBEW and, according to IBEW sources, favored IBTW men in giving promotions and in permitting IBTW organizers to solicit members on company time. By the end of 1920 the IBEW was no longer a force among telephone craftsmen in New England, and by 1923 the IBTW functioned as a company union in all essential respects.[31]

Third, the company launched a drive against the New England operators' organization, with which it had bargained annually since 1913. After 1920 the company ignored the organization's annual spring demands for wage and hour improvements and withdrew from participation in the Joint Adjustment Board. More than 7,500 of the New England company's 12,500 operators remained loyal to the union despite the company-imposed shutdown of its bargaining and grievance-handling functions, though a faction of some 1,000 members of the Boston local did secede. Finally, in June 1923, after the company once again ignored union demands for wage and hour improvements, the organization's leaders called for a vote to authorize a strike. The membership gave its approval by a union count of 6,466 to 1,133, and on June 26 about half of the New England company's operators walked out.[32]

From the start it was clear that the strike would not have the impact of the April 1919 walkout. In Maine, Vermont, and New Hampshire, very few operators left their posts; telephone service in those states remained almost normal. The effect on service was concentrated in the cities of Massachusetts and Rhode Island. But even there, service was far from halted at most telephone exchanges, in part because of short-term hiring of students and former operators, and because management personnel—some from Bell companies outside New England—put in long hours at the switchboards. Service was initially halted in Lawrence and Providence, but much of it was restored during the strike's second week as permanent replacements were hired and trained. Service in Boston was better than in most cities—in fact, nearly normal after the first few days—largely because the secessionist faction of the Boston local chose to remain on the job. Members of the IBTW also worked throughout the strike. They claimed that they were not performing the work of the striking operators, but the IBEW charged that they were, and that they were helping the company solicit replacement employees besides.[33]

The inadequately funded strike was remarkable both for its lack of violence and for the length of time the strikers were able to carry on against all odds. Finally, on July 26, following a vote to end the strike among the thirty-eight hundred remaining strikers, the union did so. There were no concessions from the company. The thirty-eight hundred were free to "apply as individuals for reinstatement" as employees, and most who did so were eventually rehired. But those most active in the walkout were not rehired, and a company union was quickly set up among the operators. Genuine telephone unionism ceased to exist in New England.[34]

After 1923 telephone unionism survived in but two small enclaves. One was downtown Chicago, where a group of Bell craftsmen, assigned to work in large buildings and at construction sites in the Loop area, retained their membership in IBEW Local 134 (which also contained nontelephone workers). This was not the result of any special tenacity on the part of Chicago telephone unionists. Rather, it was a Bell concession to the unusual strength of the unionized building trades in the area, which were ready either to shut down work or to use strong-arm tactics at job sites where nonunion craftsmen dared appear. Here the company, in allowing some of its craftsmen to remain IBEW members, was merely bowing to the fact that those craftsmen had to carry IBEW cards to do their jobs.[35]

The other enclave was Montana, where craftsmen and operators retained their membership in IBEW locals and continued to negotiate contracts with management at the local Bell exchanges. As early as 1907, bruising union-management clashes had led top management of Rocky Mountain Bell to conclude that at least part of Montana might have to become a permanent exception to Bell's nationwide open-shop rule.[36] Subsequent conflicts pointed to the same conclusion. The extraordinary political and economic strength of Montana unionism in general, plus the readiness of the Montana Federation of Labor to support the staunch telephone unionists in time of trouble, so dimmed the prospects for antiunion drives that Bell apparently forswore in Montana the kind of drives it was launching elsewhere in 1919–1920. Like the craftsmen's local in Chicago, the IBEW outposts in Montana quietly survived the 1920s and 1930s, at no time striking or threatening to strike, and making no attempt to organize beyond their pre-1920s base.[37]

Thus the field, almost everywhere, was left to the company unions. These would be the dominant telephone "labor" organizations until the mid-1930s, and they would leave a strong imprint even on the new organizations that emerged in the wake of the Wagner Act. Their dominion was in large part the result of the failure of "outside" unions. Yet as the remarks of President Thayer indicate, they owed their very existence to the fact that for a brief period outside unions enjoyed modicum of success. Had the IBEW not been strong enough to pose the possibility of widespread telephone worker organization–but at the same time too weak to carry through on it—the Bell network of company unions might never have been established.

Chapter 2

THE PROBLEM OF UNION ORGANIZATION,

1920–1935

AS THE 1920S DAWNED, the spirit of unionism in the telephone industry was alive but in deep hibernation. It could look back on a history that had been mostly defensive struggle, and losing struggle at that; and with the company union network now firmly in place, it faced truly formidable obstacles. Although some Bell workers and the IBEW national office retained a glimmer of interest in organizing telephone workers, no campaigns were initiated. They realized that prospects for success were little better than zero.

In part, of course, the difficulty of organization after 1920 stemmed from management's continued ability to use repressive tecniques, such as threatened or actual dismissal for union activity. And until 1933, conditions in the United States were such that it was probably true, as Jack Barbash has written, that "no union could organize a large employer [such as Bell] who did not want to be organized."[1] These barriers, however, were far from the whole story. Although it is true that the Wagner Act's 1935 ban on repressive techniques helped to make telephone unionization possible, the act did not make unionization inevitable. Other, more persistent difficulties discouraged the large-scale entry of legitimate unions, not only in the 1920s and early 1930s, but even in the improved political climate of the New Deal period and later. What made telephone management an especially forbidding antagonist—during and after the mid-1930s, as well as before—was the antiunion leverage it derived from the structural and technological features of the industry, the social and job attributes of the work force, and elaborate personnel measures dating back to 1913.

STRUCTURALLY, BY 1920 the Bell System controlled nearly two-thirds of the industry. In the following years its share increased, so that by 1937 the system controlled 98 percent of American long distance wires, 93 percent of telephone manufacturing, and 83 percent of telephones in service. Its overarching organization—the American Telephone and Telegraph Company—had by 1937 become the majority stockholder in all but two of the system companies, making it possible to view the results as "the largest aggregation of capital and resources that had ever been controlled by a single private company in the history of business."[2] Given this structure, most of the industry could act virtually as a unit in planning and implementing personnel or anti-union measures.

It was clear, moreover, that any sizable union breakthrough would have to occur in Bell. Much of the non-Bell telephone service was handled by more than twenty-five thousand tiny, rurally based firms and cooperatives, where most of the work was done by owners or farmer-subscribers. The remainder was in the hands of several hundred "class A" companies (those whose annual operating revenues exceeded $100,000), also typically small and rurally based, and in any event accounting for less than 7 percent of the total telephone work force.[3]

The core of the industry lay in the twenty-one Bell operating companies, which provided local service and employed over two-thirds of the industry's workers. (For the names and geographical coverage of the Bell operating companies, see Appendix A.) Within their respective areas, these companies were monopsonists in the hiring of telephone labor and monopolists with respect to telephone service, both conditions that further inhibited unionization. Workers, once they had been dismissed for union activity, would have to move from their home area to have any chance of regaining telephone employment. And should workers strike the operating companies had no need to fear what employers often fear most—the permanent loss of customers to a competitor.[4]

In addition, the technology of the operating companies made them resistant to shutdown in case of a strike. Unlike the assembly lines of production industries, which had to be halted entirely when large numbers of workers left their jobs, telephone switchboards and craft operations could be maintained individually by management employees and nonstriking workers. The conversion to dial telephones (replacing operator-connected local service), a process begun by Bell in 1920 and almost half completed by 1935, also reduced the potential impact of strikes on the industry's basic unit of service, the local telephone call. Limiting the opportunity for slowdowns or for sabotage on the job were the close observation of operators and the high degree of individual accountability among craftsmen.[5]

Important among social and job attributes was the employment of telephone workers at many widely dispersed locations, with non-Bell workers being the most dispersed, but those employed by the system also being widely scattered. In 1920 Bell operating companies maintained 5,767 central offices spread across all forty-eight states. By 1937 the number had increased to 6,945, and dispersed outside the central offices were thousands of other job sites, both permanent and temporary. The non-operating-company segments of the Bell System —or at least those segments employing large numbers of workers— were also geographically decentralized. Workers employed by AT&T Long Lines, the Bell System's conductor of intercompany long distance calls, were dispersed in job locations across forty-two states. Workers in the Western Electric installation division were on any given day scattered at hundreds of ever-shifting locations, installing new equipment in central offices and other facilities across the country. Employees of the Western Electric distributing house (later "sales") division labored in a network of twenty-nine supply and repair houses spanning the nation. Even the factory workers who built the system's telephones and other equipment, all employed by the Western Electric manufacturing division, worked at three widely separated locations: the Hawthorne plant in Chicago (completed in 1902), the Kearny plant in Kearny, New Jersey (completed in 1928), and the Point Breeze plant in Baltimore (completed in 1930).[6]

Compounding the effects of Bell's geographical dispersion, moreover, were further divisions along functional lines. As indicated above, specialized organizations handled local operations, intercompany long distance calls, installation of central office equipment, supply and repair, and manufacturing. The operating companies, along with AT&T Long Lines, were each divided into four main departments with distinct functions: plant (the employer of telephone craftsmen), accounting (handling billing, payroll, and company records), commercial (in charge of business contacts with the public), and traffic (the employer of telephone operators). And within the plant departments were further distinctions, breaking down worker groups into indoor craftsmen, linemen, telephone installers, and so on.

Reports indicate that workers performing one kind of telephone work were likely to harbor feelings of mild antipathy toward fellow employees in other lines of work. This was particularly true, it seems, of the operating companies, where, as one worker remembers, "there was a lot of departmental prejudice." Frequently "a plant man looked at a traffic girl with suspicion, and the traffic girl looked at the plant man with the same suspicion," while white-collar workers in the accounting and commercial departments looked down on both the traffic operator and the "greasy plant man out here climbing poles, with creosote all over him." Subsequent unionists remember that local management at times seemed to encourage this disaffection between worker groups. In the commercial departments, particularly, insularity was encouraged by the company practice of paying monthly or bimonthly salaries, as distinguished from weekly wages in the other departments. Along with this practice went messages designed to nourish feelings of elitism, messages stating or implying that "you have to be a little special to be a service rep [i.e., representative] in the commercial department," that "you are the telephone company in the eyes of the public" and therefore "the elite."[7]

One result of this geographical and functional dispersion was that any feeling of telephone worker solidarity had to bridge great distances and dissimilar kinds of work. Another problem was that the physical task of contacting workers for purposes of persuasion and organization was difficult, especially for outside unions, which, initially at any rate, lacked access to internal channels of communication. As the pre-1920 experience showed, the organization of one department did not readily translate into organization of other departments. Nor would a strike in one department necessarily bring out fellow employees in others; frequently fellow employees continued to work, even in one instance where they and the striking group both belonged to the same union. (In 1919 the IBEW plant men in New England continued to work for a time while the IBEW traffic operators were on strike, causing a grudge that the operators harbored for years.) In combating a strike, moreover, management could bring in employees of other Bell companies not being struck.[8]

Geographical dispersion meant that a large proportion of Bell workers lived in small cities and towns and in antiunion sections of the country, where contact with unionized workers was slight and where the generally antiunion expressions of community leaders and the media went nearly uncontested. Such workers could be hired and employed close to their homes, hence they did not experience the "uprootedness" that has been positively correlated with working-class consciousness.[9] Nor did they experience the unusual combination of circumstances conducive to unionism in industries such as mining and clothing: they did not constitute compact groups of workers living near their work under conditions of social or geographic isolation.[10]

To some degree this dispersion was offset by a large measure of social homogeneity. Despite the informality of its employee recruitment methods, based mostly on the family and friendship networks of current employees and contacts with public and parochial school officials, Bell's hiring standards were relatively systematic and stringent. The normal educational requirement in the early 1920s was completion of eighth grade; by the late 1930s it was completion of high school or trade school. Bell further required the ability to speak clear English; it generally hired only people in their late teens and early twenties; and blacks were excluded from all but the most menial work, leaving them with less than one percent of the jobs in the industry's entire pre–World War II history.[11]

One outcome of these hiring practices was that the preponderance of native-born whites was much greater in the telephone industry than in most other industries. The major telephone occupations in the operating companies ranged between 92 and 97 percent native-born white from 1920 to 1940, as compared to 1930 census figures of 72 percent for the American work force as a whole, 68 percent for "manufacturing and mechanical industries," and 86 to 91 percent for the major white-collar wage-earning groups. Another outcome was that nearly all telephone workers were alike in being well educated in comparison with most other American workers. Census returns for 1940 showed that the median number of school years completed by the largest female telephone group, the operators, was 11.8 years, while the figure for the employed female work force as a whole was 10.8 years. The comparable figure for telephone "linemen and servicemen"—representative occupations within the largest male group, plant craftsmen—was between 10 and 10.5 years, while the figure for the employed male work force as a whole was 8.7 years.[12] Possibly related to their roughly similar educational attainments was the fact that operators and plant craftsmen were perceived by outsiders as about equal in terms of their social status. Polls ranking the "prestige status" of one hundred American professions and other occupations, taken from 1938 to 1941, placed operators and linemen right next to each other, in sixty-seventh and sixty-eighth place (with structural iron workers slightly above and auto workers slightly below).[13]

On the whole, the unusual social homogeneity of the telephone workers no doubt facilitated unity and thus helped counter the effects of geographical and functional dispersion. Social homogeneity was not without its negative effects, however. The virtual absence of Russian Jewish women, for example, probably hurt the prospects for unionization.[14] And containing as it did a very high proportion of white, native-born, and well-educated Americans, the telephone work force contained a correspondingly low proportion of emigrants from the black-belt South, Appalachia, and "peasant Europe." For better or worse, this distinguished telephone workers from many of the groups unionized during the 1930s. Telephone workers were not, as Peter Friedlander says of such unionized groups in general, seeking new structures to compensate for "the collapse and/or transformation of a complex and variegated collection of prebourgeois cultures."[15] Nor were they much affected by what Herbert Gutman has called "the significant interplay between race and class that would shape so much of twentieth-century American social history."[16]

Commentators on telephone workers and their work have often emphasized two additional attributes: the largely young, female makeup of the work force and the white-collar nature of most of the work.[17] Meanwhile, commentators on the general process of unionization (normally writing without particular reference to the telephone or any other single industry) have linked those attributes with resistance to unionization, a resistance that seems to have been especially strong prior to World War II.[18] Although this general link appears well established and will not be disputed here, any attempt to apply it to the particular case of telephone workers—that is, to propose that young female and white-collar attributes served to reinforce Bell's antiunion leverage—must be carefully qualified. A great number of telephone jobs actually bore fewer of the characteristic features of white-collar work than is commonly supposed. And the largely young, female makeup of the telephone work force combined with certain peculiarities of the work and workplace in such a way as to pose opportunities as well as obstacles for any would-be union organizer. All in all, the issues here are complex enough to warrant examination on a unit-by-unit basis.

Employment in the three Western Electric (WE) divisions was neither white collar nor young female in any noteworthy degree. WE installation was almost solely the preserve of male manual workers. The range of skills and jobs was not unlike that of plant craftsmen working for the Bell operating companies and Long Lines, and the hiring standards were similar. In the WE distributing house and manufacturing divisions, meanwhile, the work and the hiring standards did not resemble those found in other telephone occupations so much as they did those prevailing in "outside" warehouses, machinery repair shops, and factories. In these two divisions, although masses of young women were at times employed in assembly work, and the proportion of office workers and "shop clerical people" sometimes rose to perhaps 20 percent, the majority of the workers were always male, and most of the work was clearly industrial blue collar in nature.[19] Together the WE divisions made up a significant proportion of total Bell System employment, though the proportion oscillated with the coming and going of equipment replacement programs—from a high of 19 percent in 1929 to a low of 7 percent in 1933, with the proportion in most years falling between 9 and 13 percent.[20]

The plant departments, whose proportion of total operating company and Long Lines employment climbed from 28 percent in the early 1920s to 34 percent in the late 1930s, were less than one-tenth female. The great majority of plant employees were men in their late twenties or older who were career telephone workers (in part because they could not market their telephone skills elsewhere). Nor was much of the work white collar. A sense of the blue-collar makeup of the outdoor plant occupations, in which most plant workers labored, is perhaps conveyed in a listing of typical job titles: cable splicer, cable splicer's helper, lineman, groundman (a lineman's assistant), telephone installer, and telephone repairman. The indoor plant jobs presented more of a spectrum. Central office repairmen were distinctly blue collar; testboardmen did work that was largely manual but clean and sedentary enough to permit the wearing of white collars and neckties; and "plant clerical" jobs (the only plant jobs frequently held by women) were distinctly white collar. But the preponderance of plant work best fit the blue-collar designation, as was evidenced in 1944 when a War Labor Board unit sought a comparative assessment of plant skills. It settled on the metal trades, clearly a blue-collar field, as embracing an array of jobs whose levels of skill were comparable to those found in the plant departments. Actually, while there is no reason to question the validity of this comparison of skills, a comparison with the construction trades might better convey the character of most plant department work: the ambulatory quality of much of the labor, the frequent autonomy of individuals and small groups, the outdoor work in all kinds of weather, and—particularly before the depression—the informal apprenticeship system, whereby young workers acquired most of their skill by watching and helping the more experienced craftsmen. A major difference, of course, was the regularity of telephone plant employment. Another difference was that among the younger plant men there was considerable movement from craft to craft, as the company changed assignments in an effort to build a largely cross-trained force.[21]

In the accounting and commercial departments, whose combined proportion of total operating company and Long Lines employment climbed from 10 percent in the early 1920s to 16 percent in the late 1930s, nearly all the jobs bore the features typically associated with white-collar work. Employees worked at clean, physically undemanding tasks, during normal business hours, usually at desks in offices, with some freedom to move about, and for the most part free of hovering supervision. In both departments women consistently held more than three-fourths of the nonmanagerial jobs—almost always the less remunerative ones. In accounting they held a range of clerical jobs, while in commercial they ordinarily dealt with the public as service representatives or tellers, or else served as clerks keeping records of commercial's transactions. A large proportion were young: in most years more than half of the female accounting workers were under twenty-five, though in commercial a tendency toward long service usually held the proportion down to between 35 and 40 percent. Taken together, accounting and commercial workers seemed to resemble closely the prototypes various commentators have advanced when describing the difficulties of organizing white-collar and young, female

workers. The difficulties seem to have been borne out in those departments' pre-1920 history, when no sign of union activity was evident
among accounting or commercial workers.[22]

The traffic departments across the country were by far the largest of
the Bell System units, ranging from 60 percent of operating company
and Long Lines employment in the early 1920s down to 47 percent in
the late 1930s.[23] It is in these departments that the most careful qualifications must be made concerning the young, female makeup of the
work force, the white-collar nature of the work, and the impact of
those traits upon the problem of union organization.

Certain facts, of course, are beyond dispute. The traffic workers
were nearly all women, and usually a majority of them were quite
young—a result of Bell's hiring of young workers and annual employee turnover rates normally between 30 and 40 percent. The proportion younger than twenty-five was 71 percent in 1920 and 56 percent in 1930. Depression layoffs of young people, coupled with
reduced hiring and low quit rates, gradually pinched the proportion
down to 28 percent by 1940, but the war economy then swelled it to
over 50 percent by the mid-1940s.[24]

As with most accounting and commercial workers, nothing in the
social makeup of these young, female traffic workers immunized them
from those influences that impeded unionization among young, female
workers in general. Like millions of young women working elsewhere
during those decades, most young traffic workers viewed their years in
the labor force as a short interval between girlhood and marriage. This
attitude, which cast wage work in an impermanent light removed from
the central concerns of life, necessarily diminished any possible importance attached to unions.[25] A further impediment was that the great
majority of these women lived at home, ordinarily with one or both
parents, though an increasing proportion were married and living with
their husbands (10 percent in 1920, 22 percent in 1930, and 33 percent
in 1940). Bell in fact preferred to hire unmarried women living at
home, and it sometimes sent investigators to check on the domestic
status of job applicants. Many traffic workers were thus enmeshed in
family networks unlikely to provide support for union activism. On the
contrary, such networks often pushed young women toward interests
that were domestic, matrimonial, maternal—an effort that found support in community and general cultural pressures. Domestic ties did
not stifle all rebellion, of course, but such active protest as arose under

these circumstances might often have found targets other than the employer. Leslie Woodcock Tentler has described, for example, certain pressures upon working daughters living with their parents that "defined the central problem in young female lives as the struggle with parents for social freedom."[26]

In important respects, moreover, the traffic employees qualified as white-collar workers, enough so to justify the U.S. Census Bureau and later the War Labor Board in grouping them among "clerical, sales, and kindred workers," as distinct from such other broad groupings as "operatives and kindred workers." In the first place, as we have seen, traffic hirees were deliberately drawn from the same labor pool generally tapped by employers of female white-collar wage earners: these workers were preponderantly young, well-educated, white, native-born, and living with their parents. Secondly, their physical surroundings amounted to something of a model for white-collar workplaces. The central offices where they worked were located in business and occasionally residential districts. According to all reports, they were clean, well lit inside and out, often contained cafeterias and well-furnished lounges, and always contained ample washrooms with good plumbing, towels, soap, and mirrors. The only major drawback was the operating rooms themselves: they were hot in the summer and poorly ventilated in the winter, which was aggravated by occasional crowding and the customary arrangement of banks of switchboards in a large U around the room, impeding the circulation of air. The summer heat was further aggravated by another "white-collar" feature of traffic employment: the mode of dress required of traffic workers was in the cumbrous fashion worn by female white-collar workers of the era. White-collar dress was feasible because traffic work was as clean as office work and less physically demanding than most blue-collar labor, though the rapid motions and frequent leaning sideways and forward did involve some physical strain.[27]

The deliberate recruitment from one broad social group joined with the pleasant surroundings and the white-collar mode of dress to produce yet another feature of white-collar employment: an atmosphere of comparatively genteel respectability—or "niceness," to use a word often chosen by traffic workers and observers. The Bell System cultivated this atmosphere in various ways, and no doubt with various motives, among them very likely the belief that it helped recruit the workers the system wanted at wages lower than it would otherwise have to pay. As Alice Kessler-Harris has pointed out, native-born white women (and some others) tended to strongly prefer fields of employment that were "respectable" in terms of surroundings, dress, and the ethnic and educational backgrounds of the jobholders already in them. They crowded into the few fields open to them that fit those preferences, thus giving employers in those fields an advantage in terms of the wages they might offer. But so too would such women crowd into fields that could be *shaped* to fit those preferences. And here there was no lack of alert managers, who were quite willing to provide pleasant surroundings, monitor the "type" of women they employed, and then offer the genteel respectability thus afforded as a partial substitute for wages. Just such a process seemed to be taking place in Bell's traffic departments (although, as we shall see, Bell also clearly had public relations considerations in mind). New York's Bureau of Women in Industry found in 1920 that "a tradition of social position, carefully fostered by the Company, surrounded the telephone operator, and many girls preferred telephone to factory or store work for this reason."[28] One acute observer, who had held several jobs before becoming an operator in the Bell company in Chicago, marveled in 1921:

> In one of the laundries where I had worked I had been paid $15.00 a week for tying up packages. I could have done that without any schooling at all, and it didn't matter how poorly I was clothed or how uncouth was my language. But the Telephone Company demanded a comparatively high standard of living from its employees, both of education and of culture, and yet it paid the same wages for a highly skilled sort of work which required self-control, patience and a certain amount of refinement. . . . Perhaps it was because there seemed to be so many girls available for telephone work that wages could be kept so low and hours so long.[29]

But in important respects, too, the work in the traffic departments was unlike white-collar work. Very few traffic workers were able to work normal office hours. Indeed, the hours worked were in many cases even less desirable than those in factories using day, night, and swing shifts, because in every central office some switchboards needed to be in service all hours of all days. And while the flow of telephone calls from businesses peaked at midmornings and midafternoons on weekdays, the flow from residences spread across the clock and calendar, rising not only during weekday midmornings but also during evening hours, Sundays, and holidays. Unusual and complicated work schedules thus abounded. Operators, who made up some 85 percent of the traffic work force, normally worked a basic term of forty-four or forty-eight hours, spread across six days of the week and slotted into one of four basic shifts. About 45 percent worked the desirable morning-afternoon shift; about 15 percent worked the less desirable afternoon-evening shift; some 7 to 10 percent worked the undesirable night shift; and some 30 to 33 percent worked the undesirable morning-and-evening shift, also called the "split trick." And there were further complications. Operators on the various shifts arrived and departed from work at dozens of different times, in such a way as to avoid interruptions in service and provide maximum switchboard coverage during peaks. All operators' schedules were disrupted by the need to work many Sundays and holidays, the average being about one out of two.[30]

The other nonmanagerial traffic positions, all filled by workers who had been promoted from operator, were for the most part still tied to the operators' schedules. Of these positions, the one held by the most workers was "supervisor"—a misleading job title, later changed to "service assistant"—which involved standing behind a group of six to fifteen operators, making sure that all calls were handled promptly and properly, and assisting with especially troublesome calls. The other jobs were those held by service observers, who worked in another room, listening in on calls and gauging performances against various indexes; senior operators, who filled in where needed at the other traffic jobs; traffic clerks; and instructors. Only the last two groups worked anything like regular office hours.[31]

Such odd-hours scheduling disrupted the lives of traffic workers, particularly those of the younger, less experienced workers. The usual practice was to share Sunday and holiday work equally, but to let workers choose among the four basic shifts according to seniority. Thus it was the younger workers, often those most concerned with pursuing active social lives in their off-duty hours, who tended to be stuck with the split tricks and night shifts, along with their share of Sunday and holiday work. Though few operators seem to have questioned the fairness of the basic allotment system, the odd hours were a source of everyday unrest, an unrest perhaps most acutely felt by precisely those young workers who might otherwise have viewed their work as the least of their concerns.[32] A group of Michigan traffic workers, later arguing their union's wage case before an agency of the War Labor Board, did not shrink from outlining the full consequences of odd-hours scheduling. "These hours of work play an extreme hardship upon those who must work them," they contended, "isolating the operator from the normal activities of friends who are employed in industries where such abnormal hours are not a necessity. Eventually the operator's circle of friends becomes smaller and smaller, as they eliminate her from their list when she is not available. It is not an exaggeration, although perhaps amusing, that the telephone industry produces more old maids than does the teaching profession."[33]

Many traffic workers would not have been amused. Indeed, they had cause for further concern. While custom determined the basic allotment of schedules, a myriad of scheduling decisions remained to be made, and these were in the hands of the chief operator. She was the one management person frequently present in the operating room—a woman who had worked her way up through the ranks, who had virtually autocratic power in matters not fixed by custom, company personnel officers, or practice manuals. In many central offices the chief operator reportedly exercised her scheduling discretion arbitrarily or in favor of her "pets," in many cases a few of the older operators with whom she had long been acquainted. Heaped on top of the unavoidable scheduling hardships, any such favoritism was of course a source of grievance among the remaining operators, young and old alike. Operators so aggrieved might be tempted to welcome any vehicle, such as a union, that promised elaborated scheduling rules coupled with avenues of appeal in case of any departure from the rules.[34]

Unlike most white-collar workers, the telephone operator's physical tie to machinery was very close. After three to four weeks of training at dummy switchboards, she entered the operating room and was seated at one of the several kinds of switchboards, donned a headset as well as a mouthpiece attached to a breastplate hanging around her neck (all connected by wire to the board), and began the work of connecting calls. The work required her to use her eyes to respond to signal lights, her ears and voice to briefly converse with customers and operators at other central offices, and both hands to plug cords and time and ticket long distance calls. Even during slack moments she had to keep her eyes on the board so as not to miss signal lights indicating incoming calls. She had to seek permission to leave her board, and she could not speak to her neighbors at adjoining boards. Everything she did was according to procedure (though the rules were relaxed somewhat on the night shift). To "talk back" to abusive or impatient customers was tantamount to inviting dismissal.[35]

The telephone operator also worked under conditions of close supervision unusual in white-collar employment. Immediately behind the operator stood the supervisor. In another room were the service observers, who might be listening in on the operator's calls at any time. And somewhere on the premises was the chief operator, who observed, listened in on calls, received written tabulations concerning the operator's performance, spoke to her about her lapses, and meted out reprimands and other forms of discipline, both formal and informal. All this helped make the operator's job an unusually nerve-wracking one, especially during peak periods, when her faculties were already taxed and when she was likely to be dealing with impatient customers. In recognition of the strain, the company provided two fifteen-minute breaks on each shift. But nervous tension ranked with odd hours as the most common complaint about traffic work, and it was often cited by women who quit to find other kinds of work.[36]

The women who stayed generally raised no objection to close supervision and observation per se. The industry's "product," after all, was local and long distance telephone calls, and operators conceded the need, present in any industry, to monitor and measure the quality of the product. But the system of observation placed them, to an unusual degree, under the discretionary power of low-level managers, some of whom were bound to be "petty tyrants and stupid disciplinarians." The young, inexperienced operators were most vulnerable in that they were most liable to make mistakes, particularly because the need for cross training required that they be moved around among the various kinds of switchboards. Like the scheduling system, the observation system thus created a legion of aggrieved operators, young and old alike, who might welcome a vehicle that promised to curb harassment and provide avenues of appeal from the many acts of correction and discipline, some warranted but some unwarranted, that the system was constantly producing.[37]

Traffic work, of course, offered some compensations. Many operators drew satisfaction from efficiently providing a useful and sometimes vital service, from surreptitiously delaying the calls of rude customers, from dealing with customers in many walks of life, and from the camaraderie afforded by working shoulder to shoulder with other "nice" people facing similar difficulties.[38] Curiously, perhaps, the camaraderie usually included the nonmanagerial workers above the operators in the traffic hierarchy, particularly the supervisors, who suffered many of the same work strains and who, in addition, were forced to stand or walk during their entire work shifts. The fact that these "supervisors" were in most respects actually closer to the operators than to management was in several ways auspicious for any potential union movement. First, the supervisors' numbers were considerable: they constituted some 9 percent of total traffic employment. Second, because of their age, experience, and tendency to stay with telephone work as a career, they provided a measure of stability and continuity amongst a total traffic group that, however strong its union loyalty and militancy might become, would ordinarily be beset by high turnover and the strong non-work-related interests characteristic of any young, female work group. Third, by virtue of their selection and their functioning as "gang leaders or working leaders" (as the War Labor Board later described their role), they tended to be the "natural leaders" among the traffic workers.[39] They had, in fact, played an important part in the New England operators' union movement from 1912 to 1923. And, to reach ahead of our story for a moment, subsequent unionists would find that the supervisors "were really the backbone in getting girls lined up to go in," and that they provided much of the local leadership so necessary in sustaining any union movement.[40]

Thus, altogether, we must not make too much of the white-collar and young female makeup of the telephone work force as a barrier to union organization. To be sure, the accounting and commercial workers fit the description, and their resistance to unionization was comparatively strong. But WE and plant department employment was predominantly male and blue collar. The work in the traffic departments, whose size made them pivotal, was white collar only in a qualified sense. And while traffic workers were female and usually predominantly young, and therefore drawn by the usual forces toward off-duty concerns, the peculiarities of traffic work—that operating was a strenuous, stressful, heavily supervised job, often performed at inconvenient hours—had a way of demanding the workers' attention and refocusing it on workplace concerns. On the other hand, the difficulties cannot be wholly discounted. The high turnover rate among Bell's largely young, female work force posed a serious problem for any union in terms of gaining and keeping members. Although the actual difficulties of organizing young, female workers were generally exaggerated by AFL unions, young women nonetheless did have the *reputation* of being very hard to unionize, and it is clear that this reputation was one of several reasons why outside unions shunned telephone organizing campaigns in the 1920s and later.[41] Moreover, even with all the necessary qualifications, the Bell work force was somewhat more white collar in makeup than that of most of the corporate giants unionized during the 1930s and 1940s.

On balance, then, the white-collar and young female attributes posed obstacles to any potential union movement, though not as severe as might be generally supposed. And if the social homogeneity of the work force could meanwhile act as a boon, its effects were in a sense countered and probably outweighed by the workers' geographical and "functional" dispersion. It is safe to say, at any rate, that insofar as the social and job attributes of the work force affected the prospects for unionization in Bell, their cumulative impact was more negative than would be the case among most of the large corporate employers unionized during the 1930s and 1940s.

Further barriers to unionization resulted from the Bell System's taking advantage, before World War I, of its centralized control to launch an elaborate, centrally directed personnel program that, according to many reports, was rather successful in convincing its workers that the Bell System was fair and deserved their loyalty.[42] Behind the program was, in part, a desire to prevent unionization. But in view of the sporadic nature of unionism in the prewar industry, it is doubtful whether the program would have been implemented so fully had it not served at least two other purposes as well. One such purpose was to promote operating efficiency. In this respect Bell was not unlike the many corporations then being led by men who, in Robert Wiebe's words, were imbued with "the values of continuity and regularity, functionality and rationality, administration and management," who wished "to draw the arbitrary powers of the foreman into the hands of a specialist in personnel," and who were thus launching "experiments in welfare capitalism, looking toward a more refined control over the labor force." Another, special Bell purpose grew from its desire, as a regulated utility monopoly, to present itself before the public in a favorable light. As early as 1907 it had assembled a large public relations apparatus, and among Bell managers the recognition had quickly dawned that the Bell workers themselves, with their considerable working contact with the public, were "potential public relations representatives"—provided, of course, that they could be persuaded to be genuinely courteous, energetic in emergencies, proud of their work, and loyal to their employer.[43]

By 1920 Bell was working hard to instill these qualities. It hired, for the most part, from among the untrained, socially "acceptable," and relatively impressionable young workers just entering the job market. In the training that followed, it exposed these people to addresses by company officials, group discussions, bulletins, and glossy company magazines. Through these media, management stressed the theme that the jobs of all workers were interdependent and that all could give a "more intelligent and whole-hearted performance" if they could understand "where they fit into the general scheme of things" and "what the other department is doing." In addition, it was stressed, Bell workers should feel a sense of special pride, and even superiority, in the public service aspect of their employment. The Bell System itself was portrayed as "a great institution devoted to public service," and employees were urged to feel that "there is one common responsibility for the president, the janitor, the operator, the lineman . . . and everyone else in the whole outfit . . . the obligation and devotion to public service."[44]

Eventually, as will be noted later, the heavy stress placed on the theme of interdependence had the unintended effect of pushing company union representatives toward an interdepartmental conception of telephone labor organization. But another effect, more in line with management aims, was to create a bias against outside unions which, when the occasion warranted, could be made explicit. A former southern California plant worker recalls, for example, that in the mid-1930s "the company went on an all-out campaign to try to convince the employees—and this involved *all* employees in whatever department they worked for—that the telephone employee was different from any other employee in other industry. Supposedly, he was a cut above the steel worker or the auto worker, any of the others who were then in unions or were becoming unionized." This was a message that "I guess all of us liked to hear . . . but the difference was always brought out in the point that *you* didn't need a union because you were better, you were different than workers who had unions."[45]

Bell also sought employee loyalty by establishing in 1913 a pioneering benefit system that included company-paid pensions, vacations, sickness and disability benefits, and an organization of retired and long-service employees. Beginning in 1915 employee stock-purchase options were added. (Eleven years later, 185,000 Bell employees were exercising such options.)[46] By the 1920s workers who had built up some seniority were being strongly encouraged to commit themselves to a career in the Bell System. Benefits were graded to reward such decisions: paid vacations, for example, generally amounted to one week after one year of service, two weeks after two years, and three weeks after fifteen years. Promotions were made almost exclusively from within, and raises were governed by extended wage progression schedules—which for the worker had distinct drawbacks, however; operators, for example, reached the top wage for their job only after fourteen years of service (the average length of the schedules in 1939), even though they had normally reached their peak efficiency within four or five years. And finally, prior to the depression, the Bell System had an apparently deserved reputation for providing secure and continuous employment.[47]

Some of the impressions Bell sought to create among its workers were tarnished a bit by the low wages it paid. During each year of the 1903–1926 period, the annual earnings of the average telephone worker amounted to about half the earnings of the average postal worker, three-fourths the earnings of the average utility worker, and from 65 to 90 percent of the earnings of the average worker in manufacturing.[48] And low wages were of course a matter of serious concern to many Bell workers. But even here Bell was careful to make the best of the situation. The workers' understanding of their low-wage position was diminished because no lines of work were closely comparable to telephone work, and because the company had a policy of concealing pertinent information from them while claiming to pay good wages. The progression schedules, for example, were not generally available to workers, and plant workers were often told of their pay raises in private, with an admonition to keep quiet about them.[49] All the while, Bell claimed that it was "establishing wages as good as and, where possible, even better than those obtaining in comparable lines of employment." It was a claim forceful enough to be believed by some scholars interested in the problem and was not authoritatively challenged until after World War II.[50]

Bell's posture as a benevolent employer was undercut more severely by its policies during the depression of the 1930s, policies that in effect placed most of the burden of retrenchment squarely on the shoulders of its workers. In the 1920s, by holding dividends at nine dollars per share of stock while net yearly income per share was sometimes as high as fifteen dollars, Bell had managed to accumulate a surplus of $540 million, a sum that might have been used to maintain job security and worker income during the depression. Yet in 1931, when confronted with a 17 percent decline in demand and a shrinkage of profits to five dollars per share, the company decided to stabilize dividends rather than employment. The corporate surplus went to maintain the stock dividend at nine dollars per share throughout the depression, while Bell workers felt the effects of retrenchment in the form of layoffs, part-timing, and reduced hourly income.[51]

Figures on the number of depression layoffs are unavailable, but the employment figures are revealing: Bell System employment fell from 454,500 at the end of 1929 to 270,500 by 1933 (and 269,000 by 1935). Some of the decline, of course, was due to voluntary resignations. But resignations represented only 12 percent of total employment during 1930 and remained below 7 percent during each of the nine following years; clearly the number of layoffs was huge.[52] While generally the younger workers were most affected, a Long Lines operator in New York recalled: "I saw girls dismissed with eighteen and twenty years' service and girls kept on who had only been there a couple of years." There were instances reported of family men with seven, twelve, fifteen, and twenty-two years of service being laid off.[53] And the New England Bell company singled out married women for dismissal. Judgment of that company should be rendered only in light of the era's prevailing practice: many reputedly progressive companies, along with the federal government and over half of the school boards in the country discriminated in the same way; a 1932 Gallup poll found 82 percent of the respondents agreeing that wives should not work if their husbands were employed. But none of this allayed the misery of those affected, which of course included still-employed women who now felt themselves pressured toward postponement of marriage, or clandestine marriage, or other "unsuitable" arrangements sustained without benefit of marriage.[54]

Part-timing or the "lack-of-work-days" system, inaugurated in 1931, was also widely applied. This scheme is estimated to have kept sixty thousand workers on the payroll who otherwise could have been laid off, but of course it considerably reduced weekly income. By 1933 the normal six-day work week had given way to a typical schedule of four or four-and-a-half days, and in some places even shorter schedules were introduced. Dallas workers, for example, were cut to alternating three- and four-day weeks, and for a brief period plant men in New Orleans were cut to three days a week.[55]

In addition, even though no cuts were made in hourly wage rates, plant and traffic workers often suffered a loss in hourly pay through the widespread sifting down of workers into jobs that paid less and through the suspension of the progression schedules. In Southwestern Bell, for example, raises in pay normally coming to an operator after the completion of each year's work were not given during a three-year period. Workers were expected to make do with less, although in some companies efforts were made to alleviate hardships through advances and loans, with liberal repayment terms.[56]

The bulk of these practices, plus the realization that the nine-dollar dividend was being maintained, generated widespread resentment among Bell workers. But it failed to spark any significant union organizing activity. Later interviews with thirty-one active telephone unionists—people who were employed by thirteen Bell companies in sixteen states during the depression—found twenty-eight of them unable to recall any internal union organizing activity during the early and mid-1930s. Two people reported secret meetings in the homes of Wisconsin Bell employees, none of which moved beyond the discussion stage, and one reported similar meetings among operators working in a New York office of AT&T Long Lines. From the interviewees came no report of organizing activities by outside unions, although from other sources came an account of sixty plant craftsmen on the West Coast signing IBEW cards proffered by a fellow plant worker in 1932, and accounts of 1933–1934 meetings of New England company operators, who decided "to establish a regular union and affiliate with the American Federation of Labor." Threats from management quickly squelched the West Coast activity, and in New England management intimidated those who had met by subjecting them to "a systematic and persistent series of personal interviews."[57]

The dearth of union activity was in part a reflection of the unwillingness of established unions and CIO organizing committees to devote substantial resources to organizing Bell workers, even in the improved political climate of the New Deal. Such organizations as the IBEW, the Commercial Telegraphers Union, the American Communications

Association, the Utility Workers Organizing Committee, and the United Electrical, Radio, and Machine Workers (UE) all preferred to concentrate on other areas.[58] Yet this preference cannot be understood apart from the other side of the equation: the failure of Bell workers to show serious interest in becoming members of such organizations. Although more dissatisfied than formerly, the people who worked for Bell were also well aware that the depression had not altered the power that the Bell System derived from its structure and technology, that union activity could lead to a swift loss of jobs and security (an especially intimidating factor to long-term workers, who now made up a larger proportion of the work force), and that work was extremely hard to find elsewhere. "The general atmosphere that I found," reported a Long Lines plant worker, "was that if somebody got a pink slip, the guy that didn't get it said, 'Well, that's one more. My chances are better of staying on.' There was no agitation for a union. It was 'every man for himself.'" And workers were well aware of the possible consequences of joining a union. "We have no rules about it," declared the president of New Jersey Bell in 1933, "and yet we all know and certainly would expect that people who belong to outside unions would not be welcome in this organization."[59]

Dissatisfaction, moreover, was still being weighed against benefits offered. Elsewhere, systems of welfare capitalism often collapsed during the depression, exploding the expectations of security that such systems had raised in workers during the 1920s and generating what David Brody has called "a profound sense of betrayal." But in Bell —with its continuing profits and its special motives for seeking employee loyalty—the system of welfare capitalism remained relatively unaffected. For workers who survived the layoffs, there were still pleasant surroundings, an elaborate benefit system and "educational" program, and hourly wage rates that were being maintained at a time of general wage cuts.[60] And while laid-off workers might well have felt a profound sense of betrayal, they had little chance to infect the remaining work force with such feelings. Unlike the automobile companies, for example, Bell was relatively immune from short-term fluctuations that led to cycles of layoffs and rehirings. Those workers that were laid off were usually out of the system for good, or, if they returned, it was not until years later. Among the thirty-one interviewees mentioned above, six were laid off during the depression and subsequently returned to Bell; but three of these layoffs were for four years;

one was for four-and-a-half years; one was for two years; and one was for six years.[61]

Thus, despite the resentment caused by Bell's depression measures, there remained severe obstacles to unionization. Bell retained much of the antiunion leverage it had traditionally derived from the structural and technological features of the industry, from the social and job attributes of the work force, and from its personnel policy. Even the passage in 1935 of the Wagner Act, with its ban on overtly repressive measures, could not destroy this leverage. Nor could it overcome the long cultivated bias against outside unions. There was still a sense of exclusive mutuality and superiority among Bell workers, one that made them highly resistant to outside organizers. When this attitude was added to the other obstacles, it created a set of conditions that made AFL and CIO unions unwilling to risk large-scale telephone organizing ventures.

STILL ANOTHER BARRIER to outside organization at the time was the network of company unions that Bell had developed and maintained during the 1919–1935 period. In operation, these organizations served to eliminate minor sources of discontent in the workplace; they offered a forum in which management could attempt to justify regressive measures during the depression; and they became vehicles through which outside organizing efforts could be depicted as alien to the "Bell way." Yet paradoxically, these same organizations, in a number of ways, enhanced the prospects for emergence of an independent national industrial union movement from within the Bell System. It is to them that we must turn if we are to understand the character of the Bell labor organizations that emerged between 1935 and 1937.

As we have seen, the policy of establishing company unions was inaugurated in June 1919, in the midst of the one sizable strike wave in the telephone industry's pre-1935 history. After being approved by Postmaster General Burleson, the policy's implementation began with letters to high officers of the various Bell companies, urging them to "encourage your employees to form associations which shall appoint representatives to discuss freely and frankly with the officials of the company questions affecting their wages and work." It is clear from the previously quoted remarks of AT&T President Thayer that the envisioned company unions (or "associations," or "employee representation plans," as they were more often called) were intended as antiunion devices, and hence were a part of the general offensive employers were launching against unions in the period following World War I. The program, in fact, was developed in consultation with such other giant corporations as Standard Oil (New Jersey) and U.S. Steel, both of which were starting antiunion drives at about the same time.[62]

Although certain features of the resulting organizations came to vary over the years, the evidence indicates that AT&T's initial approach was carefully planned and orchestrated. The first associations were established in Bell segments where there was union activity or the fear of it—ordinarily the plant and traffic departments across the country. Similar organizations did not appear in the accounting and commercial segments or in Western Electric prior to the mid-1920s.[63] In structure, moreover, most of the associations followed a characteristic pattern. Separate associations ordinarily existed for each major department in each Bell company, and, in a few large companies, such as the five-state Pacific Telephone and Telegraph (PT&T), further divisions existed along geographical lines. Each association was made up of local chapters, which normally selected chapter representatives to regional committees. These committees would select a few of their members to sit on higher-level committees—and so on through pyramided stages—with committees at each stage conferring with corresponding levels of management. Top representatives were thus selected at a level several stages removed from the association membership, but they did represent a broad range of locations and jobs. In addition, in some cases association presidents were selected by all the chapter chairmen meeting in assembly.[64]

Day-to-day operation of the associations bore many of the classic marks of company unionism. There were no membership meetings beyond those of the local chapters, and these were often perfunctory. Meeting rooms and stationery were furnished by the company. Dues were often nonexistent, and nowhere greater than twenty-five cents a month.[65] Although membership was not automatic upon joining the company, management pressures—as we have seen—made it hard not to join. In the conferences with management, airing of individual workers' grievances was discouraged. Individuals were expected to take their grievances to management before going to the association,

and, as one Bell official remarked in 1928, "This has practically eliminated individual complaints."[66] Discouraged, too, was the consideration of such matters as wages, pensions, and the lack-of-work-days
system. These topics were sometimes discussed, but the bulk of the
conferences dealt with efficiency and with comfort and safety while at
work. According to a New Jersey Bell operator,

> About the height of the complaints that ever got to management was
> that the toilet tissue in the bathrooms was too rough, or there wasn't
> enough sugar, or the food was cold in the cafeteria, and such trivial
> things as that. Nothing that had any bearing on your real working
> conditions. Elevators slow; clocks slow; not enough sheets for the
> night girls that had to work from 9 P.M. to 7 A.M. (They had a . . .
> two-hour sleeping period.)[67]

Within this general framework, moreover, a kind of management-
inspired process of subversion sometimes set in. A former Indiana Bell
plant representative recalls an incident in which a management secretary recorded notes of a conference while an association representative
was forbidden to do so, the outcome being a publicly circulated management summary that put words in the mouths of the association representatives. In some cases management influenced the selection of association officers. In others the conferences with management became
"arenas" in which the supposed representatives of the workers sought
"to gather favor with the supervisors and foremen."[68] According to
AT&T Vice-President Hall, when representatives "thought wrong,"
they were supposed to be set straight in a mild (if perhaps condescend-
ing) way: " 'The next time your suggestions will be good, old top, you
are a little off this time. We will explain to you why.' " But according
to a former plant representative in Southwestern Bell, the tone was
often more censorious. Serious complaints were countered with responses like: " 'Now, you know our working conditions are of the best,
and you evidently are the only one that's having any of this kind of
trouble.' In other words, 'What's the matter with you?' " Aggressive
complaint was sometimes dulled in other, subtler ways. A representative in another Southwestern Bell area recalls, "After you got through
talking about some safety factors and company responsibility, the
meeting broke up into a little sociability, which consisted of cards,
crap shooting, and coffee."[69]

Yet despite these shortcomings, many Bell associations had long and active lives, mostly because it was in management's interest to support them but also because they proved useful to workers. Management became convinced that the associations meshed well with their general personnel objectives—a fact that may explain why Bell, unlike many other firms, maintained (and sometimes started) its associations during periods when there was no threat from trade unions. In addition to alerting management to minor inrritants in the workplace, the associations served as a means of persuading workers that their counsel was deemed valuable, that management decisions were reasonable, and that all Bell employees were banded together in a great and vital enterprise. "The more we take time to explain to our people what orders mean, why they are issued, where they fit into the general scheme of things," an AT&T official wrote of the association conferences, "the more intelligent acquiescence we will get in the orders." And indeed, much of each conference was normally taken up by management's dissemination of information and of its own point of view. "They utilized them to discuss with representatives of the various crafts the company's plans, safety programs, sales," recalls a former plant representative in southern California. Nor was Bell's special concern with involving workers in public relations forgotten. A survey of Pennsylvania plant association conferences during 1926 and 1927 found that there were more than twice as many public relations discussions (mostly initiated by management) as there were wage discussions (mostly worker initiated).[70]

The associations also held genuine attractions for workers. In the absence of trade unions, they were the sole means by which workers could seek policy information from responsible management, discuss their working conditions on a regular basis, or compare their conditions with those of fellow employees from distant work locations. To some workers the associations represented an opportunity to develop organizational skills and to acquire experience in conferring—even though in a subservient role—with management. And for the workers as a whole, they offered a means of collective expression, usually on minor matters but sometimes on major ones. By using the associations in these various ways, Bell workers were helping to prepare themselves for unionization after 1935.

To a considerable degree the Bell associations helped overcome the effects of geographical dispersion. In their operation, worker representatives from different locales were brought together in committees and in conferences with management. And given that there was normally one representative for every twenty-five members and that companies encouraged turnover in these positions, the intermingling experience was widespread.[71] Many workers learned to think of Bell labor organization in terms as geographically broad as were the companies themselves. As the National Labor Relations Board remarked in a 1939 decision reviewing the operation of Wisconsin Bell's traffic association, "The long history of collective activity through the medium of the respondent-controlled plan has habituated the employees to a system-wide [i.e., company-wide] form of organization."[72]

The associations also helped to combat the effects of "functional dispersion" among Bell workers. Their structuring, to be sure, reflected the variety of dissimilar jobs in the plant departments. There were cable splicers' chapters, janitors' chapters, and so on. But at the same time, representatives of the various crafts were drawn together in association committees and conferences with management, the net effect being to discredit separation along craft lines rather than to reinforce it. After working together, representatives often concluded that the local chapters' separation along craft lines was artificial and ought to be discouraged. In 1936, for example, when the Illinois plant association was being converted to an "independent" labor organization, it strongly rebuffed the efforts of a group of switchmen to secure separate chapter status. As the association leadership put it:

> Our organization has become what it is because we have intermingled fellow employees of the same company. We have gotten a much wider viewpoint of what working for the Telephone Company really means because of our intermingling. It is much better for a group of men who have different crafts, working under the same supervisors, to tie their interests still closer together by belonging to an organization which gives no thought to craft divisions.[73]

Indirectly, too, the operation of the Bell associations helped to further interdepartmental integration. Occasionally it produced a frustrated association representative who, in his conferences with management, felt the need for a broadly based group standing behind him. "It looked like so useless to try to do anything if you didn't have a combined unit to back you up when you were talking," recalled a former Southwestern Bell plant representative. "You had to band together into something to get someplace."[74] Of greater importance, the company unions helped bridge departmental divisions by reinforcing the ongoing managerial theme that all Bell workers held "a common responsibility," that they were a group apart, mutually involved in "the obligation and devotion to public service." This theme emphasized not the workers' departmental status but their position as Bell employees per se—employees who should be aware of "what the other department is doing" and whose representatives were customarily taken on tours of other departments and facilities to insure that this was the case.[75] It was only a short step for association representatives to apply this theme of interdependence to their own conception of Bell labor organization, and, as early as 1926, the Illinois plant association went so far as to drop the word *plant* from its name, take on the title Illinois Bell Telephone Employees' Association, and request permission to bring traffic, commercial, and accounting workers under its aegis. Although management forced the abandonment of this "one company–one association" project, it permitted the four Illinois Bell departmental associations to cooperate in relief projects during the depression.[76]

In addition, the associations provided instruments for gathering and airing information about working conditions, wages, and company structure and operations. The occasional dissemination of wage information in conferences, usually in response to requests from association representatives, helped to counter the company practice of keeping wage scales and individual raises secret. And in a number of instances information gathered about the company's structure and operations helped to open the eyes of workers to the defects of their own organizations. In 1929, for example, a group of PT&T plant workers seeking improved vacation benefits through their association were told that "uniform vacation treatment for the entire Company was necessary and could not be bargained on an area basis." Similarly, leaders of the Ohio Bell plant organization discovered in the early 1930s that in important decisions involving labor relations—such as whether their association was to be a dues-paying organization—Ohio Bell management looked to AT&T headquarters for direction. The Illinois plant association, after requesting changes in the pension plan through the 1920s and early 1930s, eventually found that the "Pension and Benefit Plan of the A.T.&T. System" was "not confined to, nor controlled by the Plant Department of the Illinois Bell Telephone Company"; hence a "great deal of time and effort" had been consumed "in an attempt to revise something over which they have no control."[77] The information thus gathered implied a need for a broad or even systemwide labor organization. Many workers recognized this implication—and then acted upon it when the prospects for Bell's unionization were brighter.

The associations also helped workers gain experience in organizational procedure and parleys with management. Since the proportion of representatives to workers was high, and since management preferred to "settle all questions possible" in lower-level conferences—numbering thirteen hundred to fourteen hundred every month in the Bell System—this kind of experience reached a large number of workers.[78] During the depression, particularly, the associations also provided a medium in which workers gained experience in organized protest activity. In Seattle in 1931, for example, the plant association called "a big protest meeting" to register workers' objections to the lack-of-work-days system, objections that were halted only by threats from management. In 1932, discussions between PT&T plant association members and their representatives became so critical of the company that "representatives were ordered to get permission from their supervisors before talking about conditions of employment or grievances with their constituency"—and order that prompted a large number of representatives to resign their positions. And in the years from 1931 to 1934 incumbent leaders of associations in Illinois, Ohio, and PT&T were replaced by new officers running on a platform of more forceful presentation of grievances. Finally, it seems noteworthy that many of the issues that top association leaders chose to press to the point of impasse with management—such issues as vacations, pensions, the lack-of-work-days system, and association dues and structure—were matters of interest to workers throughout their respective departments.[79] Presumably the leaders thus gained skill in a field that was vital to anyone aspiring to leadership in an industrial union movement, namely, the ability to perceive and articulate the concerns of the broadest possible group.

IN VIEW of the activities described above, it should be emphasized that the Bell associations in the pre–Wagner Act period were not beginning to resemble genuine unions. It is true that they sometimes served as vehicles of worker protest, and in 1933 and 1934 their structures underwent a number of reforms, initiated by management in apparent response to the National Industrial Recovery Act. During this period associations were established in several WE and accounting units where none had existed previously, and many of the older associations now passed strict bans against the membership of management employees, or signed formal agreements with management, or adopted more independent-sounding names—the League of Ohio Telephone Workers, for example. Often, too, these changes were approved by worker referendums.[80] Yet none of this altered the basically subservient relationship to management. There was no pretense of collective bargaining; on the contrary, presentations of grievances were still couched as complaints or requests. There was no threat of strike action, or of anything more serious than verbal protest. And there was no change in basic attitude, as illustrated by the fact that the Bell associations, with company encouragement, were among the many company unions to send letters to congressmen in early 1935 disapproving the Wagner bill then being considered.[81]

Still, the pre–Wagner Act picture yielded a few bright spots for anyone interested in building a genuine union movement. Telephone workers' experience with company unionism between 1920 and 1935 would prove helpful to them in combating the severe obstacles to unionization that remained after 1935. By intermingling workers from widely separated locations and by imparting a sense of the interdependency of workers in the various operating departments, the company union experience helped to bridge geographical and functional divisions. By giving telephone workers experience in organizational work and conferences with management, it helped to develop skills that could later be turned to trade union activity. And perhaps of greatest importance, it helped to lead workers toward a conception of labor organization that, once implemented, would partially offset the advantages Bell derived from its pervasive and centralized control of the telephone industry.

Telephone workers' longstanding concern over wages and working conditions (the latter being a matter of special concern in the pivotal traffic departments), along with resentment over Bell's depression measures, would also affect the course of subsequent unionization. Overshadowed as these feelings were by other considerations, they were not strong enough to generate independent union activity before 1935. Nor could they, by themselves, transform the associations into anything resembling trade unions. Yet once circumstances had changed and the Bell System's hold on its labor organizations had been loosened by the Wagner Act, these feelings could help spur a drive for worker independence. And along with the experience workers drew from company unionism, they would help push the post-1935 Bell labor organizations in the direction of legitimate and effective unionism.

Chapter 3

THE EMERGENCE OF

AN ORGANIZATIONAL FRAMEWORK,

1935-1939

WHILE THE PERIOD from mid-1935 to mid-1937 witnessed major breakthroughs for the American union movement as a whole—including the passage of the Wagner Act and its "validation" by the Supreme Court, the emergence of the CIO, and great strides toward unionizing hitherto impregnable corporate giants—the same cannot be said of the telephone industry. Its workers, to be sure, had drawn important lessons and skills from their company union experience, as well as developing a concern about their treatment at Bell's hands during the depression (and before), all of which would eventually prove helpful to unionization. But these, by themselves, were not enough to bring forth a genuine union movement, especially in the face of the serious obstacles that remained.

Foremost was Bell's retention of much of the antiunion leverage it had long enjoyed. In addition, because genuine union activity of any sort had been smothered in Bell since 1920, the workers had done little of the preliminary agitational and organizational work needed to launch a coherent union movement. Nor could they depend on help from any outside group. The unions and organizing committees that were becoming so active elsewhere during 1935–1937 still had no taste for risking organizational campaigns in Bell.

Given these conditions, it was not the Bell workers but rather the Bell managers who were able to frame the more coherent response to the altered circumstances of 1935–1937. Some sort of management response was clearly necessary: Section 8(2) of the Wagner Act, enacted in July 1935, declared it an unfair labor practice for employers to "dominate or interfere with the formation of any labor organization or contribute financial or other support to it." It was no longer legal, in other words, for the Bell System to maintain its company unions.

Although some Bell companies moved toward desultory compliance with section 8(2) in 1935, the bulk of the system's response came in the spring of 1937, when the Supreme Court upheld the constitutionality of the Wagner Act. In essence, Bell's response was to transform its company unions into formally independent labor organizations—organizations that could claim to be genuine unions within the letter of the law but that actually remained, at first, toothless organizations bearing strong similarities to their predecessors. The main phases of this transformation were, first, to drop all formal ties with the company unions, thus shedding overt signs of employer domination; second, to encourage the then allegedly independent labor organizations to reconstitute and rename themselves; and third, to meet with the reconstituted organizations and sign recognition agreements with them.

In each phase the guiding hand of the company was evident. Illinois Bell, for example, ended formal financial aid; yet before the new plant organization got started, Bell provided it with a lump sum. Similarly, Southern Bell continued to make company meeting rooms and office equipment available free of charge and to arrange meetings with the new organization's officers at such times as were "most convenient and economical."[1] In 1937, when Western Electric manufacturing ended its formal support, the successor organization at Kearny, New Jersey, was allowed to rent an office on company premises for fifty dollars a month, use the company's telephone facilities free of charge, and at one point to solicit worker donations for the successor organization on company time.[2]

Sometimes passively and sometimes actively, the companies, which were supposed to remain strictly neutral, helped their labor organizations reconstitute themselves and sign up members. For example, ordinarily the companies did not post notice of their indifference to whether or not workers joined the "new" organizations, an omission that the National Labor Relations Board (which was responsible for enforcing the Wagner Act) criticized in subsequent cases.[3] Without such notice, workers were likely to assume that they would win favor with their employer by joining these organizations, which were in most cases clearly the successors to the old associations and officered by former association leaders. The leaders of the new organizations, moreover, were actively aided through grants of company time or leaves of absence. In Southwestern Bell an organizer for the new Southwestern Telephone Workers Union reported, "We did actually get lots of help. . . . I was granted time off to go and visit some of the boys in the outlying towns to tell them what we were doing."[4]

Under these circumstances, organizing campaigns succeeded spectacularly. Between May and November 1937, the Southwestern Telephone Workers Union increased its membership from eighty to ten thousand! And similar success stories could be told of other groups. Across the country, the 180-odd Bell labor organizations signed up a majority of the union-eligible workers within their respective units, and when they presented proof of majority status, recognition agreements came quickly.[5]

Although the effect was to remove outright company control, there can be no doubt that the new organizations' birth and initial activities were performed according to what amounted to a Bell System script. In four of the five decisions that the NLRB later rendered in Bell company-domination cases, the evidence justified findings of company domination after July 1937. In the fifth case, involving charges against the Bell company and the traffic organization in Wisconsin, there was evidence of domination before July 1937, but not after. As one of the early Bell labor organization presidents put it, in the first stages "they [the organizations] were all company dominated. There was no question about that at all—including the union that I headed."[6]

Domination, of course, could not be admitted by the Bell companies. Nor could they admit that they were attempting to prop up a weak and divided union structure in order to forestall the possibility of strong unions moving in. Yet this seems to have been the intention, and it was so assessed by an early Southwestern Telephone Workers Union official. "It is my honest belief," he declared, "that in accordance with A.T.&T. policy the Southwestern Company has consistently attempted to have a labor union strong enough to be safe from challenge by other labor organizations but too weak to stand against the company."[7]

Local-level Bell managers also tended to link the formation of the successor organizations to this same goal. The thrust of their comments to workers was, "You're superior people . . . so don't get mixed up with all that rough, tough element in labor unions. Have your own union." Or, "I think what you fellows ought to do is go out and organize a union of your own. We have always got along well together in the old employees' associations. . . . Certainly you don't want to become a part of the AF of L, or *certainly* not the CIO."[8]

In this respect, the Bell managers were acting like their counterparts in other traditionally antiunion companies. As a high NLRB official explained, the new labor law, together with the "assertiveness of the labor movement . . . and the general public sentiment that workers should have a right to organize," had accentuated the efforts of many employers to create nominally independent but friendly labor organizations.[9]

But if such was indeed the thinking of Bell management during 1935–1937, neither its hopes nor its fears were borne out subsequently. In the decade following 1937, the Bell labor organizations themselves became a much more serious threat to the status quo in Bell's labor relations than outside unions; almost immediately, many of them took steps to form the loosely knit National Federation of Telephone Workers, and, by the end of 1947, this organization and its affiliates had evolved into a vigorous, industrially structured national union. Meanwhile, large-scale organization by outside unions seems not to have been a real alternative.

During this period outside unions made only feeble attempts at organizing telephone workers. The American Communications Association, which held a CIO jurisdictional grant in telephone operating companies, did not turn its attention to Bell until it had completed its campaign in Western Union telegraph in 1942. During the remainder of World War II, its sole success was with the Order of Repeatermen and Toll Testboardmen—a small, subdepartmental group of plant craftsmen in PT&T—and not until 1946 did it gain representation rights in a department-wide unit. Similarly, IBEW efforts up to 1941 could be described not as a "mass drive" but as taking "little pecks and pieces, here and there, now and then."[10] Only in Wisconsin did IBEW prewar efforts in Bell have any success, and even there the accomplishment was limited to the splitting off of four IBEW traffic locals, leaving operators in the Wisconsin company's ninety-five other central offices to the traffic association's successor. The IBEW's main interest seemed to be in gaining for non-Bell electricians the work of pulling Bell telephone wires and cables through conduits on construction projects. This was an effort not calculated to win favor for the IBEW among Bell plant workers, and one that bespoke a low priority for its telephone organizing goals. Not until 1947 did the IBEW gain representation rights in a department-wide Bell unit. Nor were the UE and the International Association of Machinists any more successful. They started minor organizing campaigns in WE manufacturing plants during World War II, but had no success until after the war.[11]

Nor can the presence of the Bell labor organizations themselves explain the reluctance of outside unions to venture large-scale organizing attempts in Bell, at least in the years before World War II. Company domination suits before the NLRB offered a ready means by which outside unions could attack each Bell labor organization, with some prospect of destroying it through an NLRB decision ordering disbandment. Yet outside unions were not interested enough to employ this weapon vigorously, particularly in the early post–Wagner Act years, when such suits stood the best chance of success. Of the five NLRB decisions in such cases, four were rendered after 1940, and three of these four came after 1943, when most of the Bell labor organizations could truthfully deny the company domination charge. In a 1947 decision involving the WE Kearny plant, for example, the NLRB could not very well disband on grounds of company domination an organization that had just conducted a sixty-five day strike, even though the organization (like those charged in the other cases) had admittedly been company dominated early in its career.[12] Largely as a result of indifference and delay on the part of outside unions, only two of the Bell labor organizations were disbanded by the NLRB (in Southern Bell in 1943 and in the WE Point Breeze manufacturing plant in 1944), and in neither of these cases did outside unions follow up with a successful organizing campaign.

FOR THE MOST PART, then, the field was left open to the Bell labor organizations. These were the vehicles through which genuine unionism came to the industry. Yet progress came slowly, and during their first few years of operation, the organizations continued to resemble their company union predecessors more than their AFL and CIO union contemporaries. Progress, such as it was, consisted chiefly of moves to bridge separations between worker groups, the artificial nature of which the company union experience had helped expose.

These moves were of various kinds. In the PT&T plant organization in Washington, for example, separation of local groups along craft lines gave way to a system of intercraft locals;[13] in New York City, plant unions in the various boroughs formed the United Telephone Organizations; and in Illinois, groups from all four departments formed the loosely knit Illinois Federation of Telephone Workers. Employees of the WE installation units across the country managed to combine in a single organization, as did workers in the twenty-nine WE distributing houses. And while workers in the various WE manufacturing plants remained in separate organizations, leaders from these groups joined the WE installation and WE distributing house leaders in a National Committee of Communication Equipment Workers. The greatest degree of amalgamation took place in Ohio Bell, where plant, traffic, and commercial groups combined in a single union in 1937, and in Southwestern Bell, Southern Bell, and Long Lines, where, from the start, single organizations embraced workers in all four departments. It was the workers who brought about the Ohio Bell amalgamation, and it was apparently worker initiatives, too, that caused the Southwestern Telephone Workers Union to be set up as a company-wide organization, although here the issue is clouded by the participation of an attorney who may have consulted Southwestern Bell management. In Southern Bell and Long Lines, workers were merely following the somewhat unusual multidepartment structural lines of the company union predecessors. In these four organizations, as in those that undertook other forms of amalgamation, management seemed to have made no concerted attempt to block the amalgamation process.[14]

Such amalgamations, it should be noted, did not overcome all difficulties arising from geographical and functional dispersion. None of the mergers combined workers from more than one Bell company in a single organization. In each of the amalgamated unions, workers from more than one department were rarely brought together in "mixed" locals; here, as elsewhere, workers in a given area for the most part remained segregated in plant, traffic, commercial, and accounting locals. In some cases the amalgamations crumbled. But by the end of 1939 the 180 initial organizations had been reduced to fewer than 90, and after 1939 the process would continue.[15]

Of greater long-term significance were the steps that the Bell organizations took toward forming a national confederation of telephone unions. Here, too, the lessons learned from the company union experience proved important. In Illinois, for example, the plant association's inability to alter the pension plan made it "obvious that a national organization of employees was necessary to cope with this and other system-wide problems."[16] Elsewhere the same conclusion was being drawn.[17] Beyond this consideration was a desire to "maintain a solid front against rival labor organizations," to coordinate information on such matters as NLRB company-domination suits, and to cooperate in influencing federal legislation affecting telephone workers.[18]

Years later some CWA leaders were to suggest that Bell management may have instigated the early meetings that led to the formation of the national organization,[19] but this seems highly unlikely. The unions at the time had great difficulty obtaining one another's mailing addresses,[20] and once these were obtained the flow of correspondence—mostly inquiries about dues, organizational structure, contracts, and working conditions—was of a kind that suggested that meetings to exchange information might well be the logical next step.[21] Moreover, the lead in contacting other unions and covering incidental expenses of the first meeting was taken by the Ohio organization, a group that was hardly a tool of Bell management. On the contrary, the Ohio union's secretary-treasurer, Ken Blount, was almost unique among early telephone union leaders in speaking favorably of the CIO. The Ohio president, Tom Twigg, favored a national union structured along the lines of the Brotherhood of Railway Trainmen; he had learned from his experience as a company union officer that in important labor matters Ohio Bell management was "definitely instructed that under no circumstances are they to act without the approval of New York" (where AT&T headquarters was located). This, he argued, necessitated a national organization that could speak with authority to AT&T.[22]

It is true, however, that delegates to the first meetings had no trouble in securing company leaves of absence to attend, even though there were seldom contractual provisions for such absences. Management, it seems, did not regard the early meetings as a threat. Nor is this surprising when one considers the delegates, most of whom were disinclined toward a strong national organization and largely concerned with how best to avoid incursions by the NLRB, the AFL, and the CIO. As Blount was to complain after an early meeting, "Too many of the [delegates] are holdovers from old plans of representation," and "in most cases these still carry the halo of old management dominated by pink tea parties."[23]

The first meeting took place in St. Louis on December 16 and 17, 1937. Of the seventeen unions that took part, most were traffic or plant organizations. But also included were such amalgamated groups as Ohio, Southwestern, and Long Lines, as well as one commercial and two accounting organizations. The combined membership of the participating unions was 80,027, which was slightly less than one-third of Bell's union-eligible employment in 1937.[24]

Twigg was named chairman, and he soon outlined the arguments for a strong national federation. The twenty-nine delegates then exchanged information about their respective areas, a discussion unsettling to some. One Southwestern Union officer, for example, concluded that his organization had been living in a "fool's paradise" of union-management amiability. He would, he said, "go back to his own people far less satisfied" than when he had left.[25]

Rather quickly the delegates broke into a three-sided wrangle over what form a future national organization might take, if indeed there were to be any national organization. The Ohio leaders and Jerome Coughlin of the New England plant organization (still called the International Brotherhood of Telephone Workers), argued for a federation that would be a means of "united action relative to legislation, pensions, working conditions, etc." and would have national officers "in whom some genuine authority would be vested." The Northwestern and Pennsylvania plant organizations, in contrast, wanted either no national organization at all, or one that would serve merely as a clearinghouse for information. In the middle was a large group that believed that a federation coordinating information and speaking for them on pensions and legislative matters might be desirable, but that the autonomy of the affiliated unions must be paramount.[26]

By the second day the meeting was in deadlock, and although a committee was appointed to draw up a set of constitutional principles for a national organization, its report was rejected by the delegates. As the meeting approached adjournment, Twigg spoke privately to Paul Griffith of Illinois plant, one of the "middle" organizations, pressing on him the idea that he, Griffith, "was the one person who might possibly be able to hold these factions together until some kind of trust developed." Griffith subsequently took the chair and invited the delegates to meet in Chicago six months hence. Most accepted, whereupon Griffith was elected to chair the next meeting.[27]

The Chicago meeting of June 1938 was much larger. Sixty-seven delegates arrived from thirty organizations, representing a total of 137,231 members, with much of the increment coming from traffic and WE organizations that had to justify their presence and participation. Although saying little at the general sessions, the traffic delegates took care to remind "committee members that in any dues structure or expenses [of a national organization], the majority of the payments would come from the women—and they shouldn't forget that little item."[28] The WE groups, who had not been invited to the St. Louis meeting and were regarded by some as non–telephone workers, had to remind the delegates that they too worked in operating company offices, installing WE equipment, or in plants producing or repairing the industry's equipment. Where, they wanted to know, did the other delegates "think these telephones come from, if they [the WE workers] were not part of the telephone industry?"[29]

The three-sided disagreement over the form of the national organization resumed, although it soon became clear that the determination to form some kind of national organization had grown during the six-month interval. As Griffith later analyzed it, the moderate and conservative organizations were now more confident of their ability to control matters; their leaders had become convinced "that they were decidedly in the majority, that there were not enough Twiggs and Coughlins to shove anything down their throats." With these groups taking a much more active part, the people who preferred a strong national organization were now willing to modify their position, even though their numbers had grown slightly by the addition of several new WE delegates. This "strong" group was subdued by the realization that "they were strictly in the minority, and further, that if they persisted, there just wouldn't be any national organization at all."[30]

Consequently, much of the discussion moved into new and constructive paths. A Southwestern Union delegate, for example, pointed out that the NLRB looked with suspicion on labor organizations that confined their membership to workers in single companies; already, he noted, his union had begun to take in groups from non-Bell telephone companies in the southwestern territory. Thereafter, the projected names for the national organization made it clear that this was to be a *telephone* organization and not just a *Bell* organization. In addition, the delegates unanimously passed a motion by Joseph A. Beirne, of the WE distributing house workers, that "a national organization be formed" sometime in the near future. By the time the delegates adjourned, they had a tentative middle-of-the-road constitution to take home for the approval of their organizations.[31]

At New Orleans in November 1938, a slightly larger assembly modified the still tentative constitution and chose the name National Federation of Telephone Workers. The name in some ways contradicted the sense of the constitution that was now taking shape. For if the constitution envisioned an organization that would be national in scope, it also envisioned a loose confederation rather than a true federation, and constituent parts that were to be telephone unions rather than telephone workers. Before adjourning, the New Orleans assembly also formulated a questionnaire to be used in determining a union's eligibility for NFTW affiliation. Among other things, the questionnaire enabled the applying union to check its formal operations against the NLRB's emerging standards for legitimate unionism and alter its operations if necessary.[32]

The only vocal opposition to the projected organization came from Lloyd Weil, of the all-department Southern Bell organization. Probably with management encouragement, Weil argued against the formation of a national organization that would do more than meet annually and exchange information. His organization subsequently decided not to join the NFTW, and in 1943 it was disbanded after the NLRB found it to be company dominated.[33] Among the former advocates of a strong national organization, the WE unions joined the NFTW, as did the Ohio union after a period of indecision; the New England plant union did not join.[34]

At the next meeting, in New York in June 1939, the delegates put finishing touches on the constitution and brought the NFTW into formal existence, with an affiliation of twenty-seven unions totaling 92,130 members. This number represented only 37 percent of union-eligible Bell workers, a proportion that did not rise significantly until 1945. Yet the confederation that emerged in New York was in some respects truly an industry-wide organization. All four major operating-company departments were represented in the NFTW, as were Bell groups from the major nonoperating units: WE installation, WE manufacturing, WE distributing houses, and Long Lines. Even a few non-Bell telephone groups were represented, by virtue of their membership in the Southwestern Telephone Workers Union, an NFTW affiliate. In every section of the country, some telephone workers were now connected with a central labor organization, indicating clearly that problems arising from geographical dispersion had in some measure been overcome.[35]

The NFTW, moreover, was designed to be more than a paper organization. The constitution and rules adopted in New York provided for considerable personal contact among member union leaders from across the country. Aside from the annual NFTW assemblies—gatherings that would usually number between seventy-five and two hundred leaders—there were to be more frequent meetings centered in the four national regions (East, Central, West, and South), attended by member union leaders from those regions, as well as meetings of the seven-member NFTW executive board (expanded to nine members in 1940), which were to be held at least twice annually. And while the group that had met in New York assigned to the NFTW only a few specific tasks, mostly of an investigative nature, this group also defined the organization's general responsibilities in terms broad enough to allow the assumption of other, more important tasks in the future. The NFTW's responsibilities were to act as a clearinghouse for information; provide "a means for united action in relation to legislation"; serve as a "means of common counsel"; and draw the various telephone unions into "relations of mutual assistance and cooperation," both in combating outside unions and in dealing with AT&T on such matters as pensions.[36]

Yet in strong measure, too, the NFTW in 1939 reflected a continuing insularity among its affiliates, a mutual suspicion and unwillingness to unite in anything but limited kinds of action. The emphasis in the early NFTW was on the autonomy of the affiliates, as reflected in constitutional stipulations that member organizations must "remain forever autonomous and be free from interference in the conduct of their internal affairs," and further that this principle must "remain forever inviolate" and not be subject to constitutional amendment. Since the bargaining that each affiliate carried on with its respective company was considered an "internal affair," this "autonomy clause" restricted unified bargaining through the NFTW's agency. While an affiliated union might delegate certain bargaining responsibilities to the NFTW (pensions, for example), this was entirely a matter of the affiliate's own choice, and, in any event, the results had to be ratified by the individual affiliate in order to become binding upon it.[37]

Weakening the NFTW further was the power of member unions to withdraw from the organization on any pretext. Although the constitution provided that statements of withdrawal had to bear the signatures of a majority of the withdrawing union's executive board, there was no way of enforcing even this formality. Nor could new members be recruited outside the structure of the constituent groups. Individual telephone workers did not hold membership in the NFTW and were connected with it only through the affiliation of their particular union. NFTW action was restricted still further by its miserly budget. Member unions' dues were first set at ten cents per capita annually, amounting to a 1939 budget of ten thousand dollars, which allowed no full-time officers and provided the NFTW president with a salary of two hundred dollars per year.[38]

Aside from these severe restrictions on concerted action, the governmental procedures of the NFTW were not out of the ordinary. Supreme authority in matters not affecting the member unions' autonomy was lodged in the NFTW annual assembly, in which each member union possessed at least one vote, plus an additional vote for each two thousand members above the first two thousand (until 1942, when straight per capita voting was adopted). Between assemblies, authority rested with the executive board (elected annually by the full assembly), all of whose members had to have worked at least five years in the telephone industry, and all of whom had to come from different member unions. On this board, four of those chosen were to be regional members— each representing one of the national regions, each expected to concentrate on regional problems, and each selected, in practice, by a caucus of delegates from his or her region. Once the full executive board was chosen, the assembly elected from this group an NFTW president, secretary-treasurer, and vice-president (whose position was largely honorary, except in the president's absence).[39]

Paul Griffith, who had chaired each meeting since St. Louis, was elected president at the 1939 New York Assembly, and Bert Horth, of the Wisconsin plant union, was elected secretary-treasurer. Both these men were to hold their positions until 1943. Stanley Burke, of Long Lines, was elected vice-president in 1939, but he was replaced in 1940 by Joe Beirne, who was to serve as vice-president until his elevation to the presidency in 1943. Until 1941 the physical facilities of the NFTW were to consist of Griffith's desk in a corner of the Illinois plant union office in Chicago, plus Horth's small office adjoining the Wisconsin plant union headquarters in Milwaukee.[40]

THE ESTABLISHMENT of the NFTW in 1939 marked the completion of a two-level organizational framework around which telephone workers built their union movement until 1947. At the base stood the Bell labor unions—organizations that were the successors of company unions and that had been the workers' creation only in a very limited sense. Workers, to be sure, had helped put these organizations together and given them a majority acceptance that allowed them to become legally sanctioned bargaining agents. But it was the Bell managers, acting in response to the Wagner Act, who had guided these worker actions. Bell had provided a congenial atmosphere and informal financial support, and the organizations had been formed at Bell's bidding and largely according to its specifications. Even where worker initiatives had produced amalgamations between these organizations (and most, if not all, of the amalgamations were the outcome of worker initiatives), the results had not strayed from what seems to have been Bell management's fundamental design. The organizations remained numerous, generally small, separated along company lines, and usually separated along departmental lines as well.

Above these organizations, linking many of them together with bonds that were loose but capable of being tightened, stood the NFTW, an organization that *was* of the workers' own making. Bell management had tolerated, but in all likelihood had not instigated, the early meetings leading to the NFTW's formation; Lloyd Weil's behavior at the November 1938 New Orleans meeting may well have arisen from a management desire to abort the national organization in its projected form. In any case, the member union leaders had acted on their own in founding the NFTW, influenced by the lessons concerning the Bell System that workers had drawn from their company union experience; by the founders' interest in resisting incursions by the AFL, CIO, and NLRB; by the desire to influence national legislation affecting telephone workers; and, in the case of Tom Twigg and perhaps a few of the other advocates of a strong national organization, by the example of nontelephone national unions. The result, by the end of 1939, was that telephone workers possessed in the NFTW a means of at least limited cooperation on an industry-wide basis—something that had not been included in, and that in fact ran contrary to, the lines of organization Bell management had drawn up for telephone labor during 1935–1937.

In accepting and preserving the employer-inspired successor organizations and, at the same time, linking many of them together in an industry-wide confederation, telephone workers embarked on a path quite different from those taken by workers in other industries. Elsewhere, workers were either not confronted with employer-inspired company union successors, or, in the several industries where employers did launch such organizations in the wake of the Wagner Act, the workers responded differently. Employees of large firms in the steel, auto, rubber, and electrical products industries, for example, rejected employer-inspired organizations in favor of CIO national unions. By way of explanation, it need only be noted that these industries did not contain the many obstacles to unionization in general, and to the entry of outside unions in particular, that existed in the telephone industry. Employees of large chemical and oil-refining firms, in contrast, largely accepted the employer-sponsored organizations, but here the linking together of such organizations was long delayed and never approached confederation on an industry-wide scale; the workers failed, in other words, to take the first steps down a path that would eventually lead telephone workers to the formation of a national union. Although any thorough explanation of this failure must await the results of detailed investigation, comparisons with the history of telephone unionization may prove useful in arriving at such an explanation. It seems possible, for example, in view of the important part the company union experience played in telephone workers' subsequent decision to confederate, that part of the explanation may lie in the nature of chemical and oil workers' company union experience.[41]

In several respects, then, the 1935–1939 period marked a turning point in the history of telephone labor organization. The Bell company unions had been transformed into formally independent labor organizations, many of which had joined together in an industry-wide confederation. In the act of forming the NFTW, telephone workers had departed not only from the organizational lines Bell management had mapped out for them, but also from the paths of organizational development taken by workers in all other industries. As significant as these changes were, however, and notwithstanding the many efforts to paint the Bell labor organizations as legitimate unions, the events of 1935 to 1939 did not amount to unionization of the Bell System in any full sense of the term. By the end of 1939 management had suffered only minor and ineffective challenges to its control of wages and working conditions. The workers' allegiance to the Bell labor organizations and the NFTW had not been tested in an atmosphere of union-management opposition, nor was there any solid indication that their allegiance would survive such a test. And many of the Bell labor organizations were still in the process of establishing such elementary devices as steward systems and regular membership meetings. The telephone workers, in short, had barely begun the day-to-day tasks of building a genuine union movement.

Most of these tasks lay in and near the telephone workplace, among the mass of telephone workers, meaning, in effect, that those who wished to build a union movement around the existing organizational framework had to concentrate their initial efforts on the Bell labor organizations. The NFTW in 1939 neither maintained nor sought any significant presence in the telephone workplace; nor, for that matter, did any other national labor organization. Only the Bell labor organizations held forth any real prospect of touching the daily lives of the mass of workers, through their exclusive status as the workers' bargaining agents, through their claims on the workers' membership, and through their mere presence on the local scene.

Any basic change in the NFTW, moreover, could only spring from changes in the character of the Bell labor organizations. The NFTW remained the creature of these organizations, barred from acting independently by stringent constitutional and financial limitations, and subject to the direction of its affiliates' representatives on the NFTW executive board and in the national assembly. Since the development of the telephone union movement thus hinged on events within the Bell labor organizations, it is to these organizations that we must now return.

Chapter 4

DEVELOPMENT OF THE BELL LABOR

ORGANIZATIONS, 1938–1941

BY THE END OF 1937 several of the obstacles to the unionization of telephone workers had shrunk considerably. The depression had diminished Bell's reputation as a benevolent employer. The Wagner Act had shorn it of such weapons as threatening dismissal for union activity. And while outside unions still refrained from organizational campaigns, the company union successors were beginning to free themselves of company control and to bridge some of the geographical and functional divisions between worker groups. This was apparent both in the formation of the NFTW and in the amalgamation of labor organizations within Bell companies.

Yet by any standard of comparison with legitimate AFL or CIO unions, these Bell labor unions of the late 1930s were languid and toothless organizations. In some unions, meetings were held only four times a year, and in a few cases only "when and if deemed necessary." Dues in most cases were still less than fifty cents per month, while strike funds were unheard of.[1] And in bargaining sessions with management, the influence of union representatives was at first almost negligible. Much of the text of early union-management contracts was lifted directly from company practice manuals, and since most of any contract "could be loosely interpreted, with the stronger party coming out the winner," a worker with a specific grievance was often afforded little protection. When a contract expired, moreover, "it was a matter of the company coming out with new rules and regulations," which "would be incorporated into the next contract."[2] In Southwestern Bell, the bargaining sessions for the various departments and geographical areas reminded one union representative of "a harvesting combine" in which "each row of grain was cut at the same time," "all ended up in the same sack," and union representatives did not know "where the hell we were going until all contracts were signed."[3] How far the sessions were from genuine bargaining is revealed in an incident witnessed by another Southwestern Union representative. After reaching an impasse with management on plant department wages, one of the more "enthusiastic" union representatives finally insisted:

> "Well, by God, we'll get this or else!"
> The plant superintendent sat back for a little while and he said, "What do you mean by 'else'?"
> In the meantime, this old boy got to thinking, "Well, I can't strike." He says, "Well, or else we'll just keep on working for what we're working for!"[4]

Even as some of the obstacles to genuine unionization shrank, other obstacles seemed to increase. For one thing, the layoffs and reduced hirings and resignations of the depression had pushed the length of employment of the average Bell worker (excluding WE workers) up to thirteen years by 1939, compared to five-and-a-half years in 1928 and ten years in 1933.[5] This helped to spark the interest in pensions that contributed to the NFTW's formation and meant that the telephone unions of this period were not troubled by employee turnover. But longer length of employment also weakened the position of the unions in that workers were more fully exposed to Bell indoctrination; it bred caution by multiplying the penalties a worker might suffer from incurring management's displeasure. Thirteen years of Bell service entailed an accumulation of pension rights and accessibility to supervisory positions, a long climb up the wage progression schedules, and the building up of skills that would be difficult to market outside Bell. Understandably, the long-term Bell workers of the late 1930s were loath to risk all this by engaging in militant union activity.

In addition, the fears and dependencies brought on by the depression had not worn off; they were, in fact, aggravated by the recession of 1937–1938 and by Bell's continuing replacement of operator-connected local service with dial telephones. Although Bell in normal times could usually plan these dial conversions to avoid laying off operators, during the 1930s the process did involve layoffs and, more to the point here, the fear of layoffs. In explaining the lack of militancy among operators in Manhattan, an early traffic union leader remarked that "those girls are afraid of their own shadows." The company had laid off some "1,000 girls there in a period of two or three months when the dial went into about fifteen offices there, and nobody knew where the axe was going to hit next." "Suppose it was you," the traffic leader reasoned. "You would soft-pedal your remarks and a lot of things, if you needed your job and were afraid there were spotters or stooges there who were going to turn your name in."[6]

Such forces might have had less effect if telephone workers had been pressed toward militancy by raw economic necessity. But this was not so. The advanced position of most workers on the wage schedules, when combined with the maintenance of the basic wage rate through the depression years, meant that the telephone work force as a whole was a relatively well-paid group during this period. In 1939 average telephone-employee weekly earnings of $29.38 (excluding WE) ranked 22d on a standard list of 123 industry groups compiled by the Bureau of Labor Statistics, a relative position that was probably better than at any time before or since. Further, with the final dismantling of the lack-of-work-days system at the end of 1937, the standard Bell work week was set at five days rather than the predepression six.[7]

In any event, such fears, dependencies, and economic circumstances seemed to spawn attitudes that hindered the development of the new Bell unions. Those who would strengthen the new organizations found that it was hard to "wean people away from the company and the paternalistic environment that they'd had for so many years." Many still argued that "the telephone company's been here a lot longer than you fellows," or that "I worked at least three or four days a week most of the time during the depths of the depression. Union didn't pay me; the company did."[8]

Attitudes toward strikes ranged from extreme apprehension among some union members and leaders to outright rejection of the idea by many others. At the 1939 NFTW meeting in New York, there was a consensus among the delegates "that the word 'strike' is repulsive to most of our people, and that the entire subject will have to be handled very cautiously."[9] At a meeting of plant union leaders held later in the same year, some felt that strikes might be a weapon of "last resort" or that strike clauses in union constitutions might make members "more labor minded," but this was not the majority sentiment. Most held that strikes were "unnecessary."[10] In other meetings union leaders voiced fears that "we would place ourselves in a very dangerous light if we ever attempted to strike." At times, the very use of the term was avoided by substituting such euphemisms as "withdrawing your economic power."[11] Only in a few of the WE groups were strike votes conducted before 1941; in 1941, a year in which more American workers went on strike than in any previous year except 1919, there were no telephone walkouts. Nowhere in the industry did actual strikes take place until the summer of 1942.[12]

If such old attitudes persisted, however, there was also a perceptible growth in new ones, a growth that seemed to move at a pace barely "beyond the crawling stage,"[13] yet one that was gradually altering the vigor and outlook of most of the telephone unions. By 1941 activists and leaders in most of the unions were finding lines of argument and action that could gradually change the older attitudes. The result was a slow shift of loyalty from the company toward the unions.

One attack on the idea of company benevolence took the form of reminding workers that Bell had preferred to maintain its nine-dollar dividend while forcing the workers to bear the brunt of the depression's burdens. The lack-of-work-days system, as noted previously, had provoked a good deal of ill feeling, so much so that one high management official later reflected that more layoffs might have been a preferable alternative—at least "those remaining would have been happy. The way it was, with almost everyone taking LW [lack-of-work] days, *nobody* was happy."[14] The bolder unionists now appealed to memories of this experience and declaimed their view of how it had really distributed the burdens of economic contraction. In the presence of other workers, for example, they would declare to supervisors that part-timing "'didn't cost the company a penny, and you had the advantage of keeping a trained force at your fingertips [until] business picked up. . .

I don't want you to ever tell me again you helped us during the depression. You didn't. We helped each other.'"[15] Meanwhile, those workers who had been laid off and were now finally reemployed hardly needed to be reminded of the company's lack of benevolence. Indeed, among this group it was sometimes resentment of depression layoffs that led to more vigorous union activity.[16]

Such attacks reinforced an already present concern that management not be allowed to repeat the offenses against employee security that it had committed during the depression. The layoff victims were joined in this concern by those who had merely witnessed the layoffs. Here telephone workers partook of a broad, multi-industry movement among unionists who had weathered the worst of the depression and were now clinging to their jobs. Their demand was for job security in general and seniority rights in particular. Union bargaining committees became a means of expressing telephone workers' concern, and while these committees were at first too weak to achieve anything that lay beyond the narrow limits of company acquiescence, they were able to gather some of the credit for improvements in security. As early as 1938 the Ohio union secured management's oral assurance that seniority would be the governing consideration in retaining workers whenever layoffs became necessary, and similar assurances became common throughout the Bell System by the end of 1941. By that time, the drive for stronger forms of worker security was well under way. It would remain a major spur to telephone unionism into the mid-1940s.[17]

The attitude of workers toward the unions was also changed by the role that these organizations played in conflicts with the IBEW over who was to pull Bell wires and cables through conduits on construction projects. The IBEW had contended since 1913 that this work belonged to IBEW electricians employed by contractors: "Electrical work for electrical workers." To support this view, it had sometimes pressured all parties concerned in a given construction project by establishing picket lines that other AFL building trades unions would honor. And even though Bell had traditionally preferred to have its own plant department workers handle these jobs, it had, in fact, abandoned the work to IBEW locals in several cities and left the issue unresolved in most of the country. After 1938 the issue was exacerbated by the growing strength of the IBEW, the increasing number of construction starts, and the presence of the new telephone unions, which now voiced the plant workers' desire to retain all "telephone work for telephone people."[18]

In this fight against the IBEW, the telephone unions did not have much management support, but at least they had management's acquiescence. And once the unions entered the fray, plant workers found them to be effective—more so, in fact, than the unions' dealings with the company over wages and working conditions. The unions became a means of marshaling plant workers during confrontations at construction sites. (Even in nonpicketing situations, electricians and other AFL building tradesmen sometimes sought to intimidate plant workers who were performing the disputed work.) They pressed Bell to support the plant workers' claims, occasionally going so far as to threaten that unless plant workers retained the disputed work at a given construction site, they would refuse to perform the remaining, undisputed telephone installation work. And as the American economy moved toward a war footing, they offered legal and other expert help in presenting plant workers' claims before the government boards that held increasing purview over such disputes.[19]

Through such actions, the telephone unions attracted the interest and often the loyalty of plant workers who were concerned about threats to their jobs; union leaders came to regard these actions as a major factor in changing attitudes and stimulating union growth. As the president of the amalgamated Cincinnati and Suburban telephone union put it, action in a wire-pulling dispute at a large Wright airplane plant near Cincinnati "formed a rallying point, just *exactly* what we needed to generate membership interest. . . . If you looked for the single thing that caused this group to rally and get strong, that was it."[20]

Interaction between the unions and the NLRB also had the effect of changing union practices and altering worker attitudes toward them. To avoid disbandment and keep their "skirts clean with the NLRB," unionists set out not only to free themselves of "any involvement with the company,"[21] but also to "eliminate the slightest opportunity for criticism from any source with reference to Management control or support."[22] And while it is true that many of these measures were cosmetic, taking the form, for example, of changing nomenclature and formal structures in ways that a 1939 NLRB decision criticizing the Wisconsin union rendered advisable, other changes were involved as well. The NLRB-induced changes in structure sometimes became the occasion for union amalgamations, or for decisions to join the NFTW. In addition, efforts to organize outside Bell were in part a reaction to the NLRB. For example, the Southwestern Union's organization of non-Bell telephone groups was initially undertaken with an eye to the impression it would make on the NLRB, but once that union became involved in such "external" organizing, it found it attractive enough to continue in its own right. Similar considerations probably entered into the external organizing programs of at least one other union. Accompanying all this, too, were union leaders' efforts to convince the rank and file that their unions were in fact independent and in compliance with the Wagner Act, an educational exercise that undoubtedly expanded workers' awareness of the new federal law and the protection it afforded workers engaged in genuine union activity. Finally, the desire to live up to this image of independence was partially responsible for the telephone unions' decision not to subscribe to the no-strike pledges that many other unions were signing in 1941 and 1942.[23]

Also helpful in changing workers' attitudes toward the unions was use of the rudimentary grievance procedures of the period. Because of their legal standing as the workers' bargaining agents, the unions offered possible, if often unlikely, means of redressing individual workers' grievances concerning such matters as work assignments, pension computations, demotions or denied promotions, discharges, and—of special concern in traffic—shift assignments and the unremittingly close observation and supervision. Inevitably, workers used the unions for this purpose, and once involved, organizations like the Ohio union were soon reporting an "ever increasing number of cases" where the union had to "step in and correct petty grievances . . . to see that justice is done."[24] As use of the grievance procedures grew, worker attitudes began to change. Although the victories arose less from union strength than from management's willingness to take corrective action,[25] nevertheless workers were impressed with the value of the unions. In northern California traffic they "made a hit with the people," and in Indiana traffic they served to "show people that you could resist, you know; you could do something."[26]

Nor did lost grievance cases have a wholly injurious effect. On the contrary, they sometimes generated rank-and-file movements aimed at making the unions more aggressive, and in nearly all the unions they were the source of sustained drives to weight the grievance procedures more favorably toward workers. In pursuit of this goal, the unions formed corps of job stewards from among their activists, who could hear workers' grievances and initiate proceedings at the lowest management levels. The unions also sought the neutral arbitration of grievances that had been appealed to the highest management levels without being settled. Eventually their efforts along this line would produce a breakthrough. In February 1943 in a case involving a PT&T plant unit, the War Labor Board would designate arbitration as the final resort in grievances involving discharges, demotions, and releases for military service.[27]

Much of the progress of this period can be attributed to the courage and diligence of individual union activists and leaders. In a period when workers as yet had no way of knowing whether Bell would fully comply with the Wagner Act's ban on reprisals for union activity, "actual bravery" was sometimes required to perform even the most elementary union functions. In the small towns of northern Texas, for example, frightened traffic stewards were often reluctant to "stand up to a Chief Operator whom they had probably known all their lives in a close knit community, and had been taught to follow her without question. It was like talking back to one's parents, and that was not an accepted practice then." Nonetheless, many stewards did learn to press grievances and pursue their other union duties, and thus they became, in the eyes of at least one onlooker, "heroines in standing up to management."[28]

Such exercises in courage, moreover, did change attitudes. Almost always, those engaged in them went unpunished by management,[29] and this spectacle, along with the unions' reiteration of the rights workers enjoyed under the Wagner Act, helped to embolden many of the remaining workers. In Virginia, workers found "that they did have the protection of the law, that the company couldn't take any action against them for union activities." They then "began to become more individuals [i.e., independent]"; at this point, "it didn't take much . . . to wean them away from" fear and subordination to the company.[30]

The company policy of not levying reprisals was, of course, crucial, and Bell deserves credit for complying with the Wagner Act's ban on reprisals in an era when many employers did not comply. Credit, however, should be tempered by recognition that Bell had especially strong reasons for observing the law. As a publicly regulated monopoly, it had more at stake in legal confrontations with the government than did many companies; also, as noted previously, it was trying to check outside unions by fostering the relatively weak Bell unions. Management seemed to believe that repression of the Bell unions might defeat its purpose by pushing workers toward affiliation with AFL or CIO organizations.[31] And, of course, NLRB cases arising from repression could endanger the existence of the Bell unions by inviting NLRB examinations of their legitimacy.

The changing of attitudes came not only from examples of courage, but from diligent educational and representational activities carried on by other unsung heroes and heroines. In sparsely settled areas, the unions were frequently unable to pay activists for time taken off work, which meant that "some of the Plant members, working a six-day week, would travel all or most of Saturday night, hold a union meeting Sunday, travel home Sunday night, and return to work Monday morning." In other cases, leaders from far-flung locations would sometimes drive all day and all night, "to keep from paying another night's hotel bill."[32] In most instances, union officials maintained their offices in private homes, sometimes using dining room tables for desks and bushel baskets for filing cabinets. Getting paid by the unions for telephone calls and traveling expenses was also "quite a problem." "Lots of times," it was recalled, "you spent your own money."[33]

Often those engaged in organizing activities had little experience to guide them and little rank-and-file knowledge or traditions to draw upon. For most of them, genuine union activity was initially an alien enterprise set in an alien world; and as Barbash has pointed out, they were denied much of the knowledge and experience that other groups absorbed from their ties with the CIO, the AFL, or left-wing groups. Learning often had to take place "on an experimental basis; just do something and then hope it's right." Or, as a Long Lines traffic leader complained as late as 1941, "We are all learning, and learning from the ground up, and it takes time."[34] In some ways, to be sure, the company union experience had been helpful in this regard, but telephone unionists, from the rank and file to the top leadership, still had much to learn.

Initially, for example, many of the rank and file held only vague notions of why picket lines were established during strikes, why unionists were expected not to cross them, or why scabs were held in contempt. Few understood the "kind of relationships which other unions' members, with any kind of tradition in unionism at all, a background in unionism, had long ago established and never questioned." In several areas, a participant recalled, it was necessary "to establish with our local people the obligation of leaders to lead. This might seem to come naturally to other unions, but with our people, with no real experience in a union as other unions knew it, this would never occur."[35]

Union officers also suffered from a lack of experience, as was illustrated by the manner in which a 1940 bargaining deadlock was broken in Southwestern Bell's plant department. One of the union's top four plant officers, realizing that he was in no position to threaten a strike, finally proposed that the Federal Mediation and Conciliation Service be called in, even though, as he later explained, "I hardly knew how to pronounce the words 'Federal Mediation and Conciliation Service.' I didn't know what it meant or was all about. Never met any of its representatives. . . . I didn't even realize that we had the right to call them in ourselves." And when a management representative replied to the proposal by saying, "No, by God, I'll never agree to have a disinterested outsider come in and tell me how to run our business," the union officer was "stumped." "I didn't know what else to say," he recalled, "and I looked at the other guys. And nobody knew anything else to say, so we just closed up our books and said goodbye and left and accepted what had been offered."[36]

One early method of bridging the experience gap, which was probably related to concern with NLRB action, was heavy reliance upon legal advisors. A number of unions were "guided" by lawyers. Several were "actually dominated by, if not led by, local lawyers," and still others elected union officers who had attended or even completed law school. But while such union attorneys as Henry Mayer of New York worked hard and ably on behalf of various telephone unions, legal expertise was not a good substitute for union leadership and experience. Dependence upon lawyers created a structure of advisors whose pecuniary interests often lay in blocking union amalgamation and centralization.[37] It opened up opportunities for ambitious legal promoters, like the Washington attorney in 1939 who succeeded in putting together a bloc of eleven union clients and thus threatened to "split the organizations in the industry into two or more factions even before one National is set up."[38] It sometimes led to the use of legal language in bargaining sessions, which clouded the understanding of most of the union representatives present. And frequently, since the early attorneys were not ordinarily specialists in labor law, it generated advice that tended to be needlessly "safe" and inhibiting.[39]

Thus a strong need arose for leadership education, and leaders in most unions soon recognized this need and diligently began to meet it. By 1941 top union officers in Illinois, Ohio, Michigan, New York, Connecticut, New Jersey, and California had attended university extension classes in "contemporary labor problems" and other subjects. Increasingly, they sought the advice of AFL and CIO union officers, sometimes enduring gibes about their company union background while receiving it. Once established, the NFTW became a major educational device, enabling leaders from one area to draw upon the experience of those elsewhere and pool information so as to prevent the company from "putting things over" on a particular organization. The early NFTW assemblies, according to Barbash, "were as much educational institutes for the delegates as they were deliberative bodies." Along with them were preassembly panel discussions and frequent regional meetings, both involving much exchange of information about internal problems and practices. Also, special projects were undertaken for developing model contracts, and special efforts succeeded in persuading the Women's Bureau of the Department of Labor to conduct a study of the skill levels required of telephone operators. This, when finally published in 1946, challenged Bell's time-honored claim that it paid "wages as good as and, where possible, even better than those obtaining in comparable lines of employment."[40]

The most difficult problems in educating and developing leaders came at the local level. In the plant unions there was a high turnover rate among local officers, partly because of the onerous and low-paid nature of the job—even the few large locals could not afford full-time officers—and partly because management tended to promote the best ones to supervisory positions (their capabilities having been brought to management's attention through their union activities). As Paul Griffith complained, one early training program produced "about fifteen people who were pretty good," but "then Management got five of the fifteen and the wives got five more of the fifteen."[41]

There were also leadership problems in the traffic locals, some of which showed a need for education. The root problem, both in this period and later, was the unwillingness of many loyal and competent members to assume leadership responsibilities. That unwillingness was in no way surprising: in traffic locals, as in plant locals, leadership was in some respects onerous. In sparsely populated territory, where the membership of traffic locals was spread out over several towns, the steward in each office and especially the general officers of the local found that, along with carrying the normal burdens of office, they had to travel a great deal in order to conduct union business. In many city traffic locals, meanwhile, officers found that when they needed to consult the membership on important matters, three membership meetings in one day were necessary to accommodate members working the various shifts.[42] And some of the unwillingness clearly arose from circumstances that have discouraged women generally from seeking their share of local leadership posts in American unions. Even in the 1938–1941 period, much of the traffic membership was young, unmarried, and—like their female counterparts in other unions then and since —strongly attracted to nonworkplace activities that left little or no time for union leadership duties. (Young women sometimes became stewards, but their turnover in those positions was usually rapid, owing mostly to their marrying and/or leaving the company.) During this period, an unusually large proportion of the traffic membership was made up of somewhat older married women. But this group too, like their counterparts elsewhere, generally had their time taken up by nonworkplace concerns. Their lives were "pretty full with families and that sort of thing," as one traffic unionist put it. We may infer that child raising and other domestic responsibilities left them with less free time than most men who combined union membership with family responsibilities.[43] (It bears noting that in this period traffic women were *not* beset by some other difficulties that often dissuaded women from seeking local leadership posts. Since virtually no men were in the traffic locals, the women were victimized neither by male resistance to female candidacies nor by any reluctance on their own part, reportedly common among women in mixed locals of many unions, to run against men for office.[44])

Thus the full capacities of many able members were lost to the traffic locals, and leadership tended to devolve upon older, career traffic workers who did not have heavy child-raising responsibilities. This made for stability of leadership, since such women seldom left the company and the dearth of management positions open to women made it unlikely that they would be promoted into management. But women who fit this description were often not operators but "supervisors" and senior operators—people whose jobs did involve some supervisory functions. The dual role made for "tricky" situations whenever "the individual forgot which hat she was wearing at the moment." A former traffic leader in Texas (herself a supervisor for many years) recalled the example of a grievance meeting in which a steward–senior operator from a distant town rose to leave, saying "that she had to go to catch the bus home, which she must not miss because she had to 'relieve the chief operator the next day.'" In this case the meeting continued only because "the district man was a pretty good guy," and "he told the steward to continue the meeting and he would make any necessary arrangements to relieve the chief operator." Many such traffic stewards and local officers needed to be convinced that "union activities were now protected by law, and that when they were needed to represent the members who elected them, *that* representation was their first responsibility."[45]

At the local level, then, both the turnover and the dual roles of some key people seemed to require systematic and continuing education programs. By 1941 these were either operating or being developed by a number of unions, including those in Illinois, Michigan, Ohio, Wisconsin, and the territories of Northwestern and Southwestern Bell. In Illinois, for example, plant union officials, working with an expert recommended by Northwestern University, developed evening courses for local "officers and key people" in the Chicago area, and subsequently graduates from these courses launched similar programs for locals outside of Chicago. For those enrolled, there were opportunities to speak on various trade union subjects, to hold mock membership meetings where one could learn to "bring out the thoughts of men who are too quiet and . . . shut up people who are not quiet enough," and to learn the technique of allowing a management stand-in to "talk on and on, and after he is talked out, handle him then."[46]

In Michigan similar opportunities were made available. There the traffic union developed both a technical course dealing with record keeping and parliamentary procedure and a more general course concerned with "what a picket line meant; why a picket line was established; why a worker didn't report another co-worker; why it was that you didn't carry your internal disputes to the press; the sense of obligation toward a member; the sense of obligation toward the union as an institution."[47]

Such courses, it should be reiterated, were intended to educate the educators and were not aimed directly at rank-and-file members. In addition, however, some thirty-five of the telephone unions did publish monthly newspapers by 1942, most of which were distributed to the entire membership and most of which cooperated in the exchange of pertinent columns and news items, resulting in a news network across the country.[48] The educational plant was growing in size and wisdom, and the gap left by lack of experience and tradition was slowly being filled.

These changes helped account for the gradual shift in attitudes of union members and leaders, a shift that was reflected in the behavior of the unions. Looking back, one can detect notable differences between the telephone unions of 1937 and those existing at the end of 1941. As one traffic leader remarked in 1941, "We are beginning to see our way. We are beginning to walk."[49] Almost all had moved some distance along the path toward genuine trade unionism, although when it comes to estimating that distance, generalizations are difficult. Some had come much farther than others, and sharp contrasts existed in the degree of aggressiveness and labor consciousness.

The most aggressive of all the unions were three of the Western Electric groups—distributing houses, installation and Kearny manufacturing—all of whom had threatened strike action and conducted strike votes by the end of 1941, one of whom (distributing houses) had engaged in slowdowns, and one of whom (Kearny) had conducted what it called an "overtime strike" (that is, an organized refusal to work overtime).[50] The work force in these units, it may be noted, differed from that of the operating companies in several important respects. Since WE employment had undergone relatively severe cuts and rises between 1929 and 1941, the work force harbored fewer long-service workers and, no doubt, fewer illusions about company benevolence. Since WE workers did not deal directly with the public, they had adopted less of the "public service" psychology cultivated elsewhere and hence had less reluctance to use "the strike weapon." All the WE groups were predominantly blue collar, as we have seen, and while the manufacturing plants and the distributing houses were widely dispersed, workers at most of these locations at least worked "under one roof."[51] The WE installation workers, it is true, were at any given moment thinly scattered at temporary job sites across the country. But traveling, lodging, and spending idle hours together—all in rude circumstances imposed by a scanty per diem allowance—had already created in these workers a them-versus-us attitude. And now that installers had an organization around which to rally, this attitude, plus the constant issue of the per diem itself, was making them the most aggressive of all the Bell groups.[52]

In stark contrast to these three WE groups stood several other groups noted for their lack of militancy and labor mindedness. The Southern Bell union and the WE Point Breeze manufacturing union, as noted previously, were eventually declared company dominated, and there were probably others that could not have withstood NLRB scrutiny. In any event, a group of NFTW union leaders meeting in 1941 believed that several non-NFTW unions would have to "clean house" before they could be admitted, and one leader even contended that there were

NFTW affiliates "who need help in their own organizations, if they wouldn't be too proud to accept the help."[53]

Neither the WE units nor the company-dominated ones were typical, however. In most unions the degree of change fell somewhere in between, which meant that the typical union of 1941, although not as aggressive as the WE groups, was somewhat larger than it had been in 1937 (because of the widespread process of amalgamation), was more likely to contain non-Bell workers, and was benefiting from a somewhat higher dues structure (from fifty cents a month to a dollar). Typically, too, one could find a greater concern that members not violate union ethics by crossing nontelephone unions' picket lines. This had become one of the objectives of union educational activities, and by 1941 several of the unions were negotiating agreements with management that members would not be required to service telephones in strike-bound businesses. (Instead, management employees would be told to do such work.[54])

In addition, the typical union had become something of a bargaining agent, although not as yet a militant or very effective one. It was unable, for example, to prevent the relative wage return of telephone workers from deteriorating between 1939 and 1941, to establish grievance arbitration procedures, or to secure anything approaching a union shop.[55] Yet bargaining for the typical union was now something more than a pro forma exercise. There was a willingness to employ such tactics as calling in the Federal Mediation and Conciliation Service, which at least had a "nuisance value" in that "the company does not like government delving into their business."[56]

In 1941, bargaining sessions in a few non-WE units were enlivened by strike threats, although it is unlikely that the unions involved could have launched full-fledged strikes. Even in areas where no strikes were threatened, there was no longer a mute acceptance of inferior contracts. Union leaders often made it clear that workers should not be happy with the results of bargaining.[57]

Finally, during 1940–1941 the unions showed a degree of maturity in their reaction to new tactics employed by management—tactics that themselves indicated a departure from the earlier union-management amiability. In the course of bargaining, management sometimes tried to alienate local leaders and members from top union officers, or tried to prolong negotiations, presumably in the hope that impatient unionists would prefer immediate, company-offered improvements over the uncertain and long-delayed results of genuine bargaining. In some instances, the unions were simply too cohesive to be hurt by such tactics. In 1940, for example, when Southwestern Bell tried to hold down traffic department wage increases by offering immediate raises on a local-by-local basis, it failed to undermine a unified bargaining team of top union officers. The locals remained loyal to the bargaining team, and the result was a department-wide contract that provided some locals with more than the company had initially offered. In 1941 bargaining for southern California traffic, when management insisted that its offer be referred to workers, the result was a vote backing the union position and eventually producing an improved contract. In other instances the unions met such tactics by complaining to the NLRB, either on grounds of company interference with internal union affairs or (in the case of management delays in bargaining) on grounds of the company's "refusal to bargain."[58] These complaints were in themselves a sign of progress in unions that had lived in fear of the NLRB only a few years earlier.

Thus despite obstacles within the industry and despite the absence of sustained guidance by outside groups, the Bell unions made significant progress during the 1938–1941 period. And unlike the changes of 1935–1937, when the reconstitution of the organizations sprang primarily from the Wagner Act and the Bell System's response to it, the changes of 1938–1941 were largely of the workers' own making. Of course the Wagner Act, with its enforcing agent, the NLRB, played a part from 1938 to 1941. Their offstage presence spurred unionists to drop any of the remaining visible trappings of company unionism, and they protected the bolder unionists in their exercise of legitimate union functions. But the principal actors were the thousands of union leaders and activists who were finding appeals that could change older attitudes, who were willing to learn, to teach, to make personal sacrifices, and sometimes to act as models of boldness. Through their efforts the telephone unions of 1941 had for the most part become conscientious bargaining organizations, with a substantial claim on their members' loyalty, with some knowledge of trade union traditions and tactics, and with an ability to serve workers in fields that had no strong conflict with management. They were especially useful, for example, in the establishment of a modicum of job security based on seniority, in the protection of jobs from IBEW encroachment, and in grievance procedures.

This was no mean achievement. Yet it bears repeating that the progress of this period was slow, and by the end of 1941 the telephone unions as a whole still fell short of most other unions in at least one important respect. With the possible exception of the WE unions mentioned above, none of the telephone unions could be described as militant or even aggressive in bargaining; they shrank from any major test of strength with management. The idea of strike action, to be sure, was not quite the alien concept it had been a few years earlier. A Southwestern Union leader now believed that "telephone people will strike like everyone else when they get dissatisfied," and the Long Lines union president reported, "if we had talked strike in Long Lines two years ago, we would have been thrown out of office, but we are not that way at the present time."[59] Yet if there was discussion, there was still no taste for action. Outside of the WE units, strike threats by union negotiators were rare and, one suspects, not always in earnest. Union strike votes were also rare; they were usually taken within small subunits of unions; and in the two instances where the voting results were revealed in any detail, the affirmative tally was not great enough "to enable us to carry out the strike."[60] Through 1941 no actual strikes occurred in the entire Bell System, not even in the WE units.

Clearly, the union membership as a whole fell short of being militant. Commenting on the situation, union leaders tended to believe that "the average telephone man" of 1941 was "not labor-minded," that the membership needed to be further "educated in unionism," and that many members still "hate the word 'strike.' "[61] Nor was the lack of militancy surprising. These unions, after all, had had only a few years to undermine the attitudes management had long been encouraging, and despite some worsening of its status after 1939, the telephone work force as a whole remained a long-employed and—since the early 1930s—a relatively well-paid group. As one union leader remarked in early 1942, "We must give the Company credit—they give us enough to keep us fairly well satisfied. . . . We [i.e., the telephone unions] are all doing fairly well on wages."[62]

Nor were the leaders themselves militant in the sense that they wished to launch strikes in 1940 or 1941. Some leaders still had reservations about the propriety or feasibility of ever striking a public utility, preferring instead some form of compulsory arbitration. Many others did not want to be "so far out in front" as to lose their "troops," and still others felt that "we have to sell our own people the idea before the executive officers can do anything about it."[63] This lack of divergence between leaders and members on the strike issue seemed particularly pronounced in the telephone unions, whose leaders remained close to the workplace and their fellow workers. As noted previously, few of the leaders were full-time union officers. All came from within the industry (as was not the case, for example, in the CIO unions in steel and textiles), and few were in office very long. There was a rapid turnover among local plant union leaders and among the top leaders of all the unions. The presidencies of non–WE NFTW affiliates changed hands at the rate of about 32 percent annually from 1938 to 1941.[64]

Whether the general lack of militancy actually weakened the unions' bargaining position during this period must remain a subject for speculation. A few union negotiators felt that it did. They complained, for example, of an "inability to exert reasonable pressure," and of the fact that "no matter how clear a case you have, if the company says 'no,' it is 'no.' "[65] On the other hand, if union militancy had been present and had led to strikes that were subsequently broken—a likely outcome, given the unions' lack of funds and experience, as well as the structural and technological obstacles they would have faced—then the unions' bargaining position might have become even weaker.

It is certain, however, that the lack of militancy affected the structural development of telephone unionism during the 1938–1941 period. As will be seen in the next chapter, the progress made by the telephone unions during this period led to an expansion of the NFTW's activities. But at the same time, the unions' shrinking from tests of strength with management helped impose limits on the kinds of activities the national organization could undertake, and precluded the NFTW and its affiliates from evolving into a national union.

Chapter 5

THE NFTW AND THE PROBLEM

OF CENTRALIZATION, 1939–1941

BY MID-1939 the founders of the National Federation of Telephone Workers had outlined the structure of the national organization in terms as clear and indelible as they could make them. The organization, they had decided, was to be a loose confederation, and through the autonomy clause and other constitutional restraints they had tried to insure that it would not become a national telephone workers' union, or even a strong federation in which a majority could shape organizational policy in such crucial matters as bargaining with management. At the same time, however, the founders had not been clear about the responsibilities of the new organization. They agreed that it should serve as a clearinghouse for information, as a representative for the member unions on national legislation, and as a "means of common counsel" and "mutual assistance." But the nature and extent of its entry into these responsibilities remained largely undetermined. Indeed, with no full-time officers and a budget of only ten thousand dollars the NFTW could hardly make a start.

As the member unions gained experience and expanded their field of activity, however, their leaders came to recognize that some tasks were better handled by the national organization. In the years from 1939 to 1941, tasks were ceded on a piecemeal basis, with the result that NFTW responsibilities grew rapidly and its budget increased fivefold. Yet as responsibilities shifted, the structural limitations set up by the organization's founders remained intact. For a variety of reasons, unionists were unwilling to divest their local organizations of "autonomy," and no attempt was made to move beyond a loose, confederational structure into something approaching national unionism.

ALTHOUGH MOST OF the leaders who had established the NFTW constitution passed from the scene in 1940 and 1941, the idea of member-union autonomy continued to enjoy overwhelming support. The roots of this support lay in what one unionist described as feelings of "departmental or sectional pride—or prejudice, if you want to call it that,"[1] feelings that bred a reluctance to join closely with others who lived in distant areas or who performed different kinds of telephone work. Cleavages of this sort had been only partially healed by the company union experience and the events of 1935–1938, and in the meetings of 1939–1941 they were still very much in evidence. Many traffic unionists still "didn't trust plant; plant had no high regard of traffic; and both of them looked upon the commercial and accounting people as the kind of people who shouldn't even belong in a union, much less theirs." The WE groups, meanwhile, were considered "the second cousin of the whole Bell System," and there was also "a great deal of suspicion and distrust" between northerners and southerners, easterners and westerners.[2] Helping to sustain such feelings of insularity were explicit messages from management. Plant men were told, "You don't want to get mixed up with these [traffic] women" because "they don't know what they're doing." And traffic workers were advised not to have "anything to do with these cigar-smoking, tobacco-chewing old plant men. They'll only pull you down to their level."[3]

Among labor groups, as Selig Perlman and Philip Taft long ago pointed out, it is often "actual separation of interest" that accounts for "actual separation in organization." Among many telephone workers the desire for autonomy was undoubtedly based less upon prejudice or management propaganda than upon the calculation that variance of the groups' interests was indeed wide enough to warrant permanently separated organizations. Some groups prized autonomy because it allowed them to steer clear of any reckless bargaining positions that might be taken by more aggressive telephone unions.[4] Others prized it because they did not want to be held back by the less aggressive groups.[5] And in some of the plant unions, including those in New York City, New Jersey, and Illinois, an aversion to joining with traffic workers sprang mostly from the suspicion that the costs of allying with less skilled workers were apt to outweigh the benefits. It was believed that traffic workers "would be the weak links of the organization" and would lower the skill and wage levels of the average member. "If we bring in the women," the New York City plant union president cautioned, "we'll just stand still while the women catch up with us."[6] Understandably, traffic unionists "didn't like this attitude" and were inclined to reciprocate the feelings of mistrust. They were especially fearful of any structural change that might cast plant men as their representatives in bargaining, believing that "plant men can't go in and go to bat for traffic because they don't know what they're talking about. Everything is so different [in the two departments]."[7]

Another source of traffic unionist irritation was traffic's consistent underrepresentation on the NFTW executive board. With an affiliated membership ranging from 35 to 40 percent of the NFTW's total from 1939 to 1946, traffic was able to claim only one of seven board positions in 1939, one of nine in 1940, and two of nine thereafter. Irritation rose to a peak in 1940–1941, after only one of two traffic nominees had been elected at the 1940 assembly in Salt Lake City. At the 1941 assembly in Omaha, a traffic caucus made a concerted effort to place three traffic nominees on the board, and there was some talk of bolting the assembly if the effort were not successful. However, when only two of the nominees were elected, traffic delegates quickly resigned themselves to the fact. At the 1942 assembly in Baltimore, the caucus backed the election of only two traffic nominees (one other woman having unsuccessfully sought caucus support). At the 1943 assembly in Cleveland, the caucus did not meet, and only two traffic women sought election to the board. And in subsequent assemblies the issue vanished as a matter of traffic delegate concern.[8]

Part of the explanation for traffic's underrepresentation lay in the eagerness of prominent male union leaders to hold board positions, combined with an unmistakable tendency on the part of male delegates to vote for male candidates—though there is no evidence of any conspiracy to keep women off the board. (No nontraffic women were ever elected to the board.) But also important was the traffic delegates' unwillingness to push consistently and hard for executive board representation. Traffic delegates did not remain united behind the candidacies of traffic nominees for the board. And the traffic caucus's concern for the issue seemed to subside with the realization that heavy representation on the board was not important in protecting traffic's particular interests. Bargaining with management, after all, was not an executive board function. Moreover, the most important NFTW issues normally were not decided in board sessions but on the floor of the annual assemblies, where traffic representation was not the subject of complaint. When a question of special interest to traffic did come before the board, two traffic members turned out to be adequate representation, particularly since—as one of the traffic board members reported to the 1942 caucus—the male board members in these instances would say, in effect, "You two women get together, and whatever you suggest is okay with us."[9]

Equally important was the shortage of traffic candidates for board positions, especially candidates who had become prominent by speaking up on the assembly floor. The traffic delegates' readiness "to leave the oratory to the men," which had first been apparent at the 1938 Chicago meeting, continued at subsequent assemblies, despite the fact that, as one traffic delegate later put it, the men "certainly gave women who had anything to say a chance, and they had to." There was a lamentable tendency, it seems, for women to yield to men in matters of floor debate and office seeking. Or, to take the cheerier view of a perennial male delegate: the women's "group philosophy" was, "'Why do the job yourself if you can get a bright boy to do it for you?'"[10]

Perhaps one source of the traffic women's diffidence was a predisposition that has reportedly curbed women's rise to leadership in other unions: a reluctance to appear aggressive or competitive in a context that included male peers.[11] Another, more certain source was the circumstances from which these women had risen, circumstances that had produced a group of delegates who generally were not ambitious for high union office. For the most part, this was a group that had not risen to leadership in their local and regional organizations by ardently overcoming stiff competition. Rather, with so many young or married women eschewing any leadership role, leadership had devolved upon these delegates, mostly because they were capable, they were willing to serve, and they were there. A woman who had quickly risen to leadership in the Southwestern Union, for example, could truthfully say, years later, "I was not ambitious. I never campaigned for an office in my life. The jobs were there begging for somebody to take them."[12]

Nor did high-level union posts have much to offer these leaders of regional organizations. Such posts promised disrupted lives and much lonely, second-class travel to distant locations to confer with people mostly unknown to them. Far-seeing and ambitious unionists may have recognized the possibility that high-level positions offered some promise of eventually becoming permanent, full-time union posts, but this possibility was generally more attractive to men than to women. Assuming a permanent, full-time union post would almost always involve relocating, and here most women would be stymied by a problem that male unionists ordinarily did not have. As a traffic unionist bluntly put it, "The men can move their wives, but the women cannot move their husbands."[13]

Some of these circumstances that discouraged women from attaining NFTW executive board posts probably also impeded their assumption of top positions in individual telephone unions that were not, like the traffic unions, composed almost exclusively of women. Rarely did women become presidents of the commerical or accounting unions, even though the membership of these unions was normally more than three-fourths female. And in no instance was a woman ever the president of one of the multidepartment, amalgamated NFTW unions, whose number by 1945 had come to include not only Ohio, Long Lines, and the Southwestern Union, but also the unions in Northwestern Bell, Oregon, Connecticut, Virginia, West Virginia, and Cincinnati Bell, as well as a new, legitimate union in Southern Bell.[14]

While the issue of executive board representation led to no open breach, its presence in 1940–1941 did highlight and exacerbate the continuing divisions among the various groups. The persistence of insularity was also due to the lack of strong incentives for greater unity. No such incentive arose from Bell System negotiating procedures, since AT&T chose not to act as the single negotiator for the various Bell companies on matters of systemwide concern (pensions, wage schedules, military leaves of absence, and so on). Rather, it insisted that telephone unionists conduct all negotiations with the management of their respective companies, even on pension policy, a matter that unionists knew was under AT&T's direct control.[15] Consequently, unionists did not have any urgent procedural reasons for either forming a single negotiating agency of their own (possibly centered in the NFTW) or for uniting behind single sets of demands expressed through that agency.

Nor did considerations of strike strategy provide any strong incentive for greater unity. Shrinking as they did from strike action, most telephone unionists did not seriously explore the advantages that unity might provide in such a test of strength. Although questions of strike strategy were sometimes discussed, these discussions tended to remain speculative. They lacked urgency, and since strikes were not being seriously contemplated, no strong incentive to move from speculation to resolution existed.

There was, for example, the question of which workers, if any, could shut down or curtail telephone service in the event of a strike. By themselves, the accounting and commercial groups could not hope to do this; nor could plant groups hope to do so, except in a very long strike, since most of their work involved maintenance or the extension of service to new customers. Only strike action by traffic groups held forth any real promise of curtailing the industry's main revenue-producing services. They were the people necessary to connect not only the rapidly increasing number of long distance calls, but also all local calls originating from the 38 percent of the nation's telephones that remained nondial.[16] Hence, if nontraffic groups were to conduct or seriously threaten a service-curtailing strike, they would need to act in unison with traffic.

In internal discussions, moreover, there was recognition of this fact. At a June 1941 meeting of NFTW plant union leaders, an Illinois leader drew on the pre-1920 strike experience of some of his fellow plant workers to argue that "if any of our economic weapons to strike are to be successful, we must have the [traffic] women with us." "If the thing is going to be settled," he continued, "the women are the ones who are going to settle it." During the meeting no one contested his analysis, yet it did not elicit proposals for greater unity with traffic. Since questions of strike strategy were of no pressing concern, the leaders could move blithely on to another subject.[17]

Another question arose from the fact that many central offices contained several distinct groups of workers, who often belonged to separate unions. A central office building in a large city, for example, might contain plant, traffic, commercial, and accounting groups employed by the local operating company; a Long Lines group at work elsewhere in the same building; and a WE installation group temporarily at work replacing central office equipment. All or most of these groups would belong to separate unions. Consequently, if one group were to strike, the others would be faced with the question of how to respond to the picket lines established outside their place of work. Assuming they would not "scab"[18]—that is, cross the picket lines and actually perform the work of the striking group—there was still the possibility that they might cross the picket lines to perform their own jobs, thus freeing some of their supervisors to do the work of the strikers. For people who would not necessarily benefit from a successful strike and who had not had a voice in the strike decision, this behavior might appear appropriate. Yet it was also likely to invite lasting resentment and future reprisals in kind by the striking group.

If this dilemma were to be solved, the autonomy of the unions representing these groups would have to be abridged. At the very least, the groups would have to create some mechanism whereby they could review each other's decisions regarding strikes and responses to picket lines before any strike was called. And any lasting solution seemed to call for joint decisions and joint action. Yet again, the general absence of strikes and anticipated strikes kept telephone unionists from moving toward such solutions. Only once in the 1939–1941 period were they forced to explore the problem, and in this case matters did not move much beyond the exploratory stage.

The one case of exploration came in October 1941, when the entire Long Lines union threatened to strike, and this threat was discussed at a meeting attended by leaders of the NFTW's eastern affiliates. After noting the dilemma involved, the leaders arrived at a useful proposal. They agreed that when an NFTW union was "anticipating going on a strike," the NFTW executive board should have the power to "investigate the causes," "request information from other member organizations as to what support, what action, they shall take in support of this particular member organization," and then "advise the member organizations as to what support they should give them." As it turned out, however, the Long Lines strike threat had not been entirely serious, and, in any event, it did not develop into a strike. The eastern leaders' proposal was forgotten, and telephone unionists could ignore the picket line problem for the remainder of 1941.[19]

Finally, there was the question of how a group of workers in a single Bell company could offset the advantages that that company derived from its being a segment of the nationwide Bell System. If management became deeply antagonistic toward a union in a particular company, it might be willing to provoke or accept a long, bitter strike in an attempt to impose a union-breaking contract. In this kind of struggle the company would hold crucial advantages over an autonomous union. It could import management employees and nonunion workers from other companies, and any losses in revenue could be absorbed by AT&T (the majority stockholder in all Bell companies except those in Cincinnati and Connecticut). Conceivably, Bell System management might even choose to press these advantages against every union in the system, one by one, over a period of years. It might, in other words, use "whipsaw" tactics to virtually destroy unionism in the industry.

Some telephone unionists recognized this possibility and hence the need for some means of uniting in systemwide strikes or strike threats.[20] Indeed, some speculated that any telephone strike, in order to be effective, would require that "everybody in the whole darn country has to go out together."[21] Yet most unionists were still not thinking in terms of all-out confrontations, and they were devoting only scant attention to the question of how they might offset the advantages Bell would derive from its size and centralized control. In the nonmilitant atmosphere of 1939–1941, the question never reached the floor of the NFTW national assemblies,[22] and elsewhere there was no strong interest in either exploring or solving the problems of strike strategy.

Two sets of factors at work, then, were the unionists' predilection for insularity and the lack of incentives for abandoning it. Also at work were three less important factors, one being the total absence of pressure for structural change coming from the NFTW national office. The NFTW president, Paul Griffith, did not begin to serve full time until June 1941,[23] and even then his own temperament and principles barred him from exerting such pressure. As Tom Twigg had suspected at the December 1937 national meeting in St. Louis, Griffith was well suited for keeping the various "factions together until some kind of trust developed." Even those who subsequently welcomed his departure were to concede, years later, that he was "the type of man who seemed to be able to hold the controversial groups together," that he was a "necessary personality" and "good for the NFTW at this stage of our development."[24] But skill at conciliation was not leadership. Typically, he was "one who went with the group after the group voted," and being a staunch admirer of the Bell System, he had grave ethical reservations about striking and a deeply felt commitment to the autonomy clause of the NFTW constitution. Any efforts to eliminate this clause, he felt "were treasonous so far as the member organizations were concerned." It was a compact entered into, and those making it had sworn "by everything that was holy that that's the way it would stay forever."[25] Nor were there other officials willing to counter such views. The only other full-time official at the national level was the secretary-treasurer, Bert Horth. And he, like Griffith—who was his political ally—did not wish to move toward national unionism.[26]

Secondly, among those unionists who held ethical reservations about ever conducting a telephone strike were some who opposed the formation of a national telephone union precisely because they associated union bigness with strikes. (Griffith himself may have been influenced by this line of reasoning, although he never phrased his opposition to national unionism in these terms.[27])

Finally, some unionists' perception of a need for labor unity to offset Bell's centralized control was clouded by management denials that there *was* centralized control or coordination behind the companies' labor policies. Many in the union ranks seemed to feel that AT&T vice-president Cleo Craig was sincere when he declared that "the A.T.&T. did not dictate to the associated companies," and many seemed to accept the individual companies' claims that their bargaining positions were determined not by AT&T but by wage surveys of the communities in which they operated. Still receptive to these claims and to the companies' public image as locally oriented organizations, some unionists saw little need for the kind of countervailing power that a centralized national union might provide.[28]

IN SPITE OF these difficulties, the cause of national unionism remained alive, and from 1939 to 1941 the number of union leaders quietly espousing it increased slightly. Retaining their union presidencies were three of the pre-1939 proponents—Beirne of WE distributing houses, Ernest Weaver of WE installation, and George DuVal of WE Kearny manufacturing. Lost was Tom Twigg of Ohio, who died of cancer in March 1939 at the age of forty-five. But elsewhere three more proponents emerged, namely John J. Moran of Long Lines, William Dunn of the Cincinnati union, and Frances Smith of Michigan traffic. In all of these cases, the proponents' unions were either WE groups, or organizations that were themselves small nationwide unions, or unions whose members were concentrated in urban areas. And most of the leaders involved were unusual in the degree to which their union attitudes had been shaped by experiences outside the industry. Twigg had been active in a strike in his native Wales. DuVal and Moran had been members of nontelephone unions. Dunn was a law school graduate and long-time admirer of John L. Lewis. And Beirne was the son of a locomotive engineer who, in 1921, had been broken to oiler after respecting a picket line and had quit his railroad job rather than accept the demotion.[29]

Throughout the period, moreover, regional and national meetings helped to emphasize common concerns and problems. The workers, after all, were in an industry where a national company had standardized technology and vocabulary. When unionists from across the country asked each other, "What work do you do?" and, "What grade are you in?" they found that "within a very short period of time, certain key words in the industry lexicography [would] come out" and would let "you know you are with somebody who is in your own industry."[30] This lesson, repeated at dozens of meetings—and no doubt rendered more palatable by the social homogeneity that resulted from Bell's hiring policies—gradually eroded regional and departmental prejudice.

In the sprawling Southwestern Union, for example, "meetings, discussions, bickerings, fighting, misunderstandings, as well as final understandings" slowly brought the participants toward the realization that "the plant employee in Texas was no different from one in Arkansas, Kansas, Missouri. The traffic operator in Cactus Junction had the same problems, troubles, and grievances as one in St. Louis. . . . The girls and boys in Texas didn't wear horns. The ones in Missouri were not dumb mules. The ones in Arkansas were not hillbillies. The ones in Oklahoma were not riffraff Okies." Reflecting the change, the job of chairing NFTW assemblies gradually became more pleasant. By 1940, Griffith later recalled, the atmosphere of the assemblies "had less tenseness" and many of the delegates now "greeted one another as old friends or comrades."[31]

In addition, more telephone unionists were acquiring pieces of information that indicated a centralized coordination of Bell labor policies. They became aware of a report by the Federal Communications Commission confirming their long-held belief that pension policy was centrally controlled. They noticed in bargaining with Long Lines that management would sometimes adjourn in order to confer with other officials outside Long Lines. Apparently, the contracts there had become pacesetters, in certain respects, for contracts in other Bell companies.[32] And in 1941, when plant leaders from the Southwestern Union and six midwestern unions systematically compared their contracts, most of them concluded that Bell management had "set up a standard contract which permits slight variation to meet local difficulties."[33]

As yet telephone unionists had no precise knowledge of the methods or scope of Bell's centralized control. But by 1942 some suspected that local community wage schedules, far from being determined by strictly local considerations, bore a fixed relationship to telephone wage schedules in large "key" cities; that there were fixed differentials between the wage schedules of these key cities across the country; and that these differentials had "some definite tie-up" with Long Lines wage schedules in the same cities. As the NFTW magazine, *The Telephone Worker*, suggested in June 1941, "the experience of member organizations in bargaining has made it all too apparent that the A.T.&T. controlled the labor policy of the operating company" and that "A.T.&T.'s status as controlling owner of the associated companies could hardly be ignored."[34] (There can remain little doubt that this general assessment was correct. See Appendix C.)

In the long run, this awareness would combine with other factors to bring major structural change. But it was not enough to overcome the preference for autonomy that persisted during the 1939–1941 period. It could not dissipate feelings of regional and departmental mistrust. It encountered continuing resistance from those who were satisfied with decentralized bargaining procedures and from those who accepted Bell's protestations of decentralized decision-making power. And while it helped to point unionists toward the conclusion that they, too, would need centralized coordination in the event of a test of strength with management, this conclusion held no particular urgency. Most unionists still shrank from any such test.

IN EXPANDING the NFTW's responsibilities, then, the member union leaders shunned anything that might threaten the confederational structure of the NFTW or the autonomy of the affiliates in their "internal affairs." They were especially protective of their unions' autonomy in the field they considered fundamental—bargaining with management—and in this sphere they continued to look upon the NFTW primarily as a service organization. Its principal job, in other words, was to gather and distribute information that individual unions could use in their bargaining sessions. Through the secretary-treasurer's office and through its national, regional, and departmental meetings, the NFTW would serve as a clearinghouse, keeping affiliates informed of contracts and bargaining across the country, of union studies dealing with the skill levels of various telephone jobs, of Labor Department and FCC publications, and of other relevant matters. In addition, NFTW officers, especially Secretary-Treasurer Horth, stood ready to assist individual affiliates with their bargaining, and on three occasions affiliates did ask for help and offered to reimburse the NFTW.[35]

When it came to moving beyond this kind of service to the actual coordination of affiliates' bargaining, little progress was made. Not until 1941 and early 1942 were proposals even made for such action, and proposals that were made did not envision coordination through NFTW offices or sanctions against unions that refused or withdrew their cooperation.[36] Similarly, the power to bargain for improved pensions that some twenty-three unions did delegate to the NFTW was both provisional and unused. Even if AT&T agreed to bargain, each union would have to approve the results in order to be bound by them. And while some eighteen unions signed pledges against scabbing, and resolutions against it were adopted by NFTW assemblies, none of these documents offered positive help during strikes or sanctions against violators.[37]

In other fields the member-union leaders were more willing to assign responsibilities to the NFTW. This was particularly true as the unions undertook such work as resisting IBEW encroachment, keeping their "skirts clean with the NLRB," and filling the education and information gaps that resulted from the lack of trade union traditions and outside guidance. Such tasks, the leaders came to feel, could better be handled by the national organization. And where the NFTW's assumption of these tasks posed no direct threat to member-union autonomy, local leaders were willing to see them delegated.

An Ohio union leader summarized the process: "As the Ohio federation and the rest of the groups begin by thumping our noses up against problems we can't solve, we . . . look for a larger, more powerful group to solve these problems for us." The willingness to delegate problems was heightened by many leaders' already overburdened schedules and by the growth of mutual trust.[38] Once this trust developed, there was less reluctance to turn tasks over to the like-minded men and women who served as NFTW officers, executive board members, and committee members.

As it assumed such tasks, the NFTW's educational and informational role grew rapidly. The NFTW began to pool and dispense information about actions of the NLRB, IBEW, AFL, and CIO, as well as information pertaining directly to bargaining. In addition, Secretary-Treasurer Horth promoted the exchange of news items between member union newspapers, and submitted to these newspapers much of the information his own office gathered. In 1941 the NFTW began to publish *The Telephone Worker*, at first irregularly as a slick-paper magazine, and later as a monthly newspaper carrying items from the member unions and articles written by Horth. Sold in lots to the member unions, it was then distributed by them, sometimes to their entire memberships.[39]

NFTW committees also produced reports on subjects of interest to telephone unionists. One such report dealt with the advisability of pressing for a telephone labor act modeled on the 1926 Railway Labor Act. As approved by the national assembly in 1942, the report found that whatever the merits of this legislation, it would be impossible to attain. Militating against it were the telephone unions' slender resources, AT&T's expected opposition, the industry's relatively strike-free history, and the fact that telephone workers (unlike railway workers in 1926) were already covered by the Wagner Act.[40] Another committee report, begun in 1939 and completed in 1940, presented facts about AT&T stock ownership, and by doing so persuaded the telephone unions to abandon the proposal that they pool their members' stock in order to secure a voice on the AT&T board of directors — for union-eligible workers turned out to own less than 1 percent of AT&T stock.[41]

The most important committee investigations dealt with the Bell pension plan. Beginning in 1939 a series of committees assessed the plan's strengths and weaknesses, compared it with other plans, and developed a bargaining stance on pensions for the NFTW and its affiliates. At one stage this bargaining stance included demands that labor be given representation on the benefit committees that administered the plan, that pensions be raised for retirees from low-wage brackets, and that pensions be vested for those who left Bell employment, regardless of when and why they left. In 1942, however, a professional actuary hired by the 1941 committee reported that the Bell plan was "generally more liberal than those existing in most businesses." This was confirmed in detail the following year, and this assessment—along with the emergence of more pressing problems and the apparent futility of trying to bargain over pensions with either AT&T or the individual Bell companies—stifled the original enthusiasm for pension reform. After 1942, pensions assumed a smaller place in telephone union deliberations.[42]

Growing during the same period was NFTW assistance in dealing with the National Labor Relations Board. NFTW officers observed and reported on disbandment proceedings, particularly those initiated by the IBEW in 1941 against the Southern Bell labor organization (which in 1943 resulted in that organization's disbandment on grounds of company domination). In at least two instances NFTW officers helped member unions reorganize along lines that better fit the NLRB's still-emerging standards of legitimate unionism. In addition, Griffith testified several times on behalf of a small union of plant workers employed by the non–Bell Lincoln (Nebraska) Telephone and Telegraph Company. After organizing itself on the model of the Northwestern Bell plant union, this group had joined the NFTW in January 1940; eventually it succeeded in having the company-domination charges against it dismissed.[43]

Meanwhile, NFTW officers sought and won the affiliation of several other small unions in non-Bell telephone companies, mostly in the nine-state Southern Bell territory, where no NFTW affiliate was on the scene in sufficient strength to absorb these groups itself. Among their motives was the desire to enhance the standing of the NFTW and its affiliates as telephone labor organizations rather than as Bell organizations in the eyes of the NLRB. They were hoping as well to deprive the IBEW and other AFL and CIO unions of possible organizing bases in the industry.[44]

Still another growing area of NFTW activity was helping its affiliates combat the jurisdictional claims of the IBEW. On repeated occasions Griffith brought the telephone unions' slogan, "telephone work for telephone people," before government officials and boards in Washington. And in late 1941 the NFTW thwarted the Office of Production Management's formulation of rules on defense construction work that would have favored the subcontracting of telephone wire pulling to construction contractors (who would ordinarily employ IBEW members for this work). After discovering what was afoot, the NFTW reported the information to its member unions and lodged protests with the OPM, the FCC, the Truman investigating committee, and other government agencies. Member unions also threatened not to connect IBEW-pulled wire with other telephone equipment at defense construction projects. In the face of such pressures, the OPM retreated. The allocation of wire-pulling work was left to be fought out locally, and the War Labor Board subsequently ruled that pre–World War II "practice and custom in the particular area" would govern the allocation. As a result, the IBEW's control of wire-pulling work rarely expanded beyond its prewar salients.[45]

While fighting outside unions, the NFTW became engaged in more general lobbying. Beginning in early 1940 it hired a succession of attorneys to serve as its "Washington contact and information men"; in April 1941 it settled permanently on Charles V. Koons, who was first hired at one hundred dollars a month to work "five to six days a month." Subsequently, Koons became the organization's legal counsel, and in June 1942 Griffith joined him in Washington on a full-time basis. In 1941 Griffith had been appointed to the Labor Advisory Committee of the Defense Communications Board, and the NFTW now benefited from the personal contacts and information that this position afforded.[46]

As lobbyists, NFTW officers and representatives appeared before a variety of congressional committees and administrative agencies. They tried unsuccessfully, for example, to block minimum-wage exemptions for learner-operators and operators in very small exchanges. They persuaded the Women's Bureau to conduct a study of operators' skills which, as previously mentioned, ended up challenging Bell's time-honored claim that it paid good wages relative to those in "comparable lines of employment." Joining with AT&T, they helped narrow the scope of a 1941 rate reduction proceedings, block War Department plans for undertaking work that WE distributing houses could perform, and prevent the transfer of AT&T Long Lines teletype and leased-wire facilities to a proposed Postal Telegraph–Western Union telegraph monopoly. This transfer would have jeopardized the telephone union affiliation of some four thousand Bell System workers.[47]

On pension matters, cooperative NFTW and AT&T lobbying met with mixed success. On the one hand, it failed to halt an FCC order requiring Bell companies to report a designated portion of their pension fund payments as taxable profits. On the other hand, it helped in blocking Treasury-backed legislation that would have imposed prohibitive taxes on pension plans falling below certain standards. Under the projected measure, acceptable plans would have to give employees a vested interest, and when AT&T argued that meeting these standards would cost so much that it might have to drop its pension plan entirely or at least require direct employee contributions, the NFTW joined in opposing the legislation.[48]

Some of this joint lobbying was probably unwise. Barbash has called the years from 1939 through 1941 the "dabbling period" in the NFTW's history, and those instances where the organization lobbied alongside AT&T are particularly vulnerable to the "dabbling" charge. Typically, the union efforts became a mere appendage to AT&T's operation, and, in the eyes of the government officials concerned, they probably blurred the distinction that telephone unionists had been trying to draw between their current status and their company union past.[49] Furthermore, the lobbying efforts aggravated the NFTW's growing financial difficulties. By mid-1942 nearly half of the salary portion of its budget was going to Koons and Griffith, who devoted most of their time to lobbying. It may be said in the NFTW's defense, however, that these efforts were backed by strong urgings and support from the affiliates.[50] And in the OPM affair, at least, the lobbying undoubtedly worked to the benefit of telephone workers.

As these activities grew, the NFTW's budget underwent rapid expansion. For the year beginning July 1, 1939, it budgeted $10,000. Two years later it budgeted $47,000, with most of the increase going toward mailing, printing, clerical expenses, compensation for travel, time away from telephone jobs, and payments to a hired actuary ($4,212) and the Washington counsel (set at $2,500 annually by the end of 1941). Griffith and Horth had also become full-time officers now, each earning $4,800 a year. And although Horth's full-time status allowed him to leave Milwaukee and combine his office with Griffith's in Chicago, this saving would be eliminated in August 1942, when a larger office was secured in Baltimore (after a failure to find space in Washington, D.C.). To fund these increases, the member unions raised their annual dues from ten cents per capita in 1939 to thirty-six cents in 1940 (and to sixty cents in mid-1942). Nor was this enough. By late 1941 the NFTW's expenditures were outstripping its income, and it was relying on loans from its affiliates to cover the deficit.[51]

The general tendency, it seems, was for the unions to confer more tasks than funds. NFTW executive board members complained of the assemblies' "entering every field that comes up" by "passing one thousand and five resolutions directing the executive board to do this or that."[52] As Griffith put it, dues increases were being resisted, yet the NFTW was being asked to "protect the pension; to contact the AT&T Company; to hold our own in Washington; to fight other unions; to help member organizations; and to carry on organization campaigns." In addition, there were unexpected losses in income: in 1941 the plant unions in New York City and New Jersey disaffiliated. At the same time there were unexpected expenses connected with observing the company-domination case against Southern Bell, and on repeated occasions affiliates were late in paying their dues.[53]

Secretary-Treasurer Horth's bookkeeping, moreover, appears to have suffered from his moves from city to city, his attempt to write a fresh copy of the ledgers, and his being overburdened by many other tasks. Whatever the cause of Horth's difficulties—he had no formal training in accounting, and a certified public accountant later reported that "we do not feel that this is the result of any dishonesty"[54]—by late 1941 member union leaders were beginning to complain about his chaotic bookkeeping and imprecise financial reports. And in late 1942 it would become clear that the NFTW was some twenty-five thousand dollars in debt.[55]

THESE FINANCIAL DIFFICULTIES would eventually undermine many unionists' confidence in Horth's and Griffith's abilities and, in so doing, swell a political unrest that was to rack the NFTW after 1941 and drive both men from office by mid-1943. The core of the unrest was not to lie in the financial difficulties themselves, however, nor even in Horth's and Griffith's general performance as administrators. Rather, it would lie in the collapse of the old consensus favoring union autonomy, and in the resulting efforts of many unionists to restructure telephone unionism in a new, more unified system.

The idea of union autonomy—"autonomania" as its critics termed it[56]—had retained most of its strength from 1939 through 1941. While telephone unionists had been willing to cede an increasing number of tasks to the NFTW, thus expanding its budget and its role as a service organization, they had not altered its basic confederational structure. Nor had they allowed it to interfere with such crucial "internal" union concerns as bargaining with management. A large majority had preferred a national organization that posed no threat to union autonomy, and this was the kind of organization over which Griffith and Horth had been content to preside.

As widespread as the sentiment for autonomy was, however, and as rooted as it was in longstanding feelings of departmental and sectional insularity, its survival depended in large degree on the continuing lack of strong incentives for greater unity. And, as will be seen in the next chapter, the American entry into World War II was followed by vast changes in the telephone industry, changes that combined to produce growing militancy among its workers. Militancy, in turn, would force unionists to explore the problem of how to enhance their bargaining and strike power; and this exploration would finally bring forth strong and clear incentives for moving toward national unionism.

Chapter 6

DEPRIVATION, MILITANCY, AND NATIONAL

UNIONISM, 1942–1944

IN 1941 no one could have foreseen the rapid dwindling of the telephone workers' penchant for union autonomy. Autonomania, it seemed, was firmly rooted in the attitudes of a relatively long-serviced and highly paid group with no taste for the kind of union-management confrontations that could underscore the need for unity. Given these attitudes, the sentiments and pressures for national unionism seemed likely to achieve only gradual and incremental gains. As Paul Griffith later remarked, without the intervention of some stronger force it might well have taken "two or three decades, or a generation, before there would be any marked change of opinion."[1] Certainly Griffith himself was temperamentally and philosophically an improbable leader of any move toward national unionism. Indeed, NFTW leadership in 1941 seemed as wary of structural reform as were the rank and file.

American entry into the war, however, rapidly altered all this. By the end of 1942, telephone workers found themselves confronted with deteriorating working conditions, wages that were now comparatively low, and incomes that bought less and less. Relief was needed, and since neither their employer nor the newly established War Labor Board seemed inclined to grant it, many telephone unionists became determined to use any available means of bringing pressure, including strike threats and strike action. Under such conditions, they became increasingly willing to subordinate considerations of union autonomy.

AS THE ECONOMY MOVED toward a war footing after December 7, 1941, sweeping adjustments were required on the part of the telephone industry, adjustments that changed both the conditions of labor and the makeup of the work force itself. Expansion of service now became imperative. Yet at the same time, replacement and enlargement of telephone plant had to be held to a minimum.

The expanded demand for service was not so much evident in local telephone calls. Held down by patriotic appeals to the public, these rose gradually from 37.1 billion in 1941 to 38.7 billion in 1944. But the number of long distance calls—all of which required extensive service by operators—rose from 85 million to 175 million, and the number of telephones in service rose from 20.8 million to 23.9 million.[2] Meanwhile, as a result of raw material shortages and decisions by management and the War Production Board, the industry had to make do, for the most part, with the plant equipment on hand in 1941. Total Bell expenditures for new plant were $154 million in 1943 and $170 million in 1944, as compared with $420 million in 1941. Little in the way of central office equipment was manufactured or installed after 1941, and 1943–1944 additions to long distance circuitry amounted to less than half of what normally would have been added to accommodate the increased traffic. In addition, AT&T reported that there was "some deferment of maintenance activities," and it freely admitted that the effect of all this was an "overloading of telephone plant."[3]

This new emphasis on service at the expense of plant changed the nature of the industry's labor requirements. In the Bell operating companies and Long Lines, the number of manual workers in the plant departments fell from 74,500 in late 1941 to 55,000 in late 1944; the number of clerical workers in commercial and accounting rose from 60,000 to 67,000; and the number of traffic operators jumped from 143,500 to 177,000. Fewer orders for installation of new plant produced a sharp decline in WE installation employment, from over 10,000 in late 1941 to less than 3,000 in 1944. But in the WE manufacturing and WE distributing house divisions, the decline in operating companies' orders was more than offset by war orders for communications equipment, the result being an increase in total WE employment from 61,000 in late 1941 to 94,000 in late 1944.[4]

Broadly speaking, the industry's labor requirements increased in those segments where it habitually employed workers who were less experienced, less well paid, and female. Included were traffic, most notably, but also commercial and accounting, and even WE manufacturing, if its wartime shift from a mostly male to a mostly female labor force is taken into account. Where the industry employed workers who were more experienced, better paid, male, and generally more highly skilled—notably in the plant departments—its labor requirements dwindled.[5]

At the same time, the war economy was tightening the labor market, creating recruitment problems for all employers. Even in an industry where the most pressing need was for unskilled women, many of whom could be quickly trained to handle the traffic switchboards, this tightening was sorely felt. When potential hirees found that they would have to begin at the low-paying end of lengthy wage progression schedules, many chose to work for higher starting wages now frequently offered in other industries. Even after management lowered its hiring standards and began "intensified recruiting," it still found that many women were "leaving the service of the company and going into defense work and higher paying jobs." As hiring increased, so did the number of departures, and one result, by mid-1944, was that some 53 percent of the traffic work force had less than two years' service.[6]

Even in the plant departments the reduced need for labor failed to prevent recruitment and turnover problems. Here such difficulties were aggravated by the lure of higher-paying jobs elsewhere, by 61,500 male Bell workers leaving to join the armed forces during the course of the war, and by management's reluctance to hire women for plant jobs, even for those requiring relatively little training. During the war, the proportion of women in manual plant jobs never exceeded 1 percent.[7]

Annual Bell turnover, to be sure, did not reach the rates prevailing in the manufacturing workforce as a whole, but it did increase rapidly. From 1931 to 1940 it had never exceeded 11 percent, but in 1941 it was 19 percent, in 1942 some 35 percent, and in 1943 and 1944 it was 41 and 42 percent respectively.[8] At the end of 1939 the proportion of workers who had less than one year's service had been 5 percent, and at the end of 1940 only 11 percent. Subsequently it reached 22 percent by the end of 1941 and 25 percent by the end of 1942.[9]

Thus the war economy, with its tight labor market and its demand for service at the expense of plant, not only concentrated telephone workers in job categories that paid less and required less skill and experience, but also concentrated them at the lower-paying end of the wage progression schedules. The major effect was to reduce average telephone wages, but along with this came deteriorating working conditions. For workers in all departments there were difficulties, sometimes "extreme difficulties," arising from having "more business to handle than facilities to handle it with."[10] And it was the burgeoning traffic departments that were particularly affected. Summer heat was now made worse by crowding. In addition, wartime separation of American families tended to swell the long distance workload during the undesirable Sunday and holiday shifts, so that where an operator had previously worked two such days out of four, she now worked three out of four or seven out of ten. And given the constant influx of new operators, the older workers were forced to compensate for the newcomers' inexperience. As one traffic unionist complained, "We have so many young girls . . . that it is making the job exceptionally hard for the older girl. She is carrying almost a load and a half."[11]

Especially irritating was a plan that management devised to circumvent the tight labor markets in such war boom cities as San Diego, San Francisco, Detroit, Washington, and Dayton. In these areas, the expanded traffic load joined with the lure of higher-paying jobs in war industries to produce severe labor shortages in the traffic departments. Rather than raise wages to levels sufficient to attract and hold an adequate force, management devised the plan of importing just enough operators from other locations to relieve the labor shortage. These transferees came from nonshortage areas and were offered the inducement of full living expenses in addition to wages. At first, when management estimated that the plan would last three to six months and presented it to the receiving cities' regular employees in informal conferences (not in contract negotiations), it was accepted as a temporary expedient. But as the months stretched into years, the typical regular employee came to recognize the plan's wage-restraining implications, and she came to resent the "inequity" of "two girls working side by side, and one of them getting more in supplementary money for living expenses than she [the regular employee] was making in salary."[12]

Finally, adding to the wage-restraining impact of such changes, was the employment policy that Bell pursued in its commercial and accounting departments. Here, as federal agencies later determined, management assigned women to some jobs held previously by men

—and then paid the women less. Officially, to be sure, the job definitions were different, but the U.S. Women's Bureau later found, with respect to commercial department work in particular, that "the definitions differed chiefly in the use of befuddling words." In reality, there were "separate wage schedules for men and women covering the same or very similar jobs." (Such problems did not arise in the plant and traffic departments during the war because there the lines separating men's from women's jobs shifted hardly at all.[13])

Taken together, these various changes had a devastating impact on the average telephone wage. The average real wage (expressed in 1935–1939 dollars) fell from $.78 hourly and $31.12 weekly in 1941 to $.70 hourly and $29.37 weekly in 1943. Although average real earnings rose slightly during 1944–1945, the 1945 figures ($.74 hourly and $31.16 weekly) still compared unfavorably with those of 1941, and even less favorably with those of 1939 ($.83 hourly and $32.14 weekly). In a 1946 survey of nonmanufacturing industries, the War Labor Board could find only two industries in which the average weekly wage had not kept pace with the wartime increase in the cost of living—telephone and insurance.[14]

Even more marked was the decline of telephone wages in relation to those in other industries. From the mid-1930s through 1941, average earnings in the telephone industry had been much higher than those for the manufacturing workforce as a whole. In January 1941 average straight-time hourly earnings had been $.82, with average weekly earnings of $32.52 (expressed in contemporary dollars), as compared to figures of $.66 hourly and $26.64 weekly for the manufacturing workforce as a whole. But in 1942 average wages in manufacturing leaped ahead of those in telephone, and manufacturing wage gains continued to outpace those in telephone during 1943–1944. By March 1945 the average telephone worker earned only $.90 per hour and $40.60 per week, while the average factory worker earned $.97 per hour and $47.51 per week. According to a *Business Week* survey, compiling data for fifty-five industries, telephone's relative wage ranking declined further than that of any other industry: In January 1941 telephone workers stood twelfth in average straight-time hourly earnings and twentieth in average weekly earnings. By March 1945 they were thirty-second in hourly earnings and thirty-third in weekly earnings.[15]

During the war, in short, the telephone industry changed from a high-wage to a low-wage industry. And although most of this decline was caused by the aforementioned shifts in the composition of the work force, some of it stemmed from the companies' refusal to raise wage rates as much as they were being raised elsewhere. After 1941 (a year in which most telephone workers received wage boosts of $1 or $2 weekly) telephone wage levels became the object of War Labor Board and other governmental directives, as well as of union-management negotiations, and the outcome was a series of $2 and occasional $1 raises—the so-called two-dollar formula—given more or less annually from 1942 through 1944. For long-service workers, the cumulative December 1940 to December 1944 gain was $6 to $7 weekly for most operators, and $7 to $8 for most plant workers. In addition, there were small increments produced by shortening the wage progression schedules, and for those beginning service there were special adjustments to facilitate recruiting. But no large telephone group won gains that even approached the concurrent $13.60 rise in manufacturing as a whole.[16]

AFL and CIO unionists became increasingly angry with federal wage policy during the war years, and the weight of recent scholarship suggests this anger was justified. But if organized workers in general were treated unfairly by their government and employers, then the treatment accorded telephone workers, at least until November 1944, was downright iniquitous. Raises given under the telephone workers' two-dollar formula were not nearly as large as those being given other workers. Among the many AFL and CIO union representatives in Washington who were winning superior gains for their members, the hapless telephone union representatives came to be known as the "two-buck kids."[17]

In part, the disparity in wage gains can be explained by the telephone workers' unusual position with respect to the War Labor Board. As established in January 1942, following a labor-management conference at the White House and no-strike pledges by the leaders of the AFL and CIO unions, the national board and its twelve regional subsidiaries were set up as tripartite bodies with equal representation from the public, management, and labor. All labor representatives, however, came from AFL and CIO unions, which meant, from the beginning, that the interests of telephone labor were to be represented by men who had no official connection with telephone unions and no particularly friendly feelings toward them. Such representation was not an insignificant matter. Initially responsible for adjudicating virtually all union-management disputes, the WLB was subsequently given an official role in wage-price stabilization, whereupon it also assumed the responsibility for allowing or disallowing wage increases to which employers had voluntarily agreed.[18]

Denied representation on the WLB and fearing what this could mean, the presidents of the telephone unions, meeting in Chicago in January 1942, decided not to sign no-strike pledges. Although having no intention of actually striking, they believed that their organizations, unlike the AFL and CIO unions, were not being offered a quid pro quo for their pledge.[19] Some of them believed, too, that a refusal to sign would help to lift the lingering onus of company unionism. And a small group of national unionists held the additional conviction that to forswear strike action was to give up a tool that might become useful in building a national union. As Joe Beirne put it, "We had no idea that we'd have a strike. But we did have a pretty long agenda . . . in the building of the union. We didn't want to give away any options, and one option would be a strike."[20]

In 1942 and early 1943 the WLB's treatment of telephone unionists was better than it would later become. Workers in the industry did benefit from the occasional imposition of arbitration as the last step in grievance cases involving discharges. They also benefited from a WLB ruling that prewar "practice and custom" would govern the allocation of telephone wire pulling—a ruling that halted IBEW encroachments upon this work.[21] And like unionists in other areas of relatively weak union power, they benefited from the board's general policy of imposing "maintenance of membership" where no stronger form of union security existed. Before 1942 the telephone unions had only been able to obtain union security agreements whereby dues were automatically deducted from paychecks of consenting workers, but now they were also assured than once an employee had joined the union, he or she could not leave it until the current contract had expired.[22]

In addition, the WLB's basic wage policy of 1942 and early 1943 was the relatively straightforward one of allowing straight-time wage rates to rise 15 percent above the rates of January 1, 1941. Unlike subsequent WLB wage policies, this "Little Steel formula" could at least be applied to the telephone industry without generating a welter of technical difficulties and delays arising from the peculiarly monopolistic character of the industry and the unique skills of its work force. Once telephone "dispute" cases were adjudicated, the workers involved usually did receive raises in accordance with the basic policy, and some workers received more, in accordance with a subsidiary policy aimed at eliminating "substandards of living."[23]

Even during this period, however, there were problems. Unlike the many employers who were anxious to grant the maximum allowable increases in order to attract and hold scarce labor, Bell sought to hold wages down through resistance and delays in negotiations and through using avenues of appeal within the WLB. This was particularly true when other than beginning workers were involved, when retroactive application of wage increases was being sought, and when nonformula increases to raise substandards of living could not be "chalked up against" the 15 percent increases of the entire group.[24]

In part, Bell's closefistedness arose from the fact that it was not principally engaged in war production; it could not pass its wage bill on to the government, as many of the more generous employers were doing. On the contrary, wage increases would have to be paid from earnings that were already subnormal, down to 5.5 percent on invested capital for the 1942–1944 period—the lowest in the system's history, except for the worst years of the depression. Increased business and temporary economies resulting from the overloading of plant were more than offset by increased federal taxes and the effects of federal price stabilization policies beginning in 1942. (The stabilizing efforts of the Office of Price Administration were not always successful elsewhere, but in the telephone industry, subject as it already was to public regulation and scrutiny, they were. Bowing to reality, Bell eschewed attempts at rate increases for the duration and indeed, under pressure from the FCC, reduced long distance rates in 1943 and 1944.) Under the circumstances, the benefits of a tight wage policy seemed to outweigh its costs.[25] In 1942 and 1943 the grumbling of the workers had not yet erupted in widespread militancy, and the system's indexes for the quality of telephone service were declining only slightly.[26]

In disputed cases, then, delay became the norm, a situation attributable partly to management policies, partly to crowded WLB dockets, partly to the tendency of the board's labor members to push telephone cases aside while expediting cases involving AFL and CIO unions. Once telephone dispute cases had passed out of union-management negotiations and into the offices of the WLB, union representatives could only ascertain that they were "'somewhere in Washington,' which seems to mean the same as 'somewhere in Africa' so far as definite information is concerned." The cases became "lost to the sight of man," and there seemed to be "little anyone could do about the situation" except wait "patiently for the WLB . . . to act."[27] By April 1943 NFTW unions had fourteen dispute cases pending before the board, some of them a year old. And in 1944, long after most groups had collected the increases due them under the 15 percent formula, some telephone groups were still collecting theirs. To avoid such delays, union negotiators often—though reluctantly and perhaps unwisely—settled with management on subformula wage increases, which could then be approved through the WLB's much simpler procedure for handling nondispute or "voluntary" cases.[28]

A related problem for telephone unions was that the American Communications Association, a CIO union based mainly in the telegraph industry, had now entered the telephone field and was appealing to workers to join on the basis of its superior access to the WLB. In September 1942 it had won the affiliation of the Order of Repeatermen and Toll Testboardmen, a small union of toll equipment maintenance workers in the plant department of PT&T, and in a subsequent wage dispute a panel composed of six members of the national board awarded three- to five-dollar weekly raises to this group of workers. As NFTW officers were forced to admit, this was "much better with respect to wages than other Bell unions have gotten so far." Largely on the strength of the award, the ACA proceeded to make rapid headway in raiding the now restless membership of the NFTW unions. Despite the recurring charge that it was dominated by Communists—the ACA was expelled from the CIO on those grounds in 1950—it gained several hundred adherents, particularly in Michigan and in Long Lines units in the Midwest.[29]

Fortunately for the NFTW unions, two developments came to their rescue. One was a reduction of the ACA award, the result of a management appeal to the full national board.[30] The other was the CIO's decision not to provide strong support for ACA organizing. By 1943 the strategy of the CIO's organizing director, Allan Haywood, was to "work both sides of the street," hoping eventually to bring the telephone groups into the CIO as a single industrial union; he therefore allowed but did not encourage the piecemeal and fragmentizing organizational efforts of such CIO unions as the ACA and the UE. Aside from the toll maintenance workers in PT&T, CIO and AFL unions won no representation rights among Bell workers during the war.[31]

Meanwhile, the WLB had amended its formulas in April and May 1943, adopting a new "wage-bracket" approach designed to correct "gross inequities" in wage rates. Under this, the WLB examined the range (or "bracket") of wage rates paid to the various occupation in each labor market area, determined from them the minimum "sound and tested going rate" for each occupation in each area, and authorized increases for underpaid workers up to the appropriate minimum rate.[32] Telephone unions now contended that many of their members were entitled to raises under this approach, and the WLB did not disagree. But the cases based on this contention were usually delayed indefinitely, mainly because the regional and national boards found no way of rationally applying an approach whose originators—according to a 1945 investigation by a WLB panel—"did not contemplate . . . the type of situation arising from the unique characteristics of the telephone industry."[33]

One problem was that there *was* no range or bracket of rates paid for telephone jobs in each labor market area; there was only one telephone employer, with one set of wage rates. And since most telephone jobs required sets of skills that were quite different from those required of nontelephone occupations, there were no other local wage rates to which telephone rates could easily be compared. Therefore, it was hard to determine from local criteria what the "minimum" rate for any telephone job should be. Presumably, objective job evaluation studies could determine the *level* of skill required of various telephone jobs, as compared to nontelephone jobs, and appropriate wage comparisons and minimums could then be drawn. But in 1943–1944 the WLB had no wish to shoulder this burdensome task. In addition, there was the problem of taking into account "the existence of the Bell System itself." Changes in telephone wage rates—even if these were based on the most rational local criteria—could not be imposed on a locality-by-locality basis without upsetting historically stable relationships between wage rates in the various parts of the system, thus risking the creation of "instabilities" or new "inequities."[34]

Confounded by these and other technical problems, the regional boards referred nearly all telephone cases to the national board, where they met with further delays. Clearly, if they were to be adjudicated, special arrangements would have to be made, but pressure for these remained insufficient to get action. The WLB hesitated, both because it was burdened by other tasks and because such arrangements might encourage other groups to clamor for special treatment. Its labor members were also more interested in the grievances of AFL and CIO unions than in the problems of independent organizations. And perhaps most important, Bell management was for the most part satisfied with the existing arrangements and exerted no pressure to change them. Only the telephone unionists themselves were pushing for action, and their pressure seemed to accomplish little. With no special arrangements forthcoming, cases continued to pile up—125 of them by December 1944.[35]

In significant measure, then, the WLB shared in the responsibility for the plight of telephone workers. WLB delays, like Bell management's tough negotiating stance, helped to insure the continuance of existing conditions. And although WLB decisions provided some gains, notably in such nonwage areas as union security and preservation of wire-pulling work, telephone workers found relatively little relief from their regimen of low wages, deteriorating working conditions, and inferior wage increases.

EVEN THE LONG-QUIESCENT telephone workers could not be expected to endure these abuses peaceably. And indeed they did not. Confronted with the obvious failure of peaceful attempts at correction, unionists responded with an increasing number of strike threats and strike votes, several walkouts by local groups, and one brief strike involving more than two thousand plant workers. Finally, as will be seen in the next chapter, the traffic workers' anger was to erupt in November 1944 in a strike that spread from Dayton, Ohio, to Detroit, Washington, and other cities, menacing war communications, eliciting threats of government seizure, and eventually forcing the WLB to handle telephone cases in a way that hastened and enlarged wage increases.

While deteriorating wages and working conditions were clearly the major cause of this emerging militancy, other factors were also at work. Compared to the prewar work force, the workers were now younger, with fewer years of service, less exposure to company indoctrination, and less to lose from incurring management's displeasure.

The dislocations and tensions caused by the war itself may also have made them more militant. Certainly, the thousands of wartime transfers, as well as the migration of many workers prior to accepting telephone employment, contributed to a rise in uprootedness—a phenomenon from which the telephone work force had long been relatively free.[36]

In addition, workers could now walk out with some assurance that the government would act to prevent their *staying* out in long, impoverishing strikes. As Melvin Bers has put it, the NFTW unions "had the benefit of a context in which all-out warfare could not be tolerated. The few strikes emphasized NFTW's militancy without really testing its strength." To the extent that this militancy was not counterbalanced by a reluctance to imperil war communications and production, it made for a greater willingness to strike.[37]

Finally, both the willingness and the ability to strike were strengthened by the groundwork that had been laid before 1942. Many unionists had acted as models of boldness, and other workers had seen them escape unpunished. And given the lineaments of local organization that had developed, discontented workers would not have to expend most of their energy on organizing and on attempting to gain legal recognition. Rather, they could concentrate on economic job action and the preparations for it.

As in earlier manifestations of the unions' progress, the willingness to strike developed unevenly in the various parts of the system. About one-third of the industry was untouched even by strike threats; with respect to the industry as a whole, WLB officials later noted that "in practice the wartime strike record of the telephone unions compared favorably with that of unions which subscribed to the no-strike pledge."[38] For the most part, the new militancy was confined to about a dozen unions, most of them NFTW affiliates centered in WE, Long Lines, and the operating companies of the industrialized Midwest and East.

In the groups where prostrike sentiment did develop, it came for the most part gradually. A month after Pearl Harbor, for example, leaders of the relatively advanced Ohio union "agreed that strikes are out of the . . . picture at this time, with a full blown war in progress and all other Labor Unions signifying their intention to refrain from striking." Five months later the atmosphere had changed slightly: a June 1942 poll of NFTW plant union leaders disclosed that "the membership advocates discretion in strikes for the duration of the war," yet the leaders believed that members would respond to strike calls arising from "jurisdictional trouble, unjustified discharges, and certain other special circumstances." In early 1943 the newspaper of the Southwestern Union described the membership's reaction to management and WLB stalling as "disgusted" and "angry." By 1944 militancy was clearly evident. Leaders of the WE distributing house union reported "a more sensitive temper," with "a demand for economic warfare quite manifest." John J. Moran, the Long Lines union president, exclaimed that the recent growth of militant unionism was "almost a miracle, and especially when it is reflected that only a few years ago there were no more than a couple of legitimate unions in the industry."[39]

The record of documented strike threats and strike votes by NFTW unions also speaks for the gradual development of the willingness to strike. In 1942 NFTW union leaders made only three strike threats and conducted one strike vote. In 1943 there were six threats and two votes, and in 1944 nine threats and six votes. In nearly every vote there was a large affirmative majority, although in each case this merely authorized leaders to call strikes if they saw fit and may therefore have reflected a desire to enhance bargaining strength more than any real taste for strike action.[40] Nevertheless, it was clear that growing numbers of workers were willing to risk the possibility of strike action. And the rising number of strike votes, which were in each case initiated by union leaders, reflected the leaders' increasing confidence in the workers' willingness to take that risk.

The incidence of actual strike action did not increase gradually, but rather proceeded sporadically. Prior to the Dayton strike of late November 1944, the major walkout was that of August 1942, involving some twenty-one hundred plant workers in Ohio Bell's northeast area, an operating unit that in this case coincided with a bargaining unit and included groups in Cleveland, Canton, Youngstown, and Akron. In this area a contract had been signed in January 1942 with a wage-reopening clause to be exercised after six months. Accordingly, negotiations were reopened in June, with the union demanding increases in line with the Little Steel formula. No agreement could be reached, even with the aid of the U.S. Conciliation Service, and on August 5 the plant men struck without a prior vote, establishing picket lines that were generally honored by AFL and CIO union members, WE workers in the area, and union members in the other Ohio Bell departments (who in this case belonged to the same union as the striking plant workers). During the strike, management claimed that telephone service remained "satisfactory" with "the exception of intrastate and information calls," and union and management agreed that "adequate forces were being maintained" to handle "all essential service to war plants, government agencies," and local emergency facilities.[41]

After two days the strike ended at the WLB's request, apparently without a clear-cut victor. The WLB eventually awarded only two-dollar weekly increases, and it withheld the standard maintenance-of-membership award because of the union's "irresponsibility" in striking. Yet participants believed that a number of things had been gained. With no dire consequences having befallen the strikers, management now lost its "influence with some of the most conservative and fearful employees."[42] The idea of striking lost "some of its strangeness." And in the words of Bob Pollock, the Cleveland strike leader, the strike

> demonstrated that an independent union could strike, that the word "strike" was not a dirty word. It was not a shameful matter. It was something that could be talked about out in the open. And that we could get the attention of the government and we could get the attention of management, and the telephone workers *would* man the picket lines and would respond to a strike call. So I think at that point the confidence of the independent unions that learned about this strike from coast to coast increased a great deal.[43]

Observers noted that the Ohio workers had conducted "the first telephone strike of any size for many years."[44] Like Bell System strikers since that time, they could claim the distinction of having struck the world's largest private employer.

From the Ohio strike of August 1942 until the explosion of late November 1944, job action by NFTW affiliates was confined to three local groups. In late 1943 Canton plant workers ceased all installation work for twenty-seven days as a result of Ohio Bell's decision to give local installation work in new war plants to the IBEW. The work stoppage ended after the issue was certified to the WLB, which later gave the disputed work to the plant workers. In August 1944 operators in a Washington, D.C., exchange walked out in support of a demand that their "arbitrary" and "abusive" chief operator be removed. They returned to work thirty-four hours later, after management agreed to transfer the chief operator. And in early November 1944 operators in Peoria walked out during peak evening hours to protest the demotion of a fellow worker. Illinois Bell subsequently rescinded the demotion.[45]

Among non–NFTW telephone unions, there were also strike threats and walkouts during the 1942–1944 period, five of which seem worth noting. One came in March 1942, when 150 truck drivers in the New York City plant union staged a one-day walkout to protest a cut in night supply truck crews from three men to two. A second, by far the most serious of the five, was a racially motivated action occurring in December 1943—a strike conducted by the Point Breeze Employees Association (PBEA), which represented workers in the WE Point Breeze manufacturing complex in and near Baltimore. A third and fourth came in 1944, when the New York City traffic union and the Illinois plant union (which had left the NFTW in 1943) made strike threats and conducted strike votes in connection with wage issues. And a fifth came during the same year, when the Southern Federation of Telephone Workers, an organization that had recently replaced the NRLB-disbanded company union in Southern Bell, threatened to strike in an attempt to hasten NLRB certification.[46]

The December 1943 strike, one of the largest of the racial "hate strikes" that scarred the country that year, requires special mention. Earlier in 1943 the PBEA had been brought before the NLRB on grounds of continuing company domination; it was one of the two Bell labor organizations that were eventually disbanded on those grounds. The issue at stake in December was the WLB's refusal to order separate toilet facilities for white and black workers. The refusal produced a prostrike vote at a meeting attended by 350 of the complex's 6,300 workers. At the height of the subsequent strike, war production was undoubtedly affected. The PBEA claimed that 90 to 95 percent of the force was not working, while management claimed that half the force was out. It is clear, at least, that most white workers stayed off the job while most black workers stayed on. The episode ended a week after the strike was called, terminated by an army take-over of the complex and the failure of the PBEA to achieve its demand.[47]

It should be emphasized that this racial episode was exceptional and that nothing of this sort occurred where telephone workers were represented by legitimate unions. In many northern cities, small numbers of blacks were now being hired as traffic operators, thus ending the prewar policy of confining blacks to the most menial jobs—and occasionally producing stiff objections from white operators. But generally speaking, this small-scale integration of the traffic departments went smoothly, thanks in part to the cooperation of unions and local management toward that end.[48]

Viewed in retrospect, then, the 1942–1944 period saw large numbers of telephone unionists, concentrated for the most part in a dozen or so NFTW unions, lose their dread of strike action and come to regard it as a legitimate economic weapon. Once they had been unwilling to fight and thus had seen no need to mobilize and arm. But with increasing agreement on "the value of the strike weapon,"[49] with a record of scant accomplishment through peaceful protest and uncoordinated threats and action, and with their problems aggravated by a closefisted employer, an impassive government, and rival CIO unions, their attention was now shifting to questions of how to plan and order concerted strike efforts. In short, as they became willing to use their economic weaponry, they found ample cause to seek—and embrace—means of arraying that weaponry effectively. This search, once it was undertaken in earnest, finally provided telephone unionists with a strong incentive for abandoning union autonomy.

AS UNIONISTS BEGAN to explore the problems of mounting forceful, effective pressure, they were guided in part by information and perceptions acquired earlier. Deemed especially pertinent now was the prewar recognition that "A.T.&T. controlled the labor policy of the operating company." Deemed pertinent, too, was the perception, gained in the course of rebuffs by the WLB, that this agency bore certain similarities to the Bell System, that like Bell it understood only the language of "pressure and force" and had to be dealt with as a centrally controlled unit.[50] In the battle over representation, for example, NFTW representatives had concluded that "the only way to secure membership on the WLB would be through the offices of the Chief Executive."[51]

Telephone unionists had come to recognize, in other words, that confrontation with Bell or the WLB was confrontation with a unified, centralized institution. To many this now bespoke a need for countervailing unity on their own part, a need for "us all being together in order to compete with the Bell System." "Little organizations," they believed, stood little chance against an organization like Bell. Their strike actions could easily be thwarted by the tactic that "the A.T.&T. System had long since adopted, the rule of 'divide and conquer.'" Against the WLB they were similarly handicapped—capable, it seemed, of becoming occasional nuisances to federal officials but not of developing any real "political pressure." As Moran argued in February 1943, "If we do not get together now and get a national organization that can exert political power in Washington, we are going to continue to be behind the eight ball so far as the government is concerned."[52]

When unionists turned from this broad contemplation of structural problems to the practical details of strike strategy, they could also see a need for greater unity and more centralized authority. With genuine strike threats and strikes now taking place, they could no longer ignore the problem of coordination posed by separate unions and separate responses to picket lines. As NFTW unionists struggled with this problem from 1942 through 1944, they came to realize that it could not be solved by a loose confederation of autonomous unions.

The struggle began with committee discussions during the latter half of 1942 and with the meeting, in February 1943, of a special assembly in Cincinnati. There a solution was attempted through the erection of moral commitments: it was resolved that any affiliate going on strike was to notify NFTW headquarters of its intention to do so; headquarters was to "notify all member organizations of the contemplated action"; and "all member organizations and their members" were to "respect picket lines and refrain from passing such picket lines unless permission is given by the union on strike.'

That these commitments would be honored, however, seemed doubtful. In the first place, the moral weight of the resolution was diminished by its dubious constitutional status. The resolution seemed to violate the autonomy clause and its ban on such regulation of affiliates' behavior.[54] Secondly, everyone knew that the NFTW had no material leverage to compel honoring of picket lines—a major consideration in a situation where strong competing interests and feelings were likely to exist. Finally, the resolution failed to account for the legitimate concerns of nonstriking unions confronted with the picket lines of a striking affiliate.

For the resolution demanded, in effect, that nonstriking groups leave their jobs in support of a strike that they had had no voice in calling, that might be unwise or even frivolous in conception, and that offered them no immediate benefits even if brought to a successful conclusion. This was a great deal to demand, and the demand could be reasonable only if the groups being told to honor picket lines could expect, in the future, roughly equal benefit from similar action by the group now striking. For many this was not the case. Most commercial and accounting groups did not expect to engage in much strike action on their own volition. And while traffic groups could greatly aid other groups by honoring their picket lines (because of traffic's key position in the rendering of telephone service), they could not expect to receive equal benefit from reciprocal action by other groups in the future.

Concerns of this kind were brought into sharp focus in March 1944, when the three thousand members of the WE installation union threatened to strike. Spread thinly at central offices across the country, such workers could erect picket lines that approximately one hundred thousand operating company workers would have to face. If honored these could be a potent weapon. Operating groups, on the other hand, would not benefit directly; they could expect relatively little future benefit even if the installation workers were to reciprocate; and given the installation group's reputation for militancy, the greater frequency of its strikes seemed likely to accentuate the unequal exchange. Consequently, while some operating company groups did promise picket line support, others "indicated that complete support was impossible."[55]

As it happened, the threatened WE installation strike did not materialize. But the strike threat and the weaknesses it had exposed sharpened the realization that strike solidarity could not be achieved merely by demanding it. In Denver in June 1944 the NFTW assembly voted a partial salary for its previously designated "strike director," I. R. Hudson, thus enabling him to take time off from his Ohio Bell plant job and "improve that part of the Strike Manual which relates to crossing picket lines." By January 1945 his advice and their own widening experience had made the NFTW executive board "cognizant . . . that safeguards should be erected to protect member organizations from having sympathy strikes imposed upon them without first having the issues made clear and approval of the NFTW given."[56] By the end of 1945 this recognition was to produce a resolution that "NFTW affiliates shall not be obligated to support any striking affiliate unless prior approval of strike has been obtained [i.e., from NFTW headquarters]."[57]

Increasingly, unionists were moving toward the view that strike solidarity required some form of centralized coordination and authority, and along with this went the realization that these things could not be provided by a weak confederation like the NFTW. As Hudson noted in June 1944, "because of structure and contract provisions, a high degree of solidarity of strike action within the membership of the NFTW becomes most difficult." As the NFTW executive board put it, rules under which the national organization would determine which strikes legitimately commanded picket line support were unenforceable unless appropriate delegations of "constitutional authority" were made.[58] Exploration of the strike-picket-line problem was leading to the obvious conclusion that strike effectiveness required abridgement of union autonomy.

Discussion of a proposed central strike fund led unionists toward the same conclusion. First suggested by an NFTW constitutional committee in September 1942, this proposal recognized and sought to offset one of management's advantages, namely the ability of any struck Bell company to draw financial support from a central source. Although it was subsequently rejected as desirable but not practical in view of the hard-pressed finances of the NFTW and its affiliates,[59] discussion of the proposal went far enough to convince unionists that any future implementation would require some centralizing of authority. If it was to work, there would have to be swift, authoritative decisions as to which strikes merited central funding, which nonstriking unions were honoring picket lines and therefore deserved central funding, and which unions had failed to support past strikes to the point where they should be denied central funding during their own strikes. In other words, a type of centralization would have to prevail that would diminish the autonomy of NFTW affiliates and thus require "a new constitution or constitutional changes."[60]

Finally, as interunion attempts at joint action increased during this period, so did the episodes in which leaders of individual NFTW unions undercut these attempts, thus demonstrating to many unionists the need for more centralized authority. The most dramatic episode of this kind occurred in the wake of federal revisions in wage policy, ordered on April 8, 1943. Until their clarification a month later, these revisions seemed to prohibit standard 15 percent wage increases for the 175,000 telephone workers whose wage cases were then pending before the WLB. On April 10 Vice-President Beirne, who was then acting as the NFTW's president by virtue of Griffith's recent entry into the army, responded with veiled threats of a national telephone strike. In telegrams to William H. Davis, chairman of the WLB, and to Economic Stabilization Director James F. Byrnes, he declared that the revised policy "will unquestionably lead to serious dislocation of communication services" unless NFTW leaders could have "a personal conference with you so that the viewpoint of our member organizations can be properly given."[61]

To knowledgeable observers there was little doubt that Beirne was bluffing—and what doubt did exist was quickly dispelled by affiliates' violations of an NFTW resolution to "refrain from publicizing adverse comments with respect to any . . . strike or strike threat." On April 11 the leaders of four NFTW affiliates in Illinois publicly declared that the threatened action "would be a strike against the government," that it "should be called only after a membership vote," and that Beirne's statement should be "corrected so as not to convey an impression that telephone workers would openly defy the government." Leaders of two of these unions added that they had "no intention of striking."[62] Thus undercut, Beirne was unable to secure a conference with Davis and Byrnes.

A less dramatic but equally damaging form of undercutting occurred in connection with union efforts to build a united front in contract bargaining, especially an effort to arrive at a common termination date for the unions' contracts with the various Bell companies, which would facilitate the submission of identical demands and the development of multiunion strike threats and strikes. The effort began in 1941 and early 1942, after plant leaders from the Southwestern Union and six midwestern plant unions had informally agreed to seek a common date. At the Cleveland assembly of June 1943, it became an official project of the NFTW.[63] But throughout the war period the effort was consistently frustrated by leaders of the individual unions, whose autonomy in bargaining remained constitutionally guaranteed, and whose desions on contract signing were shaped less by earlier interunion agreements than by immediate pressures from the membership and Bell management. An Ohio leader later described the pressures that beset the Southwestern and midwestern plant leaders in 1941–1942:

We thought we had something and we probably did, and . . . management was more interested in that common termination date than anything else we ever did. . . . They called in three or four of our unions three and four months before their contracts expired, and offered them increases, and at the same time, through their supervisors, went out through the field and let the [members] know there was money for them if they wanted it. . . . One of the parts of the proposition was to write a new contract as of that day. After it was all over, we found our plan again had the dates spread all over the year. A.T.&T. is still laughing.[64]

And such pressures continued. As Beirne remarked in May 1943, "It is easy to agree on a termination date which is common to all, and it is equally easy to find reasons, commonly looked upon as alibis, for not fulfilling the agreement." By June 1944 only three NFTW unions had managed to win contracts that expired on the agreed-upon date of March 31 or the adjacent dates.[65]

Similarly, leaders of the various unions sometimes undercut agreements to press for identical contract improvements. Prior to 1945 these took the form of model contracts, developed in regional and departmental conferences and relying for implementation on informal interunion agreements that usually proved to be weak reeds. As a New Jersey traffic leader later explained: "You could sit in conference and make a decision, and we'd all swear '*by God*' that we would stand by it. The next day somebody would go off and sign a sub-standard contract, and that, of course, I think had the fine fingers of the industry in it, and it certainly did break our back every time it happened." This, in fact, was to remain a serious problem as long as the NFTW existed. Even in 1946–1947, a southern California plant leader was to recall, "each of the unions was left to go their own separate way if they so desired. If a company made an offer to them wagewise that was acceptable to them, they could accept that, regardless of what sort of a goal had been established by the Federation or by the convention."[66]

The difficulty was that agreements to form a united front, including NFTW resolutions to that effect, amounted to nothing more than fragile exercises in mutual exhortation. So long as the NFTW constitution stipulated that member unions must "remain forever autonomous and be free from interference in the conduct of their internal affairs," the NFTW could hold no power of ratification over the contents or termination dates of union-management contracts. Nor could it effectively discipline member unions for breaches of unity. It was not at all certain, for example, that the NFTW possessed the power to expel the Illinois unions for their actions of April 11, 1943—and this penalty, in any case, would have been self-defeating. As the NFTW's constitutional committee expressed the difficulty in late 1942, there was no way to "crack down on member organizations who may be fooled into the belief that the Federation needs them more than they need the Federation."[67]

All of these experiences, then, when joined with the discontent arising from deteriorating wages and working conditions, eroded the old consensus in favor of union autonomy and sharply enhanced the sentiment for some form of national unionism. The climate of opinion was changing, and reflecting this change was a growing volume of critical comment about the federation's structure. One traffic leader asserted that "the National should have some power, and we had better start giving it to them." Another argued that "the NFTW is outmoded. It is neither constructed nor fitted to do the things that we want it to do." A plant leader remarked that "member organizations must give up some of their autonomy if we are to have a strong federation," that his union in Indiana "would like to be known as Local Number One of the NFTW." And from the executive board of the Long Lines union came a declaration that "only an industrial union, national in scope, can hope to accomplish what many small unions are now inefficiently trying to accomplish."[68]

Such views found quick and frequent expression in NFTW assemblies, in part because many newcomers to union leadership were now attending, and these newcomers had no prior commitment to the prewar orthodoxies. One result of wartime change was to accelerate the already rapid turnover among NFTW union presidents. Between 1941 and 1944 the turnover rate averaged 38 percent annually (compared to 28 percent annually from 1938 to 1941); in the twenty-two months from April 1941 to February 1943, the presidencies of more than half of the NFTW unions changed hands.[69] Emerging now was a new generation of union presidents, leaders like Pollock of Ohio, Mary Gannon of Washington, D.C. traffic, and D. L. McCowen of the Southwestern Union. Drawing lessons from their union experience, these leaders were convinced that Bell's structure and policies necessitated forming a national telephone union that could counter Bell's centralized organization—a union structurally different from the NFTW.[70]

By 1943, moreover, such leaders were beginning their bid for control of the NFTW assemblies. Added now to the earlier proponents of national unionism—Long Lines, Cincinnati, Michigan traffic, WE installation, WE supply and repair, and WE Kearny manufacturing—were the Delaware, West Virginia, and Washington, D.C., traffic unions; frequently supporting the cause were such groups as Ohio, Indiana plant, and Illinois traffic (which should be distinguished from another NFTW affiliate, the Chicago traffic union). In addition, McCowen and such allies as John Crull and Ione Trice could usually carry the Southwestern Union delegations. And the relative voting strength of the national unionists was further augmented by the tendency of some of the autonomaniac unions to drop out of the NFTW, either temporarily or permanently.[71]

Meanwhile, some of the discontent had taken the form of challenges to the old guard national officers, Griffith and Horth. In the eyes of his critics, Griffith was "ineffective," and in May 1942 a caucus of such critics sought to displace him by taking advantage of the constitutional provision that no two NFTW executive board members could come from the same affiliate. Meeting in Chicago, they nominated C. W. "Slim" Werkau, who like Griffith was an Illinois plant unionist, to be their regional board member. Having installed him in that post at the Baltimore assembly in June, they claimed that Griffith could not be a board member and was therefore ineligible for the NFTW presidency. The stratagem was defeated by constitutional revisions that allowed both Werkau and Griffith to sit on the board, with Griffith retaining his traditional at-large slot and his presidential eligibility. He was re-elected president, but clearly the mutual trust that had once prevailed was now a thing of the past. Nor was he the only one under attack. Horth, too, was being blamed for the NFTW's spending its way into debt and—more fairly—for his failure to report the extent of indebtedness. Reflecting this criticism was the passage of a resolution demanding that the NFTW "live within its income."[72]

The proponents of national unionism were not in the forefront of the attacks on Griffith and Horth. But as the attacks continued, they were able to install one of their number, Frances Smith of Michigan traffic, on the executive board. With the backing of the traffic caucus, Smith replaced Patricia Harris of southern California traffic, a strong defender of union autonomy. The result was an almost evenly balanced board. Smith joined Beirne and Moran on the still unassertive "national unionist" wing; Griffith, Horth, and Floyd Maize of the Mountain States union remained on the autonomist wing; and the other three members stood in between.[73]

During the latter half of 1942 the position of Griffith and Horth grew weaker, partly because of rapidly growing militancy and national union sentiment, partly because they lost the support of their home unions. A year earlier their acceptance of full-time positions had rendered them ineligible to hold local offices, thus facilitating the rise of hostile factions in their home organizations. Now, with the move of NFTW headquarters from Chicago to Baltimore, they lost what contact they had with supporters in Illinois and Wisconsin. As Griffith later complained,"The secretary-treasurer and president were *entirely* separated from their own organizations. We had no access whatsoever to the facilities of our respective organizations."[74]

Then in October 1942, thanks in part to Werkau's and George Du-Val's probing of ledgers that a CPA later described as showing a "lack of bookkeeping knowledge,"[75] the NFTW executive board discovered that the national organization was some twenty-five thousand dollars in debt, that "some of the bills which weren't paid dated back a number of years," and that some disbursements had been contrary to the board's explicit instructions.[76] These revelations created a furor, not because any malfeasance was charged or found, but because—as various unionists exclaimed—"most of us are broke in our own organizations," "a true financial picture has never been given to the National Assembly," and "our people are very conscious of mishandling of money."[77] Many affiliates castigated Griffith and Horth. On October 17 the NFTW executive board, itself shaken by these findings, responded with strong measures: a call for a special assembly to meet in Cincinnati in early 1943, revision of the 1942–1943 budget, and drastic cuts in current expenditures, among them a unanimous decision to take Griffith off full time. His lobby work, it was argued, was no longer essential, particularly with General Counsel Koons doing similar work. Horth, however, was retained full time to help clear up the financial crisis.[78]

These developments prompted Griffith to consider resigning. Having to go back to his Illinois Bell job, he thought, was an "intolerable" blow to the proper performance of his NFTW duties, and, considering the damage done by the financial revelations, he and Horth might have difficulty in getting reelected in 1943. Horth, to be sure, thought they stood a good chance. Given the reluctance of Beirne and McCowen,

Griffith's strongest potential challengers, to leave the relative security of their home unions, plus the strong support Griffith retained in some affiliates, the votes could probably be mustered. But it could not be done without a bitter internal fight, a fight that might easily combine with the looming struggle over structural questions to "wreck the organization and cause two organizations to be formed." In Griffith's view, a full-scale battle for the presidency would provoke the losers, whether they were the national unionists or the autonomists, to "split off and go their own way."[79]

With these considerations in mind, and perhaps with a temperamental reluctance to ride a "stormy sea," Griffith requested a leave of absence in December 1942. He thereupon accepted a captain's commission in the Army Signal Corps, whose chief officers he had become acquainted with during his lobby activities.[80] The organization was now without a president, and on January 29, 1943, the executive board decided that all questions concerning the presidential succession should be settled by the special NFTW assembly, which was to convene in Cincinnati three days later.[81] The prestige of the national leadership was at a low ebb; as it developed, neither Griffith nor Horth was even to attend the assembly. Ironically, it was this "leaderless" group that was to engineer the most significant move thus far toward the establishment of a national union.

FROM THE MOMENT the gavel fell on Monday, February 1, 1943, the special assembly was, in Vice-President Beirne's phrase, a "gutbuster." Among the assembly's problems was the matter of Griffith's absence; it had to decide whether to consider him "resigned" and then elect a new president, or to accept his leave-of-absence request and have the vice-president serve as "acting president" until the regular elections in June. In addition, many of the ninety-odd delegates were angry about the past and present state of NFTW finances, a few angry enough to support a dissolution motion being prepared by the Illinois plant union. Adding to the turmoil was the absence of Secretary-Treasurer Horth: two days before the assembly, after an executive board session in which a majority had severely criticized him, he had fallen ill and was now reported to be in a Cincinnati hospital suffering from pneumonia. And finally, there was the structural issue. Many of the national unionists were planning to use the upcoming discussion of a constitutional committee report to propose sweeping structural changes.[82]

Somewhat to the assembly's own surprise, it was able to deal with these problems without shattering the NFTW. On the question of presidential succession a compromise was reached. After Griffith's request for a leave had been tabled, Beirne was able to inform his national unionist supporters that he did not wish to become NFTW president, although he was willing to continue as vice-president and acting president on a part-time basis. The delegates then granted Griffith his leave of absence, to last until the regular June assembly, and when he subsequently sent a telegram offering to resign, they rejected the offer.[83]

At the same time, Horth's absence was coverted into an asset. With the assembly in need of a secretary to record the proceedings, Beirne appointed Werkau, the Illinois plant leader, to serve as "secretary-treasurer *pro tem*, to act only until Mr. Horth's return." Werkau had been a leading critic of the handling of NFTW finances, but, as Beirne later explained, "When he came up to the platform, the thing I told him was, 'Now, Slim, you've just changed sides.' And he knew he did. He knew he was mouse-trapped, and he was, for now he had to act like an acting secretary-treasurer." His acceptance, moreover, meant that Illinois plant's inclination to break up the NFTW was "not as hard" as expected. Somewhat mollified, it offered no dissolution motion.[84]

So reinforced, Beirne, Werkau, and the other executive board members were able to withstand a two-day onslaught of criticism and questions concerning NFTW finances. They acknowledged past mistakes, stressed their strong corrective measures of October 1942, and held out hope that the budget could be balanced by June. Werkau also distributed Horth's financial report, explaining it as best he could and offering to seek out the answers to questions the board could not answer immediately. Gradually the storm subsided, and finally, as Beirne later recalled, most of the delegates accepted the situation, with the implied warning that "we had from February until June to clean up everything that might be wrong." In addition, they voted a temporary increase in per capita dues, from five cents to nine cents monthly.[85]

There remained the issue of structural change, specifically the report of the constitutional committee that had been appointed in June 1942 and had formulated its proposals during the summer of that year. The proposals were relatively moderate. On the one hand, they would empower the NFTW to suspend or expel member unions and to expand its jurisdiction over the entire communications field. At the same time, they would not scrap the autonomy clause or expand NFTW bargaining responsibilities, and they would retain a national organization whose members were labor unions rather than individual workers.[86]

At first the discussion of structural matters focused on the committee proposals. But quickly it became clear that the national unionists were a force to be reckoned with and that the committee proposals now fell far short of representing their aspirations. For the first time since the founding of the NFTW, the issue of national unionism itself became a subject for full floor debate, with Moran, McCowen, and Frances Smith leading the national union proponents, and Patricia Harris and L. B. Grew, of the Connecticut union, leading the autonomists. As the debate proceeded, two facts became apparent. One was that the autonomists were—as Griffith had surmised—adamantly opposed to any swift, fundamental change. The second was that the national unionists had not come equipped to offer a new constitution or a coherent set of constitutional amendments that would convert the NFTW into a national union. Toward the end of the debate, when McCowen moved that the autonomy clause be stricken, Beirne had to rule the motion out of order. It was in clear conflict with that section of the constitution that declared that "no amendments affecting the autonomy of a member organization . . . may be made." A few moments later the national unionists moved that General Counsel Koons be summoned from Washington, presumably so that they could seek his help in finding a way around the autonomy clause. This motion passed, and structural questions were tabled until Koons's arrival.[87]

As it turned out, however, Koons had little input. By the time he arrived the resolutions committee, headed by DuVal, had already fashioned a sweeping proposal aimed at "crystallizing the thinking of the Assembly" and preventing a fatal split over questions of structure. Entitled "Resolution Number One: National Union," it adopted much of the national unionist argument, declaring that "there presently exists no proper . . . designation of authority," and that "the history of the NFTW the past several years indicates that certain fundamental changes are necessary." It then spelled out the principles of a desirable organization, specifying that it must be one in which the member organizations would be chartered locals, the membership would consist of individuals, the national organization would be "empowered to bargain collectively on all matters," and "supreme authority" would be "contained in the said national union, its Constitution and bylaws." Finally, it proposed "that a Constitutional Committee be appointed with the purpose of writing a Constitution and bylaws in accordance with the above principles." By adopting Resolution One, the NFTW would in effect promise to move, at an undetermined speed, toward the eventual formation of a national union. For the defenders of autonomy, this deferring of change was the proposal's only virtue.[88]

Once introduced, the resolution drew the endorsement of the national unionists and was also revealed to have the support of six of the seven executive board members present. The task now was to placate the autonomists; this was done by arguing that the resolution projected national unionism as an "ultimate goal" that "could not be obtained in a short period" and would take "a considerable length of time" to implement.[89] The first major test came on Grew's motion to table: unions totaling 68,904 members cast votes favoring Resolution One; unions totaling 50,353 cast unfavorable votes; and unions totaling 26,706 did not vote. A short while later, on the question of formal adoption, the favorable vote mushroomed to 114,947 with 27,374 opposed and 3,941 not voting.[90]

This was not, of course, the definitive national unionist victory that it may have seemed to those outside the assembly. In the first place, there was no guarantee as to when a national union would be formed, the national unionists themselves having made assurances that national unionism would not come quickly. In the second place, the overwhelming majority by which the resolution was formally adopted was misleading. A large section of it was lukewarm and liable to reverse itself later. Some delegates had voted personal preferences that might not stand up in circumstances where they received instructions from their organizations,[91] and some had undoubtedly been carried along by the euphoria stemming from the assembly's unexpected success in handling its other problems.[92]

The shaky quality of the majority vote was recognized at the time. Beirne, who favored the resolution, remarked soon after its adoption that it reflected "the thinking of representatives gathered here, which may or may not be confirmed by our constituents." The events of the next four months did, in fact, reveal that some proresolution delegates had gone beyond the wishes of their home unions. After all the member unions had weighed the resolution and passed judgment upon it, a substantial number of delegates appeared in the June assembly in Cleveland, ready to reverse the position taken earlier. When a motion to rescind Resolution One was introduced, it failed only because it lacked the necessary two-thirds majority, the proresolution vote being only 57,304, with 65,558 opposed and 4,791 not voting.[93] In all likelihood this vote and the Cincinnati vote on Grew's motion to table (with slightly more than 50 percent favoring Resolution One) were really the best measures of the strength of national union sentiment in early 1943.

Nonetheless, participants in the Cincinnati assembly were justified in later describing the adoption of the resolution as a landmark in the development of a national telephone workers' union. The votes on it were the first solid sign that the sentiment for national unionism had grown tremendously since 1941. The national unionists could now proceed with the assurance that their position commanded about half the affiliated membership's electoral strength and with some reason to suspect that support would continue to grow. Also, by placing national unionism on the NFTW's agenda, the resolution made it an apt subject for discussion at all future NFTW and member union gatherings. It became something, as Beirne put it, that "we didn't let people forget."[94] Finally, the principles expressed in the resolution were to guide the work of the NFTW constitutional committees of 1943–1946—work that was to play an essential part in the establishment of the CWA in 1947.

With the adoption of Resolution One, then, the telephone workers were clearly beginning to move toward the type of centralism characteristic of other modern unions. Yet in their case the movement seemed to owe little to the type of bureaucratization often stressed in studies of labor unions' history. At the national level, bureaucratic aspirations and resources were minimal. Aside from narrow service functions, few responsibilities had accrued to the national office; as for Griffith and Horth, its only full-time occupants, they were not only poorly situated to push the NFTW toward national unionism, they were without any desire to do so. They had both opposed national unionism from the NFTW's beginning. If they contributed at all to the consolidation of national union sentiment and its expression in Resolution One, the contribution lay in their absence from the Cincinnati assembly. Beirne's and DuVal's contributions at Cincinnati were more positive, but Beirne's handling of office-holding questions and DuVal's formulation of Resolution One in no way relied on bureaucratic talents or resources. These were straightforward political compromises, aimed mainly at avoiding fatal splits in the NFTW. General Counsel Koons was not present while the resolution was being formulated, and he did not participate in the debate on it.[95]

The member union leaders seemed to prefer national unionism in somewhat greater proportion than did the membership in 1943. It could be asserted, of course, that their preference may have owed something to a wish to convert their own precarious elective positions into secure, nonelective posts as regional officials of a national union. In other words, perhaps they were trying to bureaucratize their own offices. But no evidence supports this assertion. During the entire 1943–1947 discussion of constitutional changes aimed at creating a national union, it was assumed that local and regional offices would remain elective. And in fact, with the 1947 establishment of a national union—whose constituent "divisions" corresponded to the former member unions of the NFTW—the offices in these divisions did remain elective.

Clearly the major impetus for national unionism was the recognition by union activists and leaders of the centralized character of the Bell System and the WLB, followed by the rational conclusion that a unified, articulated labor effort was needed to confront such opponents.

These perceptions grew mainly from the unionists' frustrating wartime experience, an experience that underlined the powerlessness of the autonomous unions to represent important member interests in the face of worsening working conditions, relatively low wages, and rising prices. Confrontations generally left the telephone workers licking wounds that were, to some degree, self-inflicted by their own scattershot approach. Older feelings of sectional and departmental insularity came to mean less than the coalescing resentments of a younger, more fluid, less docile work force—resentments at deprivations that were highlighted by the generally flourishing wartime economy. The resulting militancy provided a climate in which a grass-roots movement toward a national union could and did develop. Subsequently, what was left to the national leadership—which thus far had done little to inspire that movement—was to hold divergent NFTW elements together so that a national union, when it was finally formed, would constitute a major force in the telephone industry.

Chapter 7

TOWARD ONE NATIONAL UNION,

1943–1946

IF THEIR FEBRUARY 1943 successes at Cincinnati had proved heady stuff for the NFTW's national unionists, the unfavorable vote on Resolution One at Cleveland four months later was a sobering draught. They were not as strong as they had hoped and believed. At best the wartime setbacks in real wages and working conditions had convinced only 50 percent of the NFTW unionists that autonomy was a luxury they could no longer afford, and a "mandate" supported by only half the membership was likely to mean little.

The possibility of stalemate loomed. Yet during the next three years, the national unionists would not only be able to bring almost all the membership to accept the idea of a single national union but, in 1946, would be ready to put the idea into practice. Conditions and events, and leaders who capitalized on them, combined to bring the membership through bargaining crises and internal strife to the brink of forming a national union.

In the spring of 1943 the national unionists could not yet capitalize on the gains of the preceding two years. The NFTW's autonomists, they realized, still held a kind of veto power over moves toward centralization. The national unionists, to be sure, could muster the votes necessary to control the executive board and national offices; and men and women sympathetic to this view continued to fill these positions. Beirne was elected president (initially on a part-time basis but after June 1945 as a full-time official); John J. Moran succeeded in winning Horth's at-large post and becoming vice-president; and Werkau, now firmly in the national unionist camp, remained as secretary-treasurer.[1]

But even with this kind of majority, the national unionists were reluctant to work their will and run the risk of having autonomist-minded unions secede. "Although we could have out-voted them at any time," noted William Dunn, "the sheer strength of out-voting them wasn't all we wanted. If you exercised the power that you actually had, why, you would just ruin the organization."[2]

For it seemed clear that a number of unions would prefer secession to centralization. During the Cleveland assembly, leaders of the Connecticut union had threatened to withdraw, as had the new leaders of the Illinois plant union. The following month, Illinois plant did withdraw, soon to be joined by Illinois accounting and southern California traffic. Behind this group loomed a larger group, unions that remained in the NFTW and made no threats, yet expressed a strong desire that the NFTW not move toward national unionism. Included here were the plant unions in Maryland, Wisconsin, Washington State, and southern California, and the amalgamated unions in Oregon, Northwestern Bell, and the Mountain States company.[3] If this group withdrew, the results were certain to be crippling. Although the NFTW might then be converted into a national union of sorts, it would be no match for the heavyweights—the Bell System and the War Labor Board.

The prospect of such withdrawals was also distressing because of the anticipated effect on non-NFTW telephone unions. A major pullout, as Dunn saw it, would mean that "we wouldn't be attractive to others that we wanted in." It would shatter long-held hopes for securing the affiliation of various outside groups and the re-affiliation of some who had left over such issues as dues or alleged midwestern domination.[4] Hence such pullouts had to be prevented if at all possible, and prevention demanded a spirit of compromise and caution.

Under Beirne's leadership, moreover, the national unionists were cautious and prone to compromise. A trim, black-haired New Jerseyite of welterweight proportions, Beirne was partly an amalgam of the Irish politician's stereotypical qualities: emotional yet canny, gregarious yet introspective—and he was a captivating speaker. He had first gained prominence in 1937, when, using vacation time from his New York WE distributing house job and traveling by bus with his wife and children, he had visited the other distributing houses across the country and persuaded the workers in them to form what amounted to a small national union, with himself as president. Thereafter, the union's newspaper bore the bold slogan, addressed to all telephone workers,

"One Industry, One Union." But early in his NFTW experience, Beirne had learned how to temper his views and avoid brash statements or accusations, a skill that helped him overcome the political liabilities of being an easterner, an Irish Catholic, a WE worker, and a relatively young man (he was born in 1911). On one occasion he had joined the opponents of an early dues increase, primarily to "establish the credentials" that would allow him "later on, now, to talk their language." Though sincerely believing in the national unionist cause and vigorously pushing it at times, Beirne and his allies now consciously adopted a consensual approach designed not to "get *too* far out in front," and to make sure that other unionists "were coming with you step by step."[5] From 1943 on, Beirne personally was willing to go some distance to gain the trust of the autonomy camp. Indeed, it may well be that his February 1943 refusal to become president of the NFTW and his subsequent refusal to accept the presidency on a full-time basis were part of a general strategy for mollifying those who felt Griffith and Horth had been treated unfairly.[6]

Further strengthening Beirne's approach was a belief that unfolding events and worker experience with collective bargaining and grievances would provide the best arguments for national unionism.[7] In the end he would play an important role in nudging the bulk of telephone unionists toward national unionism, but his influence was felt less through the minor bureaucratic resources of his office than through his hortatory gifts, his skill as a political tactician (already amply demonstrated at Cincinnati), and above all his patient and consensual approach.

Also influential in the course that events took was D. L. McCowen, the man who had welded the disparate Southwestern Union membership into a unified group and in so doing had, like Beirne, learned the art of accommodation and the compromises necessary to maintain organizational unity. A brawny, bespectacled Texan, nearly six-and-a-half-feet tall, with ready command of a salty vernacular when the occasion warranted it, McCowen—when among unionists—was quiet and sincere in demeanor, courteous and intelligent in debate. Unswerving in his devotion to national unionist principles, McCowen could express them in a conciliatory way—in Southwestern Union councils, on the floor of NFTW assemblies, and in various NFTW constitutional committees. In addition, a part of his contribution lay in what he did *not* do. As widely respected as Beirne—and with Southwestern a much larger political base than the WE distributing houses—he could have become a serious contender for the NFTW presidency, thus splitting the national unionist forces. But he chose not to do so. With full confidence in Beirne, and with strong family ties in the Southwestern territory, he was content to lead the Southwestern group for the remainder of his long union career.[8]

Under such leadership, then, there was little disposition to rush matters, and the result, for a time, was a virtual stalemate on structural questions and relatively little progress in bettering wages and working conditions. Saddled with the same structural weaknesses they had borne earlier, the unionists were unable to break through the resistance of Bell management and the continuing neglect by the War Labor Board.

Stalemate on these matters, however, did not mean that no progress was made. While tolerating continued structural weaknesses, the new leadership was busy putting the organization's finances in order. In this field, thanks to curbed expenditures and the temporary dues hike voted at Cincinnati, they were relatively successful. By June 1943 the NFTW had become debt free, and a year later, at the Denver assembly, the executive board could report a surplus of thirty-seven hundred dollars. The financial health of the organization also benefited from another dues increase voted at Denver, one described as raising dues from an "absolutely inadequate" level to one that was "not quite adequate." As passed, this doubled per capita rates, raising them to $1.20 per year, with the increase to take effect at the beginning of 1945.[9] With more funds, the NFTW was able to expand its activities. In 1945 it hired three staff members, expanded its educational and organizing programs, moved its headquarters from Baltimore to a storefront office in Washington, and resumed publication of *The Telephone Worker* (with regular circulation to all NFTW union members beginning in January 1946).[10]

In addition, the constitutional committee that served from June 1943 to June 1945 moved toward solving several technical problems. Under McCowen's chairmanship, it began work on a constitution based on the principles expressed in Resolution One. And with the help of an opinion rendered by general counsel Al Kane (Koons's law partner and replacement during the latter's 1943-1945 service in the air corps), the committee managed to defeat autonomist attempts to cut off its operating funds. Also with Kane's help, it determined that the autonomy clause of the NFTW was indeed an insuperable obstacle, that to form a national union "it would be necessary for us to bring about the dissolution of the NFTW" and create "a completely new organization." Further, it began sifting through the hundreds of suggestions and preferences offered by the affiliates, seeking to find some basis for a future consensus on structure; and, despite frequent attacks of "constitutional indigestion," it was able to find some areas of agreement. The great majority seemed to agree, for example, on the need for any future national union to include all communications workers (not just telephone workers) and to incorporate Canadian as well as American workers.[11]

Perhaps most important, there was substantial progress in organizing, especially in contests with AFL and CIO unions who had now become more interested in and active among telephone workers. Although a newly opened WE manufacturing plant in St. Paul was eventually lost to the UE, the much larger Point Breeze WE plant was successfully organized following the disestablishment of the company union there. In a 1945 NLRB representation election at the Point Breeze plant, a new, NFTW-supported union defeated the UE by a vote of 1,967 to 1,082. The NFTW and its affiliates also stepped up their organizing of non-Bell companies. Representation rights were won in companies in Pennsylvania, upstate New York, Ohio, Indiana, Florida, the Southwestern territory, and southern California.[12]

The greatest organizing victory, though, came in Southern Bell. There, an NLRB order disbanding the company-dominated Southern Association of Bell Telephone Employees (SABTE) had been upheld by the Supreme Court, thus setting off a contest for a potential union membership of twenty-six thousand, spread across nine states. The IBEW responded with a full-fledged organizing campaign. The CIO was briefly interested. And the NFTW quickly put together a team of organizers from its member unions and sent it to help the Southern Federation of Telephone Workers (SFTW)—an organization of Southern Bell workers that had sprung up under the leadership of William Smallwood.[13]

From the beginning of the contest in May 1943, the NFTW and SFTW held all the high cards. IBEW organizers could not speak to Southern Bell employees as fellow telephone workers, as could the SFTW activists and the NFTW organizers. Nor could the IBEW develop personal acquaintanceships in many of Southern Bell's 949 central offices, as could the SFTW, with its network of workaday relationships, and the NFTW, with its ability to rely on Long Lines unionists in the Southern Bell territory. In addition, SFTW organizing benefited from management's tacit approval. While company officials were careful to avoid illegal gestures of favoritism, the SFTW and NFTW soon found that Southern Bell never "came out and really *fought* us," and employees became aware that management preferred the SFTW to the IBEW.[14] Even among antimanagement employees, there was a tendency to favor independence from the AFL and CIO. Strengthening the NFTW and SFTW still further was an NLRB ruling that the contest was for workers in all four departments, across the entire Southern Bell territory, a ruling that kept the IBEW from carving out the few areas where it was strong and that frustrated such splinter movements as the Carolina Telco Union and the Louisville Plant Employees' Association.[15]

By the time the representation election was held in May 1944, the IBEW had dropped out of the contest, producing a vote of 14,714 for the SFTW and 1,515 for no union. The response of the IBEW was to file charges that the SFTW was a company-instigated successor to the SABTE. Not until September, after the charges had been heard and dismissed, were the results of the election certified, enabling the new union to become an NFTW affiliate. Although SFTW activists later admitted that many SFTW locals at first behaved "like the same old vehicle with a new coat of paint," the NLRB found no evidence of actual company support or instigation.[16] With the benefit of hindsight, it is clear that the top SFTW leadership, as well as most local leaders and activists, were determined to build a strong union. The SFTW was to figure prominently in the movement toward national unionism in late 1946, and it was to become a mainstay of the 1947 nationwide strike. To Southern Bell's discomfiture and the astonishment of nearly everyone else, the Southern union group was to help lead the CWA into the CIO in 1947–1948, and in 1955 it was to conduct one of the largest, longest, and most militant strikes ever to take place in the South.[17]

Notwithstanding these gains, prospects for national unionism did not appear much brighter in late 1944 than they had in early 1943. Because "it was almost a necessity to take these things a half-step at a time," the NFTW's structural dilemma remained unsolved. And because of the intransigence of Bell and the WLB, telephone workers' smoldering frustrations were still largely ignored. Kane and the new NFTW leadership continued to ask the WLB for special arrangements for the handling of telephone wage cases, but the requests were consistently denied. Beirne "went public" in a series of radio appeals, but nobody paid much attention. While there was discussion about joining the Confederated Unions of America, a loose alliance of non-AFL-CIO unions that was lobbying for a seat on the national War Labor Board, it came to nothing.[18]

The only thing that seemed to emerge from such frustrations was a decision about the kind of special arrangements the NFTW wanted from the WLB. After trying various approaches, Kane had concluded that agitation for a telephone panel or commission, an adjunct to the board, was the most promising tack. Unlike the granting of a seat on the board itself, the creation of such a body would be politically and administratively feasible, and it seemed likely that the panel would serve telephone worker interests adequately. Kane so advised the NFTW leadership in early 1944, and accordingly, at the Denver assembly in June, a resolution was passed demanding the creation of such a body.[19]

THAT A TELEPHONE PANEL of the WLB was indeed established six months afterwards was largely due to a strike of telephone operators in Dayton, Ohio. Dayton, the site of the aircraft industry's major procurement center, was one of several boom cities where Bell had imported transferees to relieve the wartime shortage of operators. By late 1944 their number totaled 105, and from 1942 on, Ohio unionists had been protesting the policy and arguing that it would be unnecessary if adequate wages were paid. The latest dispute over the issue had gone to the WLB in August, and some three months later it had not yet been acted upon.

In early November, Jeannette Reedy, a Dayton traffic leader and president of the Ohio union's southwest traffic council, informed union president Bob Pollock that the regular traffic workers in Dayton were ready to strike, provided such action could serve a "constructive purpose." Galling them, she explained, was the presence of the transferees, who received $18.25-a-week expense money in addition to wages, and who in effect were being used to hold regular wages at low levels: 52.5 cents an hour or $21.00 a week to start, $32.00 a week after ten years. And their resentment had recently turned to fury when a group of operators, wondering why no local Dayton women were applying for jobs as operators, went to the local War Manpower Commission office to determine whether that job referral center was somehow acting as a bottleneck. What they were told had seemed to lay Bell's stinginess bare. The "female labor situation had eased," and job seekers were available, they were told. But with much better starting wages available elsewhere in Dayton, the WMC could not credibly recommend Bell as an employer; in fact it "preferred not to refer workers to employers paying less than 68 or 69 cents."[20]

Pollock, a veteran of the 1942 plant strike, gave Reedy's proposition several days' thought. Finally, he decided that strike action might serve to "shake up the War Labor Board" and possibly gain a telephone panel or commission. He not only authorized a strike in Dayton but sent a personal representative, Bill Dobscha, to insure that it would continue until he sent a coded telegram to end it. Whatever he or anyone else said or did publicly Dobscha was to ignore.[21]

The strike began with a walkout at 6 A.M. on November 17, followed, within forty-eight hours, by separate strike votes and sympathy walkouts by traffic workers in twenty-five other Ohio cities. Included were all of the largest cities except Cincinnati, which was not served by Ohio Bell. In addition, plant men in most of the affected cities either voted to join the strike or agreed to honor picket lines. By November 21 the union claimed that eight thousand workers were out, although Ohio Bell placed the number at an improbably low three thousand. The *New York Times* described the effect on all operator-connected Ohio Bell service as " crippling." Management had been forced to limit long distance calls to those falling within "emergency and war-essential" categories, and even these were not being adequately handled by twenty-three of the central offices.[22]

Meanwhile, the WLB had summoned Pollock to Washington, where, between November 17 and 23, it declared the walkout a "threat to the effective prosecution of the war," warned of government seizure of all struck work places, told Pollock it would not consider the merits of the workers' case until they went back to work, and several times ordered him to end the strike. Each time, Pollock refused, remarking at one point: "No union leader could conscientiously order a girl making $21 a week to work beside a girl making $39.25 for exactly the same work." Since he was not sharing control with the NFTW leaders, he was not amenable to pressures through them. He refused to accept Kane's recommendation that he end the strike because of its noncompliance with the War Labor Disputes Act,[23] and when war mobilizer James F. Byrnes spoke of putting NFTW president Beirne "in khaki" somewhere "across the seas," the threat was both misdirected and ineffective.[24]

The NFTW did lend such indirect support as it could. Beirne's WE distributing house unionists observed Ohio picket lines, as did Vice-President Moran's Long Lines unionists. And when Pollock appealed to individual NFTW unions for assistance, the national officers seconded these appeals. In addition, Kane quickly took advantage of the situation to "renew his request that the War Labor Board establish a panel or commission."[25]

By November 22 NFTW traffic groups in Washington and Detroit, where operators were also angry at local transferee policies, had taken strike votes and told Pollock that they were willing to help. Late that day, after rejecting Kane's advice to call off the strike, Pollock sent telegrams to NFTW and non-NFTW traffic groups in about forty cities, asking their support. The response, at least among the NFTW groups, was considerable. On November 23 the Washington and Detroit groups went on strike, Chicago traffic voted to walk out, and at least three other groups (one of them non-NFTW) initiated strike votes. Most other groups applauded the strike but took no immediate action. During the day, the number of workers actually on strike rose to an estimated ten thousand, and "war-essential" service in Washington and Detroit was clearly threatened.[26]

These developments, Pollock later recalled, "shook the government up pretty much." On the evening of November 23 he was called to a private meeting with Nathan Feinsinger, a public member of the WLB. There an unwritten agreement was suggested. If Pollock would end the strike, the WLB would hold a special hearing on the Dayton transferee issue and would form a telephone panel as soon as possible. Agreeing to these terms, Pollock returned to Ohio and called off the strike. The next morning all strike activity ended.[27]

The WLB proved as good as Feinsinger's word. In early December the Cleveland regional board began hearings on the Dayton issue, eventually producing acceptable schedules for the departure of transferees. Similar schedules were also imposed at the other transferee locations. And the Dayton wage dispute that underlay the transferee controversy—like all other union-management cases in the industry—passed to the jurisdiction of the WLB's new National Telephone Panel, a body whose makeup and functions had been ironed out in lengthy discussions among telephone management, WLB and White House representatives, and NFTW officers and counsel.[28] As established on December 29, it consisted of two public members, Pearce Davis and Henry J. Meyer; two industry members, Frank M. Stevens of Ohio Bell and R. A. Phillips from a non-Bell company in South Dakota; and two "regular" labor members, William Dunn and John J. Moran, both named by the NFTW but under the proviso that one of them would relinquish his seat in any case involving a non-NFTW union that wanted to seat its own representative. The panel was to formulate a basic telephone wage policy; once this was approved by the WLB, the panel was to hear all telephone cases and adjudicate them accordingly.[29]

Working out the policy occupied the panel for the next six weeks. The major problem was the old one—finding a way in which the WLB's local wage-bracket approach to the correction of "gross inequities" could be applied to the telephone industry. It was a complex problem, and after much study the panelists arrived at a complex solution. They agreed, first, that plant workers' skill levels were similar to those required in the metal trades and that traffic skill levels resembled those found in a "gamut" of thirteen clerical occupations; second, that equity or inequity in local telephone wages could be measured by comparing them to local wages paid for the aforementioned nontelephone skills; and third, that where they found gross inequities in local telephone wages, they would use their judgment in correcting them, giving substantial weight to the "established [wage] differentials between Bell companies" as they stood in 1940. These were the basic principles of the policy submitted to the WLB and unanimously accepted by it on February 23, 1945. Implementation remained up to the panel, subject to WLB review of decisions.[30]

In implementing the policy, the National Telephone Panel (or Commission, as it was renamed after the WLB-review provision was eliminated in June) broke through the pattern of two-dollar-a-week increases and long delays that had plagued the telephone workers since 1941. It began with the 125 cases that had been pending before the

WLB in December 1944, and by the time of its termination on December 31, 1945, it had heard 55 dispute cases involving 180,000 workers plus some 500 nondispute cases involving another 150,000 to 200,000 workers. Typically, the workers involved were awarded three- to five-dollar weekly increases, with the bulk of the awards aimed at correcting gross inequities and with the larger raises coming in areas other than the Northeast. (Wartime wage rates in general had risen faster in the West, Midwest, and South, and the panel's wage determination method was such that these faster rises were bound to be reflected in its awards.) In addition, the panel made other kinds of adjustments that affected wages, including the frequent shortening of progression schedules, particularly in the traffic departments, where the public members of the panel found "no doubt that most of the . . . schedule lengths were longer than the time necessary for an average worker to become proficient as a telephone operator." Traffic progression schedules were now shortened by two or three years, bringing the customary length down to eight or nine years by the end of 1945. Such panel practices had the general effect of raising operators' wages slightly in comparison with those of other telephone workers. In responding to the unions' claims that women were now performing commercial and accounting jobs previously held by men but were not being given equal pay for equal work, the panel followed WLB policy by stipulating that "for comparable quantity and quality of work performed, equal pay should be provided for male and female employees," and that "any claim that this principle is being violated shall be a proper matter for submission to the grievance machinery of the contract and if necessary to arbitration." On such matters as leaves of absence for union representatives and the imposing of arbitration as the last step in grievance procedures—the latter to the point where it became "fairly common"—the panel succeeded in molding telephone contracts toward "closer correspondence with contracts in outside industry," the effect being to improve the unions' position.[31]

All in all, telephone workers got much better treatment in 1945 than they had gotten earlier. Despite reductions in overtime and a new surge in the hiring of inexperienced workers that began after the war ended in August 1945, telephone workers' average real weekly earnings actually rose slightly during the year, climbing from $30.59 in 1944 to $31.16 in 1945 (compared with $31.12 in 1941). Average weekly earnings relative to those in other industries had been plummeting since 1939, falling from twenty-second place in a BLS list of 123 industries to eighty-sixth place in early 1945; but during 1945 the decline leveled off, with telephone workers standing in eighty-eighth place in February 1946. On the whole, telephone workers and their unions were less unhappy with their treatment under the panel than they had been with previous arrangements. And while the panel existed, strike sentiment abated. Only one major walkout occurred during the life of the panel, and that took place in November 1945, after the war had ended.[32]

The events leading to the formation of the National Telephone Panel, coupled with the operations of the panel itself, also spurred the growth of the NFTW. Its prestige was now enhanced in at least three ways. First, most telephone union activists, including those not connected with the NFTW, perceived the Dayton strike as a bold and effective action, and they knew it was the NFTW unions that had undertaken it. Second, the NFTW was credited with having forced (by means of the strike and otherwise) the creation of the National Telephone Panel, which in 1945 was increasingly viewed as beneficial: "the first real breakthrough," some called it. Finally, unionists knew it was NFTW representatives who sat on the panel, helping to shape its decisions.[33]

Nor was the prestige of the NFTW its only attraction. It did, after all, have two "regulars" on the panel, and once the new system began to operate, Dunn and Moran quickly became labor's "experts" on the complexities of wage policy, on case precedents, and on interrelationships with the surrounding federal agencies. While they carefully avoided overt pressures against non-NFTW unions, the latter were increasingly dependent upon them. Such unions quickly learned that designating their own representative to sit on the panel was not a realistic alternative. "After they did that a couple times," noted Dunn, "and saw how lost they were, why, they just let the commission handle [their] case."[34]

The result was the growth of subtle pressures and dispositions toward NFTW affiliation. As a direct consequence of union strike activity, Dunn and Moran had become government agents, thus assuming control of pertinent information, expertise, and other facets of bureaucratic power. And because independents desired access to this borrowed bureaucratic power, they began reconsidering the question of affiliation. One concrete example was that of the Wisconsin traffic union. As Dunn recalled, the group had

> got an attorney . . . and he came in prior to our hearing of the case. But it so happened it was the first case he had had to handle dealing with the War Labor Board or any of its agencies. So he relied heavily on Moran and myself for his presentation on the dispute case. And, by the way, because of the help we gave him, he recommended to this group that they come into the NFTW, which they did almost immediately after they came down here to Washington for the case.[35]

It may be noted that the main effect upon the NFTW of Moran and Dunn's wielding of bureaucratic power was an increase in the number of affiliates (though the Wisconsin traffic union was the only case in which such wielding was clearly a major factor in the decision to affiliate). Any effect upon the ultimate structure of telephone unionism was tenuous and probably negligible. Certainly what transpired here bore no connection with patterns of union centralization identified by either Nelson Lichtenstein or scholars working in the tradition of Robert Michels. Dunn and Moran's activities did not result in a significant shift in power from the separate telephone labor organizations to the NFTW or to any other centralized agency in the telephone union movement—although they might have, had the National Telephone Panel remained a permanent agency.[36]

The new attractions of the NFTW helped spur its growth from an affiliated membership of 125,078 in mid-1944 to slightly more than 200,000 by the end of 1945. Of the 75,000 increase, about 13,000 came from gains in the membership of the older NFTW unions, primarily as a result of expanded employment; an additional 30,000 can be attributed to special organizing efforts, mainly in the Point Breeze WE plant and Southern Bell.[37] But the remaining 32,000 can be credited, for the most part, to the Dayton strike, the operations of the Telephone Panel, the invitations of NFTW unionists, and a general disillusionment with autonomania as an outmoded luxury. New NFTW affiliates included the upstate New York plant group, the traffic groups in Indiana and Wisconsin, the accounting groups in Michigan and Indiana, and the commercial groups in Indiana and southern California.

Rejoining the NFTW were the WE Hawthorne manufacturing and Illinois accounting unions.[38]

There were still, to be sure, large groups outside the NFTW, mainly in the commercial and accounting departments across much of the country; in Illinois plant; in PT&T, where southern California traffic was the largest nonaffiliate; and in the Northeast, where old quarrels combined with resentment of the panel's less-favorable wage treatment to keep most telephone unions from affiliating. Moreover, within the units represented by NFTW unions, many union-eligible workers were nonmembers. Yet by the end of 1945, NFTW union membership, for the first time, consisted of a majority of the union-eligible workers in the Bell System.[39]

During the same period, growth in membership and the number of affiliates was also matched by growth in the strength of those advocating greater centralization. The crisis of the strike itself had "brought all the NFTW organizations a little closer together" and had demonstrated that interunion cooperation could bring results. Beyond this, the strike and its outcome succeeded in "focusing the attention of the telephone worker on where the real power was."[40] Decisions, it was now clear, were made in highly centralized institutions, in the National Telephone Panel and in a centralized management personified by Bell's man on the panel. As one national unionist leader pointed out, the arrangement "had the effect of saying, 'We got to have one union and speak with one voice,' because it was blatant that the telephone industry was speaking with one voice through Stevens on the Telephone Commission."[41]

In its reports, moreover, the panel assumed and acted as if Bell were a unified entity. In February 1945, for example, it declared that "the over-all wage structure of the Bell System reflects the centralized management policies of the A.T.&T. Company," a remark that did not escape the notice of the national unionists, who flung it before the NFTW autonomists with some relish. Since the report had been "unanimously submitted" (and thus, of course, endorsed by Stevens), the statement was further branded as Bell's own admission of a fact around which it had frequently thrown a smoke screen.[42]

At the June 1945 assembly in Chicago, the full impact of the panel's workings had not yet been felt. The national unionists, still wary of autonomist withdrawals, were not inclined to press for structural change.

But already there were signs that their strength was growing and that the two-year-old political stalemate was breaking up.

One sign was that the assembly laid down guidelines for more forthright action by a new constitutional committee. No longer satisfied with the circumspect procedures of McCowen's group, with its reluctance to move beyond discussion, it now voted to create a new committee of three members, instructed it to draft a constitution embodying an "integrated structure," and empowered the executive board to convene a constitutional convention for consideration of the draft. Selected by President Beirne, the committee consisted of Moran, Kane, and—as chairman—Frances Smith.[43]

In collective bargaining policy, also, the Chicago assembly took at least a half step toward greater centralization. Anticipating the war's end and consequent resumption of unfettered bargaining, it passed a resolution permitting the NFTW to "endorse" contracts negotiated by member unions and withhold endorsement from those not meeting common bargaining goals. In reality, this amounted to a kind of ladies' and gentlemen's agreement, for the autonomy clause of the constitution still denied the NFTW the right—and consequently any real power—to interfere with a member union's bargaining.[44] Yet the resolution indicated a wider and deeper determination to form a united front. As it turned out, the attempt at united-front bargaining that took place in late 1945 and early 1946 was to become the second great impetus toward national unionism, an impetus even stronger than that provided by the Dayton strike and the operations of the National Telephone Panel.

IN LATE 1945 and early 1946, the unions' voice in bargaining was strengthened by renewed militancy of telephone unionists, a militancy sparked in part by the same factors then igniting labor unrest elsewhere. Like other workers, those in the telephone industry were caught up in a postwar restlessness; they wanted to force wage rates up to compensate for lost overtime earnings and were anxious to act before the anticipated mass unemployment undercut labor's bargaining power. In these respects they were part of a larger movement that included more than four million workers who struck between V-J day and March 1946. Yet in other respects their problems and grievances were peculiar to the telephone industry. With the war over, the industry began spending large amounts on new construction—approximately four times as much in 1946 as in 1944. It was also straining to meet new demands for service, demands that were reflected in a 16.8 percent increase in local calls, a 16.2 percent increase in the number of toll and long distance calls, a 14.5 percent increase in the number of telephones in service, and a backlog of unfilled applications for telephones that had reached two million by the end of 1946. Somewhat surprisingly, the telephone industry had again become a major growth field—which had implications for the makeup and militancy of the work force.[45]

Employment in the industry had remained steady at about 430,000 through 1944, but by the end of 1945 it had risen to 475,000, and at the end of 1946 it stood at 617,000. Much of the increase consisted of young, inexperienced workers; and given the continuing low wages, the often trying working conditions, and the changing patterns of employment created by demobilization, the turnover rate rose to 35 percent in 1945 and held at 28 percent in 1946. All told, 400,000 people entered Bell employment in the sixteen months following the end of the war, many of them leaving it quickly. And with the exception of the 57,400 rehired war veterans, these entrants were nearly all without previous Bell experience. By late 1946 nearly half of the operating company force had less than two years of service.[46]

Such workers were bunched at the low-paying end of the wage progression schedules, a circumstance that placed Bell's average straight-time hourly wage some 7 cents below that of the manufacturing workforce as a whole. In October 1945, when average straight-time hourly earnings in manufacturing were 98 cents, the hourly wage of some 55 percent of Bell's operating company workers was less than 85 cents, the wage for 42 percent was less than 75 cents, and the wage for 24 percent was less than 65 cents.[47]

The bulk of the work force, then, was young, poorly paid, and relatively untouched by the conservatism of seniority. Compared with the prewar work force, "they were younger and they were militant." Older workers, on their part, were still smarting from their wartime treatment and from the necessity to "carry extra loads" because of burgeoning service demands and the presence of inexperienced workers. And the rehired veterans were a "new breed of people who came back from the

War" feeling that "they had lost anywhere from two to five years" and wanting "to regain those years economically." As a result, noted one local plant officer, "it was much easier to get people to walk out on strike, and it was much easier to get them to honor picket lines."[48]

This renewed aggressiveness was first manifested in a November 1945 strike by the Illinois traffic union, an organization whose 8,500 members handled all Bell traffic in that state except for local calls in Chicago (handled by the Chicago traffic union). Launched after a 6,293-to-996 vote, the five-day strike secured the union's major demand—a promise by the company to add two dollars to a four-dollar-a-week increase recently awarded by the Telephone Panel. But marring the action was the refusal of the Chicago traffic union to honor picket lines.[49]

More important, the new militancy contributed to NFTW designs for united-front bargaining, an approach that seemed especially promising because of the clustering of contract negotiations in nearly all the Bell bargaining units in the winter of 1945–1946. As noted previously, the June 1945 assembly had passed a resolution providing for NFTW endorsement of contracts. This had been followed by informal discussion of bargaining goals and their implementation, and in late September the executive board decided to call a meeting of all NFTW union presidents to discuss a national bargaining program. Convened at Milwaukee in December, the meeting came at a time when militancy was rising and bargaining was already under way in most Bell System units.[50]

The first task of the thirty-eight union presidents attending the meeting was to clarify the NFTW's picket line policy; this they proceeded to do by passing a resolution obliging all affiliates to honor each other's picket lines, provided the NFTW had approved strike action. Next came the agreement that all NFTW unions were to press for identical contract goals, the most important being a two-dollars-a-day increase or its equivalent (twenty-five cents an hour) and a sixty-five-cent minimum hourly wage. Individual unions were to hold to these demands in negotiations with their respective companies, sign no contracts without NFTW approval, and send weekly reports on negotiations to the NFTW. The hope was that such a coordination would produce common gains; but if the executive board found that "sufficient progress" had not been made by mid-February, it was to call another presidents' conference to "consider a general strike."[51]

There was, to be sure, still no way to enforce the agreement. But those entering into it did so unanimously and enthusiastically, creating what one participant called "almost a commitment signed in blood that nobody would settle off." The leaders, declared President Beirne, had vowed "that we were all going to act together, and everybody went away from Milwaukee proud and happy."[52]

Almost immediately, however, the program was threatened by precipitous strike action on the part of militant affiliates. On January 4, 1946, the three-thousand-member Washington, D.C., traffic union staged a one-hour sit-down strike, led by one of the most militant traffic leaders in the country, Mary Gannon. Six days later the union began a "continuous meeting"—a conventional strike, but without picket lines—to protest "excessive and dictatorial" supervision and "sweatshop" working conditions. Responding to this situation, the NFTW executive board urged Gannon to postpone the strike so that her union would be in compliance with the War Labor Disputes Act's thirty-day notice requirement and so that her members would be in a better position to join a national strike in case one were called in late winter. Following minor concessions by management, Gannon finally did comply.[53]

On January 10 the seven thousand members of the WE installation union struck, demanding a number of reforms, chief among which was an improved per diem system. Again the NFTW executive board urged postponement, fearing, first of all, that the government would seize the struck facilities and impose financial penalties, and secondly, that installation picketing could destroy the kind of cooperation needed if a national strike was to be effective. When the thinly spread installers began picketing their work sites (about half of the central offices across the country), most of the operating company and Long Lines workers did honor the lines. The *New York Times* headlined: "Telephone Tie Up Worst in History."[54] But prolonged picketing of this sort was bound to test such workers' patience and drain their capacity to conduct a later strike on their own behalf. And beyond this, it could sow dissension within some operating company groups since, as a Washington State plant unionist observed, the installation union did not picket all locations and hence left some working while "others were picketed out of the job." This, he continued, "caused dissension among the groups, and if it hadn't been for the settlement, I'm afraid that we would have had to start from scratch again."[55]

The "settlement"—that is, the installation union's decision to defer further strike action—came after the NFTW executive board refused to approve the strike and pleaded with installation union president Ernest Weaver to allow operating company and Long Lines workers to take mass strike action on their *own* behalf, rather than be forced to continue a "sympathy strike" on the installers' behalf. "We just can't go in there on an entire sympathy strike," Frances Smith argued. "Our members will go up in the air. We have to use this thing [i.e., the strike power of operating company and Long Lines workers] to get that $2-per-day demand, and it will give the members something to strive for." Reluctantly, Weaver consented to "tie up all issues in one bundle," and on January 14 he and his own union's executive board managed to get their members back to work. The following day, in response to an executive board request, NFTW unions representing about 150,000 workers filed thirty-day strike notices.[56]

A third strike threatening united-front action was the January walkout of the seventeen-thousand-member WE Kearny manufacturing union. Here the issues were complicated by a UE company-domination suit against the Kearny union and by an initial NLRB trial examiner's report recommending disbandment. In protest, most of the NFTW affiliates had conducted a four-hour "continuous meeting" on October 5—a protest, according to NFTW estimates, involving some two hundred thousand workers and cutting service by 70 percent in affected areas. This action had impressed workers with their strike power, perhaps more than was justified; but the NLRB had not responded, and in November the Kearny union began preparations for a long strike. George DuVal, who had left the Kearny union's presidency the preceding summer prior to joining the NFTW staff, suspected that the new leaders' wish to impress the NLRB with their independence was a major motive in the decision to strike. But the strike vote of 11,069 to 637, conducted by the NLRB under War Labor Disputes Act procedures, suggests that, to the rank and file at least, wages and working conditions were more important.[57]

Once the walkout began on January 3, the NFTW leaders' first concern was not to diffuse the NFTW's strike power. Again, they urged postponement and withheld picket-legitimizing approval. But in this case, their pressure went unheeded. The strike continued for sixty-five days, ending on March 7 with a settlement that arose from the national bargaining effort. Subsequently, the Kearny union, cleared by the

NLRB, would withdraw from the NFTW—partly because of recriminations arising from the sixty-five-day strike—and affiliate with the IBEW.[58]

Meanwhile, the national bargaining program was also being threatened by numerous sign-offs. Many unions, in other words, were signing contracts with their respective companies without consulting the NFTW, and these contracts were falling far short of the demands agreed upon. The five-dollar weekly (or 12.5-cents hourly) wage increases being offered were too tempting to resist, and, in Beirne's words, after the first contract of this sort was signed, the one in Chicago traffic, "they fell over like duckpins, and everybody forgot what they had said in Milwaukee."[59] Somewhat shamefaced, leaders of most of the sign-off unions telephoned NFTW headquarters to report their action, saying, so Beirne recalled, "My members wanted it. We didn't want any strike, and we are autonomous. We can do what we please." A few also called NFTW headquarters beforehand to report their intentions and ask NFTW approval, to which Beirne could only respond, "Approval be damned! How could you do such a thing?" and "We must stick together. We must stick together." Such responses, he noted, "went no place,"[60] the result being that by early February all but seventeen NFTW unions, representing about half the total membership, had signed off.[61]

The executive board, glumly concluding that its program had indeed fallen short of "sufficient progress," now decided on a second presidents' conference, to meet in mid-February at Memphis. There, all forty-two NFTW unions with Bell memberships were represented, and, as a first order of business, the leaders of the seventeen unions who had held out proceeded to upbraid and in some cases humiliate the presidents of unions that had signed off and "ignored what they had agreed to." The seventeen unsigned unions then decided to stand firm, conceding only in private that seven dollars a week (17.5 cents an hour) would be an acceptable wage increase in lieu of the two-dollars-a-day formal demand. The entire group then empowered the executive board "to take whatever action may be necessary to enforce the demands of the telephone workers," including the launching of a March 7 strike by the seventeen unions. Taken on a union per capita basis, the vote was 121,997 to 30,791, with 26,913 not voting. In addition, twenty-three of the twenty-five sign-off unions gave pledges that they would honor picket lines. Since the potential strikers included the nationally dispersed WE installation and Long Lines unions, such pledges meant that the NFTW could still threaten what amounted to a national strike.[62]

When the leaders returned to their respective bargaining sessions on February 19, they found no further concessions being offered by management; five dollars was still the limit. Beirne then turned to Secretary of Labor Lewis Schwellenbach and other government officials, trying to persuade them that the Bell companies' bargaining was being "directed from a central source" and that "a strike would surely take place unless some concerted action was taken to bring the framers of the companies' policies into the open." On March 5 government officials agreed that negotiations in Long Lines might be useful in providing a pattern that could be applied elsewhere. And since Long Lines, a direct subsidiary of AT&T, had already begun to improve upon the five-dollar offer, these negotiations were moved from New York to Washington, where they proceeded under the scrutiny of Schwellenbach and the Conciliation Service.[63]

On March 6, with the strike now scheduled for 6 A.M. the next day, Schwellenbach summoned Cleo Craig, AT&T's vice-president for labor relations, to Washington. There Craig joined with the Conciliation Service in proposing that the NFTW postpone the strike so as to give a fact-finding board time to investigate. But the NFTW leaders refused. Their suggestion, relayed to Craig through the Conciliation Service, was that "since the long lines parties seemed to be so close to an agreement, it might provide a basis for settlement [for the other sixteen unsigned unions]."[64]

Craig spent the next several hours conferring by telephone with AT&T headquarters in New York, while at the same time receiving assurances from the NFTW leaders that they had the power to call off the strike. At about 8 P.M. on March 6, he and Beirne initialed a memorandum stating that once Long Lines reached an agreement, its "dollar pattern" of wage increases would be applied to groups in the operating companies, and its average cents-per-hour increase would be applied to WE workers. The agreement went on to state that Beirne and Craig guaranteed that this "application" would take place, even though formally the companies and unions still bargaining had the right to accept or reject such an arrangement. And it stated that once the application did take place, the NFTW would "call off [the national] strike immediately."[65]

The Long Lines union and management then quickly reached an agreement whose major feature was a weekly wage increase of five to eight dollars, amounting to an average hourly increase of 17.6 cents. For the next nine hours, however, the agreement remained unsigned, thus giving NFTW officers time to telephone the leaders of the other unsigned unions (most of whom were in bargaining sessions), outline the terms of the Long Lines wage increase, explain that it could be applied to all the unsigned groups, and advise them that now was a good time to press for settlement of local nonwage issues. In nearly all cases, the union leaders voiced enthusiastic approval. They then reached quick, informal agreements with their management counterparts, the few balky management people swinging into line after they had spoken with Craig by telephone. Finally, at about 5:35 A.M., after it was clear that the unsigned unions approved of the Long Lines agreement and were indeed applying it in their own negotiations, the Long Lines contract was signed and the NFTW executive board called off the strike.[66]

During the next several days the remaining unions signed formal contracts that adopted wage increases paralleling those in Long Lines, as well as other improvements not stipulated in the Beirne-Craig memorandum. The companies agreed, for example, to reduce all wage progression schedules to eight years or less and to grant fringe-benefit improvements amounting to an additional .7 cents per hour for the average worker. In addition, Craig voluntarily agreed to urge the Bell companies to renegotiate contracts with the sign-off unions. At stake now was Bell's traditional system of geographical differentials, the upsetting of which might generate new labor unrest. Hence the five-dollar contracts across the Bell System—those held by NFTW and non-NFTW unions alike—were reopened, and through the rest of March new contracts were signed calling for wage raises and other improvements, resembling those won by the seventeen NFTW unions.[67]

The outcome, as a whole, was a tremendous victory for the NFTW and its unions. Against initially strong management resistance, and despite breaches in unity caused by precipitate strike action and the early sign-offs, the organization had negotiated a pay increase equaling those won by the most powerful industrial unions and surpassing those won by most American unions. It had, to be sure, abandoned its initial demand for a 65-cent minimum wage. But the 17.6-cent average wage increase brought all but 1 percent of Bell workers above that level, and of the fewer than five thousand workers who remained below it, nearly all were operators in training. In a period of only moderate inflation, with the cost of living rising only 1.9 percent between August 1945 and May 1946, the NFTW had increased the average telephone worker's wage by more than 18 percent.[68]

In addition, the NFTW leaders had succeeded in bringing AT&T, in the person of Cleo Craig, "into the open." His initialing of the memorandum binding Bell companies to the Long Lines wage increases was actually a confession of AT&T's ability to control those companies' labor policies. By thus engaging in a form of systemwide or "national" bargaining, the central company had put itself in the position of contradicting every public statement it had made on the subject over the previous ten years.[69]

Why did AT&T capitulate, both in the substance and form of bargaining? Clearly, the major cause was an almost desperate desire to avoid a national strike for which it was ill prepared. The NFTW's ability to launch a credible national strike threat had come as a complete surprise, perhaps partly because of the December and January sign-offs, and Bell had done almost nothing to prepare for such an eventuality. In addition, there were the effects that a strike could have on the huge service expansion program, considered vital not only because of the revenues to be gained but also because the Bell System's public relations were suffering from its inability to meet the burgeoning demand.[70] And finally, AT&T appears to have been shaken by Schwellenbach's intervention, the more so because this was the first time a high federal official had shown a keen interest in Bell's peacetime labor relations. Indeed, Beirne in 1971 ventured the guess, based largely on his experience in dealing with AT&T after 1946, that this was a major cause of the capitulation:

> [Schwellenbach] was not identified with labor. . . . But in the discussions that Craig participated in with Schwellenbach, it was very evident early in the game that we had at least persuaded *him* about the rightness of our position. And Craig, in reporting that fact to the chairman of the board of A.T.&T., stirred up the pot which still can be stirred up today. When the big federals come in and they take a look at A.T.&T., everybody in A.T.&T. first gets scared. And if you can get an agreement out of them while they're still scared, you're ahead of the game. . . . Their first reaction is to run scared as

hell and try to work out a compromise so that they won't be in the public print . . . and so FCC and the public service commissions in the various states don't have another document.[71]

If the national unionists had themselves choreographed the events of December through March, they could not have arranged a better demonstration of the value of a national union. For new unionists and for those few older ones who still needed to be persuaded, Craig's role in the bargaining exposed the centralized control of Bell's labor policies. But much more important, the outcome proved that a large, cooperative union effort could move Bell management as it had never been moved before. The evidence was on every Bell worker's paycheck, evidence that "just flabbergasted" some of them. Equally important, the sign-offs of December and January showed that union autonomy might easily work to sabotage such a potentially rewarding effort. Had there been a few more sign-offs, the ability to launch a national strike might well have been lost, and with it the 17.6-cent wage raise.[72]

Another effect of the March bargaining was to discredit the leadership of the autonomist unions, all but two of which (Wisconsin and Northwestern) had signed off. It was plain for everyone to see that the leaders who had signed off had fallen short of the wage increases that were there to be gained. Nearly everyone now condemned them because they had been in violation of the "blood oath" taken at Milwaukee—even the sign-off leaders condemned themselves. At the Memphis meeting and later, all they could say was, "'By God, I did it once, but I'll never do that again. . . . *Mea culpa, mea culpa, mea culpa!*'"[73]

Penitence for their exercise of autonomy was hardly a promising position from which to wage a strong defense of it, either in NFTW councils or within their home unions. Many now abandoned the defense, a step made somewhat easier by the conciliatory attitude of the national unionist leaders. Dunn recalls that he and others harbored some bitterness, but the main concern was "to prove even to them that we had to have one union." Accordingly, the national unionists joined Frances Smith in deliberately focusing on the failings of autonomy itself, not on those of its defenders: "We are not condemning these affiliates for what they did," she declared. "We do, however, point to the present structure of the NFTW which made it possible for them to do it."[74]

Alluding to the March victory, the national unionists urged those unions that had faltered to reunite, with promises of more victories to come. "If seventeen can do this," they argued, "what could we do with you all in one union?" And beyond factual arguments, they moved into flights of rhetoric. "With only a fraction of our latent power unleashed," said Smith, the result had been the placing of "an annual $185,000,000 into the pockets of our members." "What frontiers are yet ahead," she wanted to know, "if and when we have a genuine national union with the power and resources to mobilize us all?"[75]

DURING THE THREE YEARS from 1943 to 1946, the progress of the NFTW toward national unionism had been remarkable. For this some credit must go to the union's leadership, especially to its caution in handling structural questions, its boldness in dealing with the government and Bell, and its confidence that events themselves would provide the most telling arguments for national unionism. Pushing the cause along were wartime deprivations that made autonomy seem a luxury and a changing work force that gave the unions a more flexible and pragmatic membership. And given the opportunities created by these developments, the national unionists precipitated effective action and thus won converts to their position. It was the Dayton strike that brought the National Telephone Panel into being and gave the national leadership greater influence and prestige, and it was the success of the March 1946 bargaining, achieved despite the timidity and bad judgment of many autonomists, that dramatized the potential inherent in greater centralization. During this bargaining the national leadership had performed before a nationwide union audience in a plot providing elements of suspense, surprise, and ultimate triumph.

Finally, national unionists played the role of educators as adroitly as that of activists. They let slip no chance to point out that their Bell antagonists were a united and centralized foe, that they had used this unity to advantage in the past, and that only centralized union action could oppose them on anything like equal terms. By the spring of 1946, noted Beirne, "we had forceful examples . . . on how a centralized organization could really work better than a fragmented one,"[76] examples that pointed up how nearly every manifestation of autonomy had slowed or jeopardized progress and how the "logic of events" was indeed on the side of "one national union."

Consequently, the national unionists looked toward the 1946 national assembly with added strength and confidence. The morale and electoral strength of their opposition was crumbling, creating a situation where the national unionists were at last ready to press their advantage.[77] In April they launched a full-scale campaign for the dissolution of the NFTW and the formation of a national union—a campaign that was to preoccupy the Galveston assembly in June, reach beyond the assembly delegates to the entire NFTW membership in the summer and fall, and finally, in June 1947, culminate in the formation of the Communications Workers of America.

Chapter 8

NATIONAL STRIKE, NATIONAL UNION,

1947

FROM 1942 THROUGH MARCH 1946, events had served the national unionists well. Wartime deprivation had instilled new fire in old telephone unionists; wartime hiring had added low-paid and combative young people to the Bell work force; and both groups had been moved toward national unionism by the pragmatic experience of 1942–1944, the dramatic Dayton strike and its Telephone Panel aftermath, and the bargaining victory of 1946. In a period of mounting militancy, it was the national unionists who were in the vanguard of NFTW action, often achieving their goals without or despite the laggard apostles of autonomy. But mainly the national unionists capitalized on the events themselves, painting their own interpretations on them, and exhorting and educating the NFTW membership so that, by the spring of 1946, it finally appeared ready for the establishment of a national telephone union.

Meanwhile, however, these same events had been pushing telephone unionists toward another consequence, one that would pose grave dangers for national unionism—namely, a full-scale confrontation with the Bell System. As long as unionists had remained divided and generally quiescent, management had viewed them with forbearance. But as they became demonstrably effective in bargaining, and as they groped their way to the threshold of national unionism, forbearance gave way to alarm. A united, aggressive union movement was not at all what Bell managers had contemplated when nurturing the company union successors of 1935–1937; nor was it something to be accepted without resistance in 1946–1947. Management, according to

AT&T President Walter Gifford, was responsible "for the interest of all concerned: the millions of telephone users, the hundreds of thousands of employees and the hundreds of thousands of stockholders." Only management had "intimate knowledge" of all of the factors involved,[1] and hence it was management's task to "prevent having another John L. Lewis" (that monster of so frightful mien) in the telephone industry.[2]

Indeed, the union victory in 1946 had made a clash all but inevitable. In the unionists, the victory had bred confidence that they could again win major concessions, either by a national strike threat or, at most, by a few days of actual work stoppage. In management, it had bred resolve not only to recoup losses but to preclude future union victories by destroying labor unity. The result was the 1947 national telephone strike, an unequal, six-week struggle that was to end in a sound defeat for union negotiators; sow despair, confusion, and dissension among telephone unionists; and, in so doing, almost destroy the CWA at the moment of its birth.

IN THE SPRING OF 1946, however, prospects for national unionism looked bright. Its supporters believed that the NFTW had reached a turning point, and their arguments were meeting with little opposition in leadership and membership meetings.[3] Moreover, Frances Smith's constitutional committee was making progress. As empowered by the June 1945 assembly, it had drawn up a rough draft of a complete national unionist constitution, copies of which had circulated at the December 1945 presidents' conference in Milwaukee. In April 1946, disappointed that reaction of member unions "indicated a need for further revision" but newly encouraged by the recent national bargaining victory, the committee sent revised copies to the member unions, along with a call for the establishment of some form of national union. In May copies were sent to all NFTW union members, via the pages of *The Telephone Worker*.[4]

By the time the Galveston assembly met in early June, the national unionists were able to marshal a large majority, the result being a new committee under John Crull and the enunciation of some forty "constitutional principles" largely extracted from the Smith constitution.

After lengthy debate the delegates approved a resolution authorizing the new committee to spend the summer formulating and submitting for member-union inspection a constitution based on these principles. This action would then be followed by a special assembly to be called in the fall of 1946; that assembly, if it wished, could reconvene as the constitutional convention of a new national union. In addition, the delegates voted overwhelmingly to allow any future assembly to dissolve the federation by majority vote.[5]

After the Galveston assembly the Crull committee went to work as authorized, writing and rewriting drafts of a national unionist constitution, eliciting responses to the drafts from telephone groups across the country, and finally settling on a firm draft in October. While the committee labored, the national unionists accelerated their campaign among the membership, speaking both at regular meetings and at special gatherings called to air drafts of the constitution-in-preparation. At such meetings they urged local units to vote at least quasi-official endorsements of national unionism and to send committed national unionist delegations to the upcoming special assembly, now scheduled for Denver in November 1946. And during the summer President Beirne conducted a two-month speaking tour of locals across the country, stressing the narrowly missed pitfalls of 1946 bargaining and arguing that "you have to have a union instead of a federation. In a federation you can have no discipline other than the discipline that comes from expulsion."[6]

While the campaign and the drafts of the Crull constitution were generally well received, all did not go smoothly. For one thing, it was becoming clear that a national union could not actually be formed until some months after the Denver assembly, even if that assembly were to reconvene as a constitutional convention. The transition to national unionism would necessarily involve dissolution of the cooperating member unions as legal entities, an especially complicated process for the several unions that were incorporated and one that unions were reluctant to initiate before the Denver meeting. In addition, some union constitutions required membership referendums as part of the dissolution process. In all, the proceedings might take as long as 180 days.[7]

Secondly, an ambitious NFTW organizing project in PT&T, begun in early 1945, was going badly. The aim had been to unite the seventeen unions in PT&T—NFTW affiliates and nonaffiliates alike—into a single, NFTW-affiliated organization, the Telephone Workers Industrial Union (TWIU). But TWIU organizers were hindered from the start by the lukewarm response of the eight NFTW affiliates in PT&T; by a scarcity of money and organizers to campaign among the membership of the nonaffiliates, most of whose leaders were staunchly anti-NFTW; and by a rival organizing campaign simultaneously conducted by the ACA, a campaign that would eventually induce northern California traffic to leave the NFTW and affiliate with the ACA in early April 1947.[8] No new groups were brought into the NFTW through TWIU organizing, and the TWIU itself never became more than a paper organization.[9]

Finally, there were some disaffiliations. The autonomist Connecticut union had left the NFTW on March 1, 1946, at the time of the nationwide strike threat. The Chicago traffic union had left in late March, under pressure from Secretary-Treasurer Werkau (whose duties now included that of strike director). His request had been prompted by the union's action in crossing picket lines in November 1945 and its subsequent refusal to pledge picket line observance. In the summer and fall, three more unions departed: upstate New York plant and the WE Kearny and WE Hawthorne manufacturing groups. In each case the loss appeared virtually unavoidable, and to some extent there were offsetting gains. During the same period the NFTW gained new affiliates in New Jersey traffic, Michigan commercial, and WE's small new manufacturing complexes at Buffalo, Lincoln, and Burlington-Winston-Salem. The three new WE affiliates had been aided by NFTW organizers in successful NLRB election campaigns against the IBEW and the UE.[10]

All of this was by way of prelude to the Denver meeting of November 4–16, the largest and longest as well as the last of the NFTW's assemblies. Present were some 350 delegates representing 225,638 members in all forty-seven NFTW unions, plus observers from three nonaffiliated unions. The major item for consideration was the Crull constitution; while it was clear that official acceptance and the dissolution of most member unions must await membership referendums, the delegates were empowered to grant provisional ratification. For six days they debated the constitution, article by article, accepting in general the basic structure proposed by the Crull committee.[11]

The constitution as proposed would lodge supreme authority in an annual convention, whose delegates were each to represent approximately five hundred members. Between conventions, authority was to rest with the executive board, elected biennially at the convention and consisting of the president, vice-president, and secretary-treasurer, each elected by the whole convention; four regional directors elected by caucuses from the eastern, southern, western, and central regions; and six group directors elected by caucuses of plant, traffic, accounting, commercial, non-Bell, and manufacturing-research delegates.[12]

Beneath the convention and executive board, the organizational chart of the proposed union resembled that of the NFTW, though power was shifted and terminology changed. The subunits of the national union were to parallel the former NFTW member unions in their makeup, and with minor exceptions these were allowed to retain their old framework of locals and elective positions. Subunits would no longer be called *unions*, of course; the term *divisions* was chosen to emphasize that they were dependent parts of a larger entity. Thus the Southwestern Union would become Division 20, the Washington, D.C., plant union would become Division 36, and so on. The divisions were to collect dues and send a designated portion directly to the national office for its use. At Denver the portion was set at twenty-five cents per member per month, but this was subject to change by any future convention.[13]

The disaffiliations that had so often jarred the NFTW could not take place under the new union's constitution. Any group attempting to disaffiliate would have to resort to legal procedures involving an NLRB election among the workers involved. The divisions would retain considerable latitude in the conduct of their internal affairs, but the national union executive board could impose disciplinary measures for such infractions as financial malfeasance or allowing members to cross bona fide picket line set up by other units of the national union. The executive board could revoke or suspend a division's charter and appoint temporary administrators.[14]

The power to bargain contracts was to be shifted radically, moving from the former NFTW unions to, for the most part, the new union's national office—*not* to the new divisions. Formal negotiations, to be sure, would still take place at the level of the divisions and their management counterparts across the country. This was a concession to inescapable facts: contracts at this level were legally sanctioned, and it was clear that Bell would depart from this system of formally decentralized negotiations only under duress (as in March 1946). But real decision-making power concerning bargaining was to be centralized in the national office of the new union (as management decision-making power was believed to be centralized in the AT&T offices of the Bell System). The annual convention was to formulate bargaining objectives. No contract could be valid unless signed by a representative of the national office, meaning in effect that the union executive board would have the authority to approve or reject all contracts negotiated by the divisions and hence to disallow the sign-offs of the past. And only the executive board would have the power to call or halt strikes in which picket lines need be honored by union members, thus discouraging precipitate strike action of the kind that had occurred in the past.[15]

The delegates' only important departure from the Crull draft dealt not with structure but with clarifying membership eligibility. Rejecting the suggestion that "known Communists" be excluded from membership, the delegates stipulated that "no person, otherwise eligible for membership, shall be denied membership in the Union because of sex, race, color, creed, nationality, or political adherence."[16]

In naming the new union, the delegates accepted the words that Crull at a late moment had decided to pen in: the Communications Workers of America. In addition, they adopted a plan for bringing it into being: A constitutional convention would meet, at which the proposed constitution would be considered adopted upon the affirmative vote of delegates from unions representing 115,000 communications workers. This convention would then elect temporary officers of the projected national union, such officers being empowered to issue charters to those divisions that wished to join; after the membership of the divisions thus chartered had reached 115,000, the officers were to announce a date upon which formal operations of the CWA would begin (formal dissolution of the NFTW coming the day before). The date of June 9, 1947—the day on which the projected first annual convention of the CWA was scheduled—was the date most of the delegates had in mind.[17]

Having arrived at a sense that the constitution was satisfactory to most of the delegates, the asembly set it aside in order to develop plans for 1947 bargaining. According to plan, however, the assembly reconvened on November 13 as the constitutional convention of the Communications Workers of America, and in unrecorded votes representatives of more than 115,000 telephone workers quickly adopted the constitution and selected NFTW President Beirne, Vice-President

Moran, and Secretary-Treasurer Werkau to fill corresponding positions as temporary officers of the CWA.[18]

Once the assembly had adjourned, the national union issue lay with the NFTW unions (WE Kearny being the only non-NFTW union that showed any interest). Their response was positive and quicker than expected. By February 17, thirty-three unions totaling 185,594 members had applied for charters as CWA divisions. Only two (Maryland plant and Maryland traffic) had rejected the CWA. While the remaining NFTW unions had yet to make a decision, the largest of these (Ohio, Illinois traffic, Michigan plant, and WE installation) had sided with the national unionists in the past. The CWA's temporary officers were so encouraged by this progress that they began looking favorably on the idea of advancing the date of the CWA's formal establishment to April 1.[19]

By the time that date arrived, however, they had been forced to abandon the idea. February bargaining between the NFTW unions and the Bell companies had reached a state of virtual deadlock; March had passed without any sign of a peaceful settlement; and on April 1 unions and management were preparing for a national strike to begin on April 7. In the midst of this crisis, the NFTW unions had no wish to endanger their legal status as bargaining agents; nor, on the other hand, did they wish to postpone the strike while the transition to national unionism was consummated.[20] The establishment of the CWA would have to wait until the national telephone strike was over.

THE OVERRIDING ISSUE in the 1947 strike was whether an ambitious union movement—one bent on acquiring large and continuing influence over the conditions of telephone labor—could survive management's attempt to destroy it. In this respect, the strike resembled the cataclysmic labor struggles of the 1930s. The analogy, however, does not hold completely. The telephone unionists, after all, had endured ten years without a full-scale confrontation—the sort of malign neglect not permitted the upstart unionists of the thirties. And the passage of ten years had altered the kinds of questions being negotiated and the perceptions of what was at stake. The status of the telephone unions as authorized bargaining representatives was not at issue during the strike itself, as it was in the big strikes of the thirties; the unionists were largely unaware that the survival of their movement was at stake; and when the strike ended the outcome was not fully clear—as it had been, for example, at the close of the broken southern textile strike of 1930–1931 or the close of the successful auto and rubber strikes of 1936–1937.[21]

Prior to the strike, the NFTW unionists believed that the struggle would center on their own major objectives: a large wage increase and systemwide bargaining. The first, they argued, was necessary because of the rising living costs and because the wages of telephone workers continued to lag behind those in other industries. The galloping inflation that had followed the lifting of price controls in June 1946 had cost the average telephone worker some $7.40 per week in purchasing power, thus wiping out the gains of 1946 bargaining. And telephone earnings in March 1947 averaged only $1.12 hourly and $43.31 weekly, compared with general manufacturing work force earnings of $1.18 hourly and $47.72 weekly.[22] Management, on the other hand, took the position that there was "no justification for a wage increase at this time." It contended that recent studies "showed that wages for various telephone jobs compare well with wages paid by others for comparable jobs"; after the strike was over, a Southern Bell vice-president maintained that the added cost of union demands "would have been many million dollars more than this company collected in revenue."[23] It was only behind the scenes that managers speculated that a moderate increase, given after a hard-fought strike, might improve Bell's position in the many telephone rate increase cases then being brought before state regulatory bodies.[24]

The second NFTW objective—systemwide bargaining—was an open issue in 1947, the Beirne-Craig agreement having committed AT&T to it for 1946 but not for the future. As the NFTW saw it, this kind of bargaining would protect unionists against management's whipsaw tactics. And it would also allow union negotiators to use their powers of persuasion upon AT&T officials who had the real power to negotiate on behalf of the Bell System, rather than upon dozens of associated Bell company officials across the country who were deemed mere mouthpieces for AT&T. Systemwide bargaining would thus provide greater material benefits, according to the NFTW reasoning, and with the NFTW-CWA group negotiating what amounted to contracts for all Bell System labor, membership in that group would become increasingly attractive to those unions and workers who remained outside it. Management opposed the proposal, undoubtedly with the same considerations in mind, and with the fear as well that it might call into question the validity of decentralized rate-making procedures.[25]

The NFTW's plans for concerted bargaining were shaped by the Denver assembly in November and polished by the executive board in December and January. (As in 1946, the plans were backed only by oral commitments of union leaders; written commitments would still be an obvious breach of the constitution's autonomy clause.) The plans dictated that by February 1, the member unions would place before their respective companies a uniform set of demands, the most important of which was a twelve-dollar weekly wage increase, but also including a union shop, reduction of progression schedules to five years, narrowing of geographic wage differentials, and doubling of the minimum pension to one hundred dollars a month. No union was to settle for less, and the executive board could disallow (in the interest of the systemwide bargaining principle) even those individual settlements that met the demands. If the parties were still in disagreement on March 1—as they undoubtedly would be, given the magnitude of union demands—the unions were to file notice of their intention to strike on April 7. Strike votes would then be taken; with a strike authorized, the unions' bargaining authority would pass to a policy committee, which would hold "full and sole" power to sign a systemwide agreement. This committee, composed of one representative from each of the NFTW unions, was to assemble in Washington in late March and use a seven-member "coordinated bargaining committee" as its negotiating arm in dealing with AT&T.[26]

While union leaders did not expect to fully achieve their demands, most of them did believe some form of systemwide bargaining could be won, as well as a large wage increase—perhaps six to nine dollars weekly. Their confidence was based partly upon signs of militancy among the membership, for much the same forces that had produced aggressiveness in 1946 were at work again in 1947. In addition, leaders and members alike were heavily influenced by management's response to the 1946 national strike threat. Most expected another prestrike capitulation; further, they expected that if an actual walkout occurred, the traffic unionists' departure would cause a nearly total shutdown of operator-connected local service, as well as long distance service (all of which was operator connected), thus forcing management or perhaps the federal government to produce a settlement within two or three days.[27] Even in the unlikely event of a longer strike, they were confident that they could win. In the absence of any experience to the contrary, they estimated that dial and other equipment would break down after ten to twenty days if not maintained by plant unionists, and that this would shut down *all* telephone service.[28]

In February, negotiations opened according to plan. The NFTW unionists made identical demands in their respective bargaining sessions; and, as expected, their management counterparts rejected or ignored the demands. Several large nonaffiliates also made similar demands, with the apparent intention of timing strike threats and walkouts to coincide with NFTW action. From the start, however, there were disturbing signs. Management was not merely disdaining union demands; it was rejecting the idea of any wage increase at all, and making demands of its own, including the cutting of seniority provisions, sick-pay benefits, and the number of paid holidays. In addition, managers were talking about "holding out until Christmas,"[29] and this time they were preparing for the possibility of a long strike. Management employees were being trained to operate the switchboards; overtime work was being used to put equipment in top shape; precautions were being taken to prevent sabotage; and, according to union allegations, the proportion of supervisors to union-eligible workers was being increased and efforts were being made to lure union officers into management positions.[30]

By March 1 neither side had budged. The unions then filed strike notices, began strike votes, and, as planned, passed their bargaining authority to the central policy committee. During the first three weeks in March, the strike votes were tallied, with every union's membership favoring a strike and with the overall margin reported to be fifteen to one. Meanwhile, Beirne met several times with Cleo Craig in New York, where he invited AT&T to begin systemwide bargaining with NFTW's coordinated bargaining committee. Craig, however, was noncommittal. When the forty-nine-member policy committee met in Washington on March 24, it too invited AT&T to begin systemwide bargaining, but the only reply was a telegram from Craig saying that the message had been relayed to the local Bell companies.[31]

On March 24 the policy committee also discussed whether to exercise its option of declaring a strike for April 7. In a secret session, Beirne and Werkau, who were not members of the committee, spoke against the declaration, warning of Bell's preparations for the strike and arguing that any strike action should wait until after the CWA was in full operation. Strike sentiment, however, was overwhelming. When Pollock moved that the NFTW strike on April 7 unless acceptable offers were forthcoming, his motion passed unanimously.[32]

In the days that followed little movement occurred on any of the bargaining fronts. Government conciliators succeeded in bringing the stalled Long Lines and Southwestern Bell negotiations to Washington. But the only proposal acceptable to the Bell companies—a plan whereby arbitration boards chosen by state governors would determine local company wages according to Bell's community-wage principle—was rejected by the NFTW. The only concession came on March 27, when government conciliators got the telephone unionists to agree that AT&T would not have to deal with the NFTW so long as the offers made by the Bell companies were uniform on the major issues. To this proposal neither AT&T nor the companies responded.[33]

As the strike date drew near, the NFTW sent telegrams to AT&T offering to maintain emergency service during the strike as long as management did not assign management employees to fill strikers' jobs. AT&T relayed the messages to the Bell companies, but no responses were forthcoming. Secretary of Labor Schwellenbach then made a last-minute appeal to postpone the strike. The NFTW refused.[34]

At 6 A.M. on April 7 a total of 294,000 telephone workers walked out or refused to cross union picket lines, and by afternoon of the next day some 340,000 workers were off the job. It was the first nationwide telephone strike, the largest strike of 1947, a strike that reached into more communities than any strike in American history, and —since nearly two-thirds of the participants were females—the biggest walkout in the history of American women.[35] Joining the NFTW unions were eight large nonaffiliates: New Jersey plant, Pennsylvania plant and traffic, and five of the eight unions in New York Telephone. And where the nonaffiliates chose not to strike, many of their members at least refused to cross NFTW union picket lines, which were generally maintained around the clock and en masse at central offices during daylight hours. The only states not affected, or only slightly affected, were Montana, where Bell workers had been IBEW members since before World War I; Virginia and Indiana, where utility antistrike laws were backed by prohibitive penalties; and the New England states, where nonstriking, non-NFTW unionists in the local operating companies far outnumbered the Long Lines and WE installation strikers.[36]

Union leaders were heartened by the numbers and the conduct of the strikers. Erased were all doubts about the largely untried membership's willingness to strike, as well as doubts about the willingness of female strikers to picket. And somewhat unexpectedly, many nonmembers in the struck units had joined the initial walkout and were now signing up as union members. The immediate effect on service, however, was less than leaders and members had anticipated. It was no surprise, of course, that local service remained nearly normal for the 65 percent of telephones that were dial; operators were not needed for this kind of service, and here there could be no reduction until plant equipment broke down. What was surprising was the extent to which operator-connected service was being maintained. With management, nonstriking employees, and recalled retirees working long hours and often living in telephone exchanges, the Bell system was completing about 33 percent of local calls from nondial telephones, and the completion rate for long distance calls was 20 percent and rising. Rather than cutting total service to less than 65 percent of the normal volume, the strike had only cut it to about 80 percent.[37]

Considering the size of the strike and the Bell System's attempt to maintain operations, there was remarkably little violence. In contrast to several later telephone strikes, particularly the Southern Bell strike of 1955, only occasional sabotage occurred, consisting of isolated acts of cable cutting, with little legal action arising from it. Pickets often tried to discourage scabs from passing through their lines, but persuasion was confined to verbal abuse, hurled eggs and tomatoes, fists, and an occasional hat pin. No one was badly hurt, although some pickets were arrested and fined.[38]

On balance, the conduct of police and local authorities was anti-union, but only mildly, and not in a way that affected the outcome of the strike (barring the possibility of a totally free rein for the picketers). In Florida a statewide injunction against all picketing was in effect. In Miami and several towns in Utah, fire hoses were turned against pickets. In Louisville and Cleveland there were arbitrary arrests. But for the most part, police confined themselves to suppressing union violence at picket sites and enforcing ordinances requiring pickets to parade continuously. At times unionists were somewhat surprised by the mildness and evenhandedness, especially in such reputedly antiunion cities as Memphis, Tennessee; Macon, Georgia; and Gadsden and Jasper, Alabama.[39]

In part, this comparatively mild treatment may have been a reflection of public sympathy for the strikers. During the first and second weeks of the strike, when Gallup surveyors asked, "Are your sympathies on the side of the telephone company or on the side of the workers?" the response was 44 to 24 percent in favor of the workers (32 percent had no opinion). The public, it seems, was favorably impressed by the strikers because of their relatively decorous behavior and high social status in small towns and cities, because telephone workers were familiar figures everywhere, and because most strikers were women or war veterans—a fact the unions stressed at every opportunity.[40] In addition, Bell workers had long been trained to project an image of courtesy and helpfulness, an image that was not to be wiped out in a matter of weeks. Finally, much of the public's sympathy for the strikers undoubtedly rested with the fact that it was not being greatly inconvenienced.

For the strikers, of course, this absence of public inconvenience bore more dangers than benefits. During the second and third weeks of the strike, dial and other equipment did not break down as unionists had expected. The companies were still maintaining service at some 80 percent of the normal total volume, and for telephone subscribers this was apparently tolerable. They did not pressure the companies to reach a settlement. On the contrary, as one union leader put it, they seemed inclined to "cooperate with the System," putting up "with the inconvenience of not getting [some] calls through" and with "being billed for the same amount of money practically as if they were getting full-time service." Subscribers even went to some trouble to pay their telephone bills, mailing them in when the commercial offices were closed "instead of going down and paying them." This is not to say that the strike inflicted no financial damage on Bell. Largely because of overtime payments to scabs and the still shrunken long distance service (now running at about 40 percent of the normal volume), the system's profits for April 1947 fell to $17 million as compared with $43 million for April 1946.[41] In addition, hidden costs undoubtedly accrued from the undermaintenance of equipment. Yet clearly these were losses that could be sustained for a long period. They fell far short of the scale necessary to shake the Bell System.

With the system willing and now clearly able to sustain a long strike, the NFTW sought another means of pressure: federal intervention. On April 17 it halved its wage demand, calling now for a six-dollar weekly increase, a figure in line with the 1947 gains of the large industrial unions. It then sent résumés of its position to President Truman and Congress, calling on the government to "use pressure to make the telephone companies . . . give wage increases." But here too the unionists were blocked by their inability to discommode the public. There was little popular pressure on behalf of a federally forced settlement. Even if the government had wished to intervene vigorously —and no evidence exists that it did—the maintenance of 80 percent of service left it with little excuse for using its main tool: threatened or actual seizure of the system.[42] The NFTW could only fall back on ingenious but ineffective schemes for stimulating pressure, one being a suggestion that regulatory bodies require rebates to those suffering from a disruption of telephone service, another seeking to generate subscriber complaints about lapses in service, and a third requesting letters from CIO unionists demanding full reinstatement of service.[43]

From the third week of the strike onward, large numbers of strikers—particularly young family men and widowed or divorced women with children—began to suffer hardship and even distress. Many strikers could not afford groceries, and often they could not obtain credit or commercial loans. Some families went hungry until they could sell their furniture, or obtain loans from friends, or find some form of charity. The few strike funds among the NFTW unions were quickly drained; other funds of the NFTW and its affiliates also ran out; and most of the unions lacked the organization, experience, and community liaison necessary to aid strikers in obtaining outside help. Although strikers were encouraged to seek temporary jobs, and a hastily erected Telephone Workers Defense Committee managed to raise some $225,000 (including a $100,000 loan from the United Mine Workers), conditions continued to worsen. While the CIO staff and local officers in CIO unions were helpful in securing meeting halls, intervening with creditors and relief agencies, and raising local relief funds, the NFTW strikers were mostly on their own.[44]

In the absence of adequate organization or finances, maintenance of the strike hinged almost solely on striker morale, and by the end of April morale had suffered many severe blows. Along with the failure to shut down service, the halving of the wage demand, the failure to secure government intervention, and the onset of material hardship, there were the effects of management initiatives. Back-to-work movements, sometimes real and sometimes imaginary, were publicized by company spokesmen. Telephone calls to individual strikers urged them to return to work. And accompanying the rigidity at the bargaining table were veiled threats that strikers might lose their seniority or even their jobs.[45]

Under the impact of such blows, the strike "began to crumble around the edges." Many nonstrikers who had been honoring picket lines returned to work, followed by individual strikers. Then, with the strike about three weeks old, some fairly large groups voted to join the returning procession, among them the plant engineering group in Wisconsin, the commercial group in Ohio, and many locals in southern California plant. By May 1 the number of strikers had fallen only slightly in WE installation, Southwestern Bell, Washington, D.C., traffic, and the plant and traffic units in Michigan and Ohio. In Southern Bell their numbers had fallen only 15 percent. But in Maryland, Wisconsin, and PT&T, a majority had returned to work, and elsewhere the losses ranged from 20 to 30 percent. The number of workers off the job had fallen from 340,000 to an estimated 250,000, and their numbers were still dwindling.[46]

As the strike began to deteriorate, Bell moved to destroy NFTW unity. Between April 22 and 28, negotiators for the various Bell companies began dropping their original demands and offering the possibility of "reasonable" wage increases if affiliated unions would break away from the NFTW's coordinated bargaining program and give proof of their authority to sign contracts.[47] Informed of these proposals, the policy committee debated whether any such contracts should be approved, but the debate was becoming increasingly pointless. With locals and entire unions being torn apart by back-to-work movements, union leaders seemed increasingly inclined to end the strike with at least some wage gains for their constituents. On April 25 the Northwestern Bell union broke away from coordinated bargaining, and in the days that followed one affiliate after another took similar action. On May 6 the policy committee bowed to the inevitable. It voted to disband and to approve independent negotiations and contract signing on the part of the affiliates.[48]

Having fulfilled their part of the company proposals, however, the unions were discovering that company offers amounted to only a two-and-a-half dollars per week increase, with no improvements in nonwage areas. Reluctant to accept, they continued the strike. Since Bell was now anxious to end the strike and consolidate its victory over systemwide bargaining, the unions were able to secure better terms than these initial offers. Between April 30 and May 2 the unaffiliated New York and Pennsylvania unions and the NFTW affiliates in Illinois commercial and accounting all signed contracts. Nearly all the other striking unions signed between May 4 and May 18. With WE installation's settlement on May 20, what remained of the national telephone strike came to an end. Wage increases averaged four dollars weekly, with the diehard unions receiving slightly more. With a few minor exceptions, there were no improvements in nonwage sections of the contracts.[49]

Was the strike a mistake? The question is largely beside the point, for under the circumstances it could hardly have been avoided. The Bell companies, in a period of severe inflation, made no wage-increase offers until the national strike was in its third week. No self-respecting union movement could have accepted the companies' original terms without a strike. And aside from Bell's provocative posture, the unionists were not to be dissuaded from striking in pursuit of their own ambitious goals. McCowen, reflecting years later upon Beirne's and Werkau's eleventh-hour attempt to delay the strike, remarked that "no one could have persuaded us not to have had that strike." As the Michigan plant union president, Walter Schaar, explained, "That was a very unfortunate thing we did, but there was no stopping it. . . . It had to be. Everybody was flexing their muscles and 'We'll have them crawling in ten days' time,' and that kind of stuff. Only they didn't crawl."[50]

If the strike was unavoidable, there were tactical mistakes aplenty. It was clearly a mistake to formulate public plans months ahead of the strike, thus giving the Bell System every opportunity to prepare a coordinated response. It was a mistake to peg the initial wage demand at a lofty twelve dollars, thus contributing to the members' subsequent view that the four-dollar settlement was a disaster—even though four dollars was not in itself an ignominious figure, constituting as it did two-thirds of the 1947 "packages" won by the large industrial unions and one-and-a-half dollars more than Bell had wanted to give. It was probably a mistake as well to show such restraint on the picket lines. As a union attorney sarcastically observed, such restraint made a "wonderful strike from the public's point of view," but public approbation was "no good in a fight like this."[51] And finally, it was a mistake to undertake such strike activity without better preparations for worker relief.[52]

In addition, the NFTW policy committee probably erred in not heeding the Beirne-Werkau appeal to postpone the strike until after the CWA was in operation. It is true that the organizational change would have risked the withdrawal of representation rights, but this was a risk that would have to be taken whenever the transition to the CWA occurred. It it true, too, that if NFTW unionists had entered the strike as the Communications Workers of America, the results could not have been very different in terms of contract gains: while a fledgling national union might have better coordinated the national strike, this could not have made enough difference in so unequal a contest. But a prestrike transition to the CWA would have produced a genuine national structure that could have weathered failure and, it seems fair to say, would have left the CWA in better shape in terms of membership and unity than, a year later, it proved to be. At the very least, it would have eased the agonies that nearly aborted the creation of a national union altogether.

BY THE WINTER OF 1946–1947, NFTW unionists had almost bridged the divisions that had long kept them in separate unions — divisions by geography, kind of work, sex, and attitudes toward union militancy and centralization. But they had paused just short of uniting in a single union, and now, in May and June of 1947, they were divided in yet another way, this time by their differing responses to the searing strike. Broadly speaking, every NFTW unionist responded in one of two ways: with despair for the prospects of ever building an effective union movement, or with zeal to redouble union strength. Both responses posed distinct threats to the formation of the CWA.

In many unions, confusion and despair prevailed. Members who had returned to work during the strike had often been jeered by the remaining strikers and had promptly torn up their union cards. Strikebreakers by the thousands had resigned, and where they dared to renew or retain their membership, locals were reported "torn up due to scabbing during the strike."[53] Some unionists had remained on strike for the duration on principle, only to resign once the strike was over. A widow and mother in Dallas, for example, had sold the French doors in her small home for groceries rather than return to work during the strike. "If I belong to the union, I'll support it," she declared, "but I can't ever go through that again, so I just can't be a member."[54] In the months immediately following the strike, most unions dared not reveal their membership figures, since doing so might lead to a loss of representation rights. But in several units the membership clearly fell below half of those who were union eligible; as late as December 1947 total membership of the units that had struck had climbed back to only 90 percent of the prestrike level.[55]

Among those who remained members, many were so discouraged by Bell's show of strength that they questioned the utility of militant unionism or of national unionism—particularly since systemwide bargaining now seemed impossible. Nor were the leaders immune to such discouragement. A Washington State plant unionist found that in the closing days of the strike, the union's officers "had *had* it." The strike was "just more than they wanted." They were reluctant "to stay in office" and it was difficult to "find many people that wanted the darn jobs." Discouragement also infected the NFTW policy committee, meeting for the last time on May 6. A majority of the committee felt that the convention in which the CWA was to be established, scheduled for Miami Beach on June 9, should be postponed until the fall of 1947 or later. They pleaded uncertainty as to whether their constituents now even wanted a national union; in any case, they argued, hardly anyone, including the leaders, who had gone unpaid during the strike, had the money to travel to Miami Beach. In response to such arguments, Beirne insisted that the convention would be held on June 9, just as the CWA constitution stipulated. But his insistence was no guarantee that a significant number of delegates would attend. In many unions, including even the once stalwart Ohio organization, large groups were arguing that discretion lay in having nothing to do with the convention or with the CWA.[56]

The response of other unionists was entirely different. Many who had walked the picket lines and made Spartan sacrifices for a cause they thought just were bitter toward Bell and more determined than ever to build a strong and militant union movement. "You can't walk a picket line for three or four weeks," a local leader in Minneapolis observed, "and not benefit by it for your own good, your own militancy, because you remember it."[57] "Up until that time," a former local leader in Montgomery, Alabama, recalled, "the activity was interesting" and "building a functioning organization locally was a challenge." But the 1947 strike "was the birth of whatever dedication I have. I guess it came out of the desperate economic circumstances of other people, as well as myself." In many of the NFTW affiliates, these strike-hardened unionists were now gaining or consolidating control, a process that was hastened by the departure of less dedicated members and officers. In PT&T, for example, "pasteboard members" were giving way to a "substantial group of real down-to-earth unionists"; and in Maryland accounting, those who had "really got the bug" and become imbued with "true unionism" were now running things.[58]

For such groups, the strike had pointed up "the obvious weakness of trying to stand alone," and in Long Lines, WE installation, Southern Bell, Illinois traffic, Michigan, Maryland, PT&T, and elsewhere, many unionists "began to look for additional strength."[59] Even as they did so, the CIO launched a major organizing campaign among telephone unionists, one that promised added strength through "the effective support of other workers in other industries."[60] Begun on May 24, this campaign threatened to draw off about half of those telephone groups that otherwise would have been the CWA's strongest adherents.

CIO organizing, of course, had been something of a threat earlier. The ACA-CIO had made inroads in some NFTW groups in 1943; the Long Lines union had pondered CIO affiliation in the same year; and shortly after the war, an NFTW committee had explored the terms under which NFTW unions might affiliate with the CIO or AFL. Yet prior to 1947 the threat of an exodus to the CIO or AFL had never been major. Most NFTW unionists favored independence, some because they felt that building a national union was the first priority, others because they still cherished their autonomy.[61] Their inclinations toward independence were strengthened when they learned that the AFL proposed to confine them in the IBEW—which offered only "class B" membership to many telephone workers—and that the CIO would accept piecemeal affiliation only through the ACA or UE. (The NFTW groups could have full status as a separate CIO union if they entered the CIO en masse, but this was a political impossibility in 1945–1946.)[62]

Now, though, attitudes had changed drastically. The strike experience had made CIO affiliation attractive to many, and in connection with its new campaign the CIO provided an avenue of affiliation that did not require joining the ACA or UE. This was the Telephone Workers Organizing Committee (TWOC), an interim organization that was to enlist members and eventually be converted into a full-fledged telephone workers' union.

Special circumstances, moreover, gave the CIO an edge in several affiliates. In WE installation, for example, it benefited from the disgust that members felt for operating company unionists who had joined the back-to-work movements and from the belief that joining the CIO now would not violate the principle of telephone worker unity, since the NFTW would soon be dissolved in any case. In the Long Lines union, leaders had long been weighing the merits of CIO affiliation, and the union's president, John J. Moran, now hoped to lead a mass movement of telephone unionists into the organization. And within the Southern Federation of Telephone Workers were many unionists who appreciated the aid that CIO staff and local officers had proffered during the strike and looked to CIO affiliation as a way of regaining lost strength. In the closing days of the strike, when SFTW negotiators had half-seriously threatened to poll their membership on CIO affiliation if a better wage offer were not forthcoming, Southern Bell management had appeared deeply disturbed and had indeed raised its "final" offer. In each of these unions, strong movements for TWOC affiliation were under way, and in another half-dozen, including the large and ostensibly pro-CWA organizations in Illinois traffic and Michigan plant and traffic, similar movements seemed to be developing.[63]

On May 24 Moran resigned his NFTW and CWA vice-presidencies; and during the next two weeks he and other leaders of the Long Lines and WE installation unions joined the TWOC as individuals. They also initiated membership referendums, which would enable them to bring their entire organizations into the TWOC by the end of the summer. As a result, two organization's that had long been among national unionism's strongest supporters were now lost to the CWA. And by this time the Southern Bell, West Virginia, Illinois traffic, and Michigan plant and traffic unions were considering similar action.[64]

As these events unfolded, Beirne considered the possibility of leading the CWA itself into the CIO. To this he had no personal aversion. But after surveying the situation, he came to the conclusion that doing so, even if it were possible, would mean a further diminution of the union's actual or potential membership. It would drive away the cautious groups that were wavering between the CWA and total independence, and it would encounter strong opposition from several unions that were among the CWA's staunchest supporters—unions such as Southwestern, Mountain States, Indiana plant, and Washington, D.C., traffic.[65]

With the old NFTW unions threatening to split into three roughly equal camps—one favoring cautious independence, one the TWOC, and one the CWA—Beirne and what remained of the national unionist leadership directed most of their persuasive efforts toward the first group. In a whirlwind series of trips and telephone calls, Beirne restressed the merits of national unionism; further, as he later recalled, "I took all of the cakes I had in their ovens out and said, 'Okay, call it what you want. You agreed to this and, God damn it, you are going to be *held* to it.'" This hard line reportedly had some effect. But Beirne, of course, had no material hold over the decisions of union leaders and activists, and he acknowledged that the upcoming convention still looked as though "it could have been a wake." *Time* magazine, assessing the fragmenting impact of the strike, declared in late May: "To NFTW president Joe Beirne, the breakup was the end of a dream to weld his loose confederation into a single, tight union at the Miami convention next month."[66]

National unionism, however, proved to be more resilient than *Time* and other prognosticators had supposed. Rooted as it now was in the thinking of thousands of union leaders and activists, its survival did not hinge on the power of the NFTW leaders or anyone else to exert pressure on its behalf. Its basic strength, as always, lay in the perception —in some cases gained only after years of experience—that workers needed unity if they were to successfully confront a centralized management. And while the disheartening effect of the strike and the TWOC's promise of quickly added strength distracted many unionists from this perception, nothing in either of these developments called the perception itself into serious question. As the opening day of the CWA convention drew near, leaders and activists appear to have refocused their attention on the national unionism issue. At any rate, national unionism began to regain many of its earlier supporters.

The revival was especially pronounced in the unions that had been leaning toward the TWOC. There a number of unionists were now arguing that the greatest advantage could be gained by first joining the CWA and then helping to lead it into the CIO. Within the SFTW, for example, CWA support was rekindled by "the same thing that drove our people toward the CIO: a recognition that we had to have some sort of unity, nationwide, to ever accomplish anything." While a large group in the SFTW remained in favor of TWOC affiliation, many who were most attracted by the CIO reasserted their "underlying determination" to "stay with the national union, the idea of a national union. And we believed that we could bring all of CWA into CIO and that we could do it best by staying in [the CWA]."[67]

Similar views were advanced in Illinois traffic, where a majority of the union's executive board looked favorably upon the CIO. The board finally agreed that "whichever road [telephone workers] took, we should do it together"; in June 1947 this meant joining the CWA and working within it for CIO affiliation. In Michigan plant and traffic there was no such agreement. There, TWOC partisans went so far as to charge that CWA had been devised specifically to keep telephone workers out of the CIO. But the unionists who wished to work for the CIO within the CWA eventually prevailed. As plant union president Schaar later exclaimed, "We had no business [i.e., we had no reasonable hope of] holding [the CWA] together, just no business whatsoever, and yet it stayed. . . . I attribute it to the fact that the people we represent, they're just maybe a little smarter than we give them credit for being. Because I think here in Michigan, at least, they saw the wisdom of one national union."[68]

Even among those unions that had been leaning toward total independence, a revival of pro-CWA sentiment was evident. Beirne's forceful personality played a role in swaying the uncertain, as did the repeated declarations of the Southwestern Union leaders that their large and respected union would enter the CWA, no matter what course other unions pursued.[69] Probably more important, however, was the fact that many telephone workers, once given the chance to reflect on their strike experience, were finding that it confirmed rather than clouded their earlier perceptions of the need for unity. According to a southern California plant leader, for example, those in his union "who really looked at the strike on a nation-wide basis"—including such features as the "gradual whittling off of the unions, the settlements ahead of time that were made, the loss of the clout that a nation-wide strike would bring"—were now reaffirming their belief that "we needed a much better, much tighter organization than we had." And in Washington, D.C., a leader of the plant-accounting-commercial union—Glenn Watts, who was to succeed Beirne as CWA president in 1974—recalled that "the people that came out of that strike still trying to lead a union became completely convinced that the loose kind of an organization that had existed prior to that time just was *not* the tool that you needed to deal with the Bell System, that you had to have something that was a tighter organization, that had greater organizational discipline. . . . That certainly was the turning point in my own feeling."[70]

On the eve of the June 9 opening of the convention, delegations representing nearly three-fourths of the total NFTW union membership gathered in Miami Beach. Present were representatives of thirty-six unions, including five relatively large unions that had pondered TWOC affiliation and some seven unions that had flirted with total independence. The turnout itself was an encouraging sign, but the successful outcome of the convention was not yet assured. Several unions had only reluctantly decided to join the CWA. Delegations from at least two unions, Michigan plant and the SFTW (together containing nearly one-fourth of all members represented at Miami Beach), were still undecided. And while Beirne and other CWA advocates were furiously lobbying undecided delegates, TWOC organizers from Long Lines and WE installation were equally active.[71]

Soon after the gavel fell, however, it became clear that a national union could and would be formed. Seated were some two hundred delegates representing thirty-four unions, all of whom quickly declared their readiness to enroll their organizations in the CWA. As officially reckoned by membership dues paid in March, these delegates by themselves represented more than the 115,000 members required by the CWA constitution to bring the organization to life.[72] Shortly after the convention opened, the SFTW delegates also entered the meeting hall and enrolled their union in the CWA. They were "not going TWOC," they said, but they would "work inside the group for affiliation with CIO."[73] The divided Michigan plant union chose not to enter the CWA at the June convention but did join two months later.[74]

No ceremonies attended the birth of the CWA on June 9. Once the delegates had enrolled their organizations, the CWA immediately went into operation and, as its first action, elected an executive board and officers, including Beirne as president, Werkau as secretary-treasurer, and Crull of the Southwestern Union as vice-president. (Frances Smith would easily have been elected vice-president in place of Crull had she chosen to run, but she decided to remain in Detroit because her family was settled there and her health was uncertain. She died of cancer in 1951, at the age of thirty-nine.)[75] The delegates then turned to the real and huge problems confronting the new union, particularly its bargaining weakness in coming negotiations, the hostility that could be expected from Bell management,[76] and the continuing disunity in the telephone union movement as a whole. Although the CWA was by far the largest single union, a majority of telephone unionists were distributed among a variety of organizations that were either independent (as was now the case with Ohio and many other unions), or TWOC affiliated (Long Lines and WE installation), or ACA affiliated (Northern California traffic and the ORTT), or even IBEW affiliated (Illinois plant voted to join the IBEW the same month that the CWA was formed.)[77]

Since organizing campaigns were clearly needed, particularly in those CWA units being threatened by decertification or by TWOC campaigns, the delegates declared organizing to be the CWA's prime objective for the coming year. Upon such activity it would soon be spending about half of its budget.[78] But aside from this action, the delegates showed little disposition to meet problems head on. There was almost no discussion, for example, of strike strategy or new attempts to force systemwide bargaining upon Bell. The only action on collective bargaining was a resolution authorizing the executive board to put "into operation whatever program or plan may be deemed by it to be in the best interests of the members." And rather than risk the ire of members whose money had been drained by the strike, the portion of the per capita monthly dues that was to go to the national union was kept at twenty-five cents instead of the fifty cents proposed by Beirne.[79]

On the issue of CIO affiliation, the majority also moved gingerly. On the one hand, no serious proposals were put forth for recapturing TWOC defectors; on the other, votes related to CIO affiliation clearly indicated that a majority of the delegates were in no hurry to enroll. The key vote was over a clause in the constitution requiring that a majority of the entire membership, voting in a referendum, must approve of affiliation before the CWA could join the CIO or AFL. Some of those favoring CIO affiliation sought to smooth the way by offering a constitutional amendment stipulating that affiliation could take place if it were approved merely by a majority of *those voting* in the referendum. The amendment failed by a margin of 96,911 representative votes to 63,880. But this outcome, as interpreted by the union's new monthly newspaper, the *CWA News*, was "not to be construed as a rejection of the idea of ultimate affiliation." Many of the delegates who voted with the majority, said the paper, merely believed that hasty moves toward affiliation might alienate actual or potential CWA members, and that "we should strengthen and build up CWA before doing anything about the matter of going into the AFL or CIO."[80] In short, the delegates—in this matter as well as in others—favored a holding action.

WHAT SORT OF ORGANIZATION had been established by the time the convention was gaveled to a close? The CWA was a subdued and anxious group of telephone unionists, well aware of its manifold problems and of pitfalls lying ahead. But it was also a national union. The fledgling CWA, uncertain as its status was in many respects, emerged from Miami Beach not only centralized in structure but "national" in size of membership and geographic scope. With the enrollment of the SFTW and Michigan plant unions, its dues-paying membership amounted to some 135,000—about 73 percent of the total membership of the former NFTW unions at the time—with members and representation rights in forty-one of the forty-eight states. Included were workers in sixteen of the twenty-one Bell operating companies, as well as in Western Electric, Bell Telephone Laboratories, and thirty-three non-Bell telephone companies.[81] The union was genuinely industrial as well as national in structure, representing as it did workers in virtually every occupation of the telephone industry.[82]

It was a union whose leaders and members had already shown fortitude simply by forming the organization amidst the harrowing effects of the national strike. And while the CWA's first few steps were cautious, they reflected the immensity of the problems facing the union rather than lack of ambition to overcome them. The search for increased strength would continue, and within two years that search would carry CWA unionists into the CIO, a move that united them not only with other industrial unionists, but with their departed TWOC brethren as well.

Finally, the CWA was a union whose structure enabled it to use the full economic strength of its membership. For the time being, to be sure, that strength left a great deal to be desired. Bell could virtually dictate the form and even the results of bargaining. But the new union's constitution assured that there would be no more sign-offs. Unionists would remain united in bargaining, not only in forming demands but in holding to or retreating from those demands. Though the CWA was in no position to fully test its powers in 1947, the organization then formed provided the means that union labor would eventually use in asserting its interests effectively in the telephone industry.

CONCLUSION

THE EVENTS OF SPRING 1947 marked a turning point in the history of telephone unionism. The national strike of April and May was the culmination of the ultimately reckless militancy that had risen during World War II and been nourished by postwar economic conditions and the bargaining victory of 1946. Establishment of the CWA in June 1947 represented the triumph of national unionist aspirations, aspirations inextricably linked to the rise of militancy but nearly blighted by the strike which that militancy had produced. Both the strike and the establishment of the CWA were to shape the course of telephone unionism in the years to come.

The strike had important and long-lasting effects, most of them hurtful to the unionists' cause. While its corrosive outcome did not prevent the formation of the CWA, it did deflect some unionists from earlier commitments to national unionism and curtail the CWA's bargaining power for the rest of the 1940s. From it Bell seemed to draw the lesson that aggressive resistance to national telephone unionism was a feasible long-term response. The strike was followed by a decade-long struggle in which Bell sought, at various times, to decertify the union in most of its bargaining units, to withhold the union dues that Bell deducted from workers' paychecks, to change wages and working conditions without prior bargaining, and to impose no-strike contract clauses and agreements whereby unionists refusing to cross picket lines could be disciplined by management.[1]

In the long run, however, the effects of the actions at Miami Beach outweighed those of the strike. Despite the CWA's initial weakness and Bell's strenuous efforts, the system was unable to sunder the CWA groups during the course of bargaining or at any other time; the CWA was never wracked by the withdrawals and fear of withdrawals that had so damaged and inhibited the NFTW. It not only remained intact but gradually established itself as the bulwark of union strength in the communications industry, in part through a series of disruptive strikes, beginning with the "hit-and-run" strikes of 1950–1952 (in which roving groups of WE installation strikers would halt operating-company work at a few selected locations by picketing those sites, then move on to other locations by the time local management had taken remedial action), and culminating in the tumultuous Southern Bell strike of 1955.[2]

By 1959 Bell management had clearly decided that the CWA was a union it would have to live with and that agreements were better than showdowns. A form of "pattern" bargaining was inaugurated in 1959, and in the ensuing years the CWA won contracts whose benefits increasingly resembled those being negotiated between other large unions and corporations. The patterns negotiated between the CWA and Bell were extended not only to Bell units in the CWA orbit but to those outside it as well, that is, to those units represented by independent unions—including such large units as New York traffic, Pennsylvania traffic, and Connecticut—and those units affiliated with the IBEW.[3] The IBEW units eventually came to include, in addition to the older units in Montana and Illinois, the New Jersey and Pennsylvania plant units, the majority of WE manufacturing plants, and finally the New England traffic unit (in September 1970, forty-seven years after Bell had first driven the IBEW out of that unit). IBEW affiliation, it should be noted, remained a step quite unlike that of joining the CWA; the organizations so affiliated continued, for the most part, to operate independently of one another and the IBEW national office.[4]

Meanwhile the CWA's membership grew, in part through the expansion of telephone employment and the organizing of non-Bell companies in telephone and other communications industries, but also through the entry of more Bell groups. The 1949 affiliation with the CIO brought in Long Lines and WE installation, as well as northern California plant and traffic (which had joined the TWOC in 1948). By 1951 the CWA had also enrolled the former NFTW groups in Ohio, Oregon, Washington–Northern Idaho, and Maryland plant; and subsequently it brought in New York plant (1961), Chicago traffic (1963), southern California traffic (1974), and several smaller units.[5] Membership grew from 145,000 in early 1948 to 233,000 in 1952, to 260,000 in 1960, to 357,000 in 1968, to 483,000 in 1976. By 1980 membership had passed the half-million mark, and the CWA had come to represent more than two-thirds of the union-eligible workers in the Bell System.[6]

In short, the national union proved a hardy and reasonably effective instrument, well suited for the forceful representation of labor's interests in an industry where management still held many advantages. Yet this outcome was never a foreordained one, and given other leaders and circumstances, the outcome might have been quite different. In 1947 it looked for a short time as if the doorway to national unionism would be shut just as the telephone workers were finally prepared to step through it—a bitter outcome for unionists who had waged their struggle in a setting where social and job attributes of the work force, as well as the structure and technology of the industry, had long favored their managerial adversary. Indeed, during the earlier period from 1920 to 1937, the obstacles in the way of building a CWA-type organization had appeared all but insurmountable.

But telephone unionism overcame these obstacles, initially by following paths diverging from conventional lines of development, circumventing unusual pitfalls, and drawing strength from unusual sources. On the whole, as we have seen, telephone unionists benefited from the company union experience. And like unionists elsewhere, they benefited from the Wagner Act—although, again, in unusual ways. The impact came not in allowing organization by the CIO or in permitting internal unions to rise spontaneously, but in freeing the 180 Bell labor organizations from the tether of company domination. Thus freed, they drew upon their company union experience to form the NFTW, around whose framework a national industrial union movement could be built.

True, the NFTW lacked militancy and recognition of strong mutual interests. These would come later. During World War II the once-placid work force became a restless and aggrieved one, its younger members underpaid, its older ones overworked, and all working under conditions that left much to be desired. Telephone workers who had found the word *strike* repulsive in 1939 did indeed strike in the summer of 1942, at a time when most nontelephone unions had bound themselves by wartime no-strike pledges. And as militancy grew, the search for greater bargaining strength took precedence over the longing for autonomy and the previous disdain for cooperation with other departmental or geographical groups.

For those conducting the search, experience in the bargaining arena pointed to the high costs of autonomy and the advantages of centralization. The costs of autonomy, it became clear, included the failure of unions to stand by resolutions calling for common contract terms and common termination dates, the undercutting of NFTW spokesmen when they assumed a militant stance, and the inability to erect systems of mutual picket line observance that would equitably serve the various departmental groups. The advantages of centralization became apparent as serious strike threats and strikes began to occur, for while the Bell company involved could claim access to the resources of the entire Bell System, the union involved lacked comparable support. In the case of telephone unionism, the impulse toward centralization came with the *advent* of militancy, not—as Lichtenstein and others have suggested was the case elsewhere—with militancy's wartime suppression. Telephone unionists, leaders and activists alike, wished to centralize their union movement not in order to tamp down conflict with the employer, but rather in order to arm for it.

There were lessons to be drawn from successes as well as failures. The Dayton strike showed that determined strike action could bring positive results. The aftermath of that strike—the establishment of the National Telephone Panel—highlighted the profitability of labor representatives speaking with a single voice and exposed more clearly than heretofore the centralized control of a Bell System labor policy. The March 1946 strike threat and its outcome served to discredit the autonomists, and it resoundingly demonstrated how unified action could win major concessions.

The 1947 strike, on the other hand, damaged the national unionist cause, and for a time even so astute a pulse taker as President Beirne was uncertain of the viability of the June 1947 convention. Yet the strike experience deepened the militancy and commitment of many national unionists, and the actions that finally brought the CWA into being suggest that the great majority had arrived at a firm belief that a centralized national union was the only answer to the centralized Bell System.

But what of the influence of bureaucratic accumulation of power within the unionists' national organization? While this may have been significant in the drift toward centralization in other labor organizations (and in the CWA itself in the 1950s and later), there is little indication that it was a major factor in the transformation of the NFTW into the CWA. In February 1943, at a time when the passage of Resolution One signaled the conversion of about half the NFTW to the national union idea, the only full-time occupants of the national office had been Griffith and Horth, and the only professional staff consisted of a part-time general counsel and a part-time actuary hired to study the Bell pension plan. The resources of such a "bureaucracy" were extremely slender; perhaps more to the point, such resources as existed had been exercised in opposition to national unionism.

After February 1943, to be sure, the national unionists controlled the national office; they had been put there by votes of unionists well aware of the autonomania of Griffith, Horth, and Patricia Harris, and of the pronational unionism of Beirne, Werkau, Moran, and Frances Smith. But the resources of that office remained meager. Other than a small clerical staff and some unionists hired temporarily for organizing campaigns among non-NFTW groups, *no one* worked full-time for the NFTW from June 1943 to January 1945. And after January 1945 the full-time bureaucracy remained small. It consisted of a research analyst and Telephone Panel member William Dunn, both put on the payroll in early 1945; President Beirne and Secretary-Treasurer Werkau, who began full-time work in Washington in June 1945; and three more full-time staff members hired between November 1945 and January 1946: a *Telephone Worker* editor, an education director, and an assistant to Beirne (George DuVal). In March of 1946, at the time of the national unionist breakthrough arising from the Beirne-Craig bargaining settlement, there were just seven full-time officers and staff working for an organization whose affiliated membership exceeded two hundred thousand.[7] None of the seven had served full time longer than fifteen months.

It seems safe to conclude that bureaucratic influence was limited. In 1970 one such "bureaucrat," Ruth Wiencek—a traffic unionist who became full-time NFTW education director in January 1946—was asked if her NFTW education program helped "pull the telephone workers themselves into a tighter organization." "I don't think so," she replied. "I think that the need for structural changes came out of their own frustrations and trying to work with each other. . . . By '46 and '47 we [i.e., NFTW unionists] began to realize that there had to be some coordination and a considerable amount of structural change."[8]

All this is not to detract from the considerable role played by the national unionist leaders, both before and after they were elected to national office. Beirne and the rest were dedicated, able, imaginative people, and Beirne in particular forcefully expounded the telephone workers' point of view. But the point of view expounded was in nearly all circumstances the consensual one. When Beirne's predecessor, Griffith, stood athwart the growing NFTW consensus favoring national unionism, the resulting threat of being voted out of office helped impel him to resign; conversely, when Beirne's vice-president, Moran, "got too far out in front" in his move toward the CIO in 1947, he failed to carry any great part of the NFTW with him. The formation of the CWA required not only the consent of the mass of union activists but more; the events of 1947 were such as to require their active participation. Also vitally important was the participation of local and regional union officers, most of whom were not career union officials and showed no signs of wanting to be.

Thus the centralization of the telephone union movement in 1947 appears as the culmination of a slow but grass-roots-based process by which the logic of events, over a period of years, was observed, interpreted, and finally acted upon. It was the telephone unionists' experience with the centralized Bell System—and, to a much lesser degree, with the federal government—that led them to recognize the need for centralization of their union movement, and this recognition was the compelling force in the transformation of the NFTW into the CWA. Put another way, it was the centralized character of the Bell System, along with telephone unionists' rational perception of and response to that characteristic, that was the primary cause of telephone union centralization.

Was employer-management centralization, along with unionists' rational perception and response, an important cause of union centralization in other industries? Telephone union history can only be suggestive, not instructive, on that point, for in important respects it is a deviant case. That is, it is doubtful whether telephone union centralization could have occurred in anything like the manner it did were it not for the unusual circumstances of the industry and its workers, among them, notably, the Bell System's ability to exclude outside unions. Unfortunately, instruction on the point is hard to come by elsewhere, too. As noted earlier, industrial relations specialists, sociologists, union officers, and others have not probed much beyond the frequent assertion that "the union mirrors the industry it serves."[9] Nor have those social scientists whose specialty is the analysis of formal organizations much explored how the structures of unions (or other institutions) are affected by interaction with surrounding institutions. "Problems of interorganizational relations have been neglected by organizational analysts," they frankly admit, despite the fact that "managers are greatly preoccupied with interorganizational relations."[10]

The lack of knowledge about the impulse toward union centralization outside the telephone industry doubtless springs in large part from the sheer difficulty of unearthing such knowledge. Insofar as American industries characterized by employer-management centralization have been unionized at all, unionization has in nearly all cases occurred since the passage of the Wagner Act. And among post–Wagner Act union movements, telephone unionism was unusual in that its "making" occurred in relatively discrete phases, over a span of more than a decade. Those phases included initial membership drives, the emergence of an organizational framework, the gaining of formal employer recognition, the building of union loyalty, the rise of militancy, the winning of substantial contract gains, a company-wide strike, and, finally, centralization. In many of the other post–Wagner Act unions, by contrast—and this is particularly true of those unions facing a centralized industry management—the phases piled upon one another in a matter of months, not years, with CIO affiliation often squeezed in besides. One result may be that historians will be unable to isolate and trace an impulse toward centralization among activists in those unions, if indeed such an impulse ever existed as a distinct and important entity.

Nonetheless, in view of the telephone union experience, it seems quite possible that in other industries union centralization gained strength from the conclusions that unionists drew from their experience with a centralized management, even in—or perhaps especially in—those industries that were organized by CIO national unions or organizing committees. The few glimpses we have of auto unionists' views on union structure in the months before the advent of the United Auto Workers–CIO would suggest this possibility. In early 1934, for example, an AFL federal local of General Motors workers in St. Louis petitioned the AFL leaders (who were then attempting to keep auto locals separated), arguing that the locals were "without a common weapon to

combat the policies of the organized industry" and urging "the formation of a National Committee to represent the Workers in the Entire Industry."[11] Similarly, when company unionists in US Steel were straining toward independence in the months before the entry of the Steel
Workers Organizing Committee–CIO, their dealings with local managers—who "often pointed out that wage matters affected general
company or corporation policy and were beyond their control"—reportedly advanced their recognition of the need for a multiplant, company-wide steel union.[12] All this suggests that the causes of centralization in post–Wagner Act unions remain a proper subject for
rigorous and possibly fruitful investigation. For too long, students of
those unions and activists within them have had to contend not only
with thickets of unfounded assertions but also with an enervating fatalism arising from what James R. Green calls "overdetermined sociological theories like [Michels's] 'iron law of oligarchy' which imply that
labor organizations must inevitably be undemocratic."[13]

But suppose that the impulse toward union centralization elsewhere
was in fact similar to that in the telephone industry in that it did draw
much of its strength from rational conclusions reached by unionists
upon the basis of experience with a centralized management. Might
this not lead us toward a fatalism of a different sort: the positing of an
irresistible mechanism, fueled by the power of human experience and
logic, through which corporate structure replicates itself in surrounding institutions, finally exerting a kind of hegemony in matters of
structure through most of the economy and society? Those who are
persuaded by Robert Wiebe's brilliant synthesis of an earlier period,
The Search for Order, 1877–1920, may be tempted to answer yes. After noting that "one giant firm after another [was] adopting some form
of administrative centralization" in the years around 1900, Wiebe goes
on to trace some of the effects upon other elements in society, including those progressive reformers who were trying to curb or counter the
new corporate power. But, Wiebe writes, these reformers' efforts were
"predicated upon the existence of the modern corporation and its myriad relationships with the rest of American society. Chronologically,
psychologically, this network had come first. It had set the terms of debate." One result, Wiebe continues, was that the institutions that reformers succeeded in erecting actually "strengthened a scheme they
disliked by weaving its basic elements into an ever-tighter national system."[14] Much the same could be said of telephone unionists struggling

with corporate power a generation later, and perhaps it could be said of other unionists as well. The existence of the corporate giant and its centralized structure: these had come first, and indeed they had set the terms of debate in the making of telephone unionism.

Yet on balance, fatalism somehow appears misplaced wherever the telephone union experience is to be our guide. As much as anything else, that experience is the story of workers who did not accept the fate that appeared to be in store for them—open shop status or, perhaps more likely, membership in numerous and quiescent labor organizations spotted across the Bell System. In a sense, it is a story of workers overcoming severe obstacles through the exercise of qualities mostly antithetical to fatalism, namely, hard work, clear thinking, patience, militancy, and courage. By exercising those qualities, telephone workers between 1920 and 1947 became the one example in the history of American labor of a single industrial group independently winning its way from company union beginnings to a full-fledged national union.

APPENDIX A

BELL OPERATING COMPANIES AND

THEIR TERRITORY,

1920–1947

THE LARGEST BELL OPERATING COMPANIES were Pacific Telephone and Telegraph, serving California, Oregon, Washington, northern Idaho, and Nevada; Southwestern Bell, which served Missouri, Arkansas, Kansas, Oklahoma, Texas (except the El Paso area), and the East St. Louis, Illinois, area; Southern Bell, which served the nine southeasternmost states, including Kentucky and North Carolina on the north and Louisiana on the west; and the New York Telephone Company.

Middle-sized companies were the Pennsylvania, Ohio, Michigan, and New Jersey companies, as well as Illinois Bell (serving most of Illinois and the northeastern corner of Indiana), the New England Telephone Company (serving the New England states, except Connecticut), Northwestern Bell (serving Minnesota, Iowa, Nebraska, and the Dakotas), and the Mountain States Telephone Company (serving the territory between the Pacific company on the west and the Northwestern and Southwestern Bell companies on the east).

Smaller companies were the Indiana, Wisconsin, and Cincinnati and Suburban companies; the Southern New England Telephone Company (serving Connecticut); the Diamond State company (serving Delaware); and the four Chesapeake and Potomac companies: C&P of Virginia, C&P of West Virginia, C&P of Maryland, and C&P of the District of Columbia.

APPENDIX B

TURNOVER AMONG NFTW UNION

PRESIDENTS

STATEMENTS IN THE TEXT concerning the turnover of top leadership in NFTW unions are drawn from a large sampling of NFTW union presidencies, the results of which are presented in table A.1 below. The sampling was governed by the following sources and limitations. Names of union presidents as of June 1938 were taken from the roster of the Chicago meeting of that month. Names of union presidents as of April 1941 were taken from an NFTW directory compiled in that month. Names of union presidents at other dates were taken from rosters of those in official attendance at the annual NFTW assemblies, held in June.[1] To be included in the findings for each period, the union presidency had to be represented (as described above) in *both* the paired years. (Thus, to be included among the twenty-six unions sampled in the June 1942 to June 1943 period, for example, a union's president would have had to be in official attendance at both the June 1942 and June 1943 NFTW assemblies.) In a few cases, in June 1939 and later, presidents of non-NFTW affiliates were on the rosters, in official attendance at assemblies as "guests" of the NFTW. Where this was the case in *both* the paired years, that union's presidency was not included in the findings for the period in question (because the sampling was principally intended to arrive at a sense of the turnover within NFTW affiliates). However, where this was the case in one of the paired years, and the union *was* an NFTW affiliate in the other paired year (as well as being represented in the manner described above), that union was included in the findings for the period in question. Where a union split or amalgamation occurred between the paired dates. presidencies of none of the organizations involved were included in the findings for that period.

TABLE A.I. *Turnover among NFTW Union Presidents*

	NFTW Unions			Non–WE NFTW Unions		
	Number of Union Presidencies in Sample	Number of Union Presidencies that Changed Hands	Percentage of Union Presidencies that Changed Hands	Number of Union Presidencies in Sample	Number of Union Presidencies that Changed Hands	Percentage of Union Presidencies that Changed Hands
June 1938 to June 1939	18	6	32	16	6	38
June 1939 to June 1940	29	8	28	25	8	32
June 1940 to April 1941	26	6	23	22	6	27
April 1941 to June 1942	31	15	48	27	15	56
June 1942 to June 1943	31	9	29	28	9	32
June 1943 to June 1944	29	9	31	26	9	35
June 1944 to June 1945	24	6	25	21	6	29
June 1945 to June 1946	32	12	38	28	9	32

APPENDIX C

AT&T CONTROL OF BELL SYSTEM

LABOR POLICY

SINCE BELL'S METHODS of centrally controlling labor policy were often informal, sometimes labyrinthine, and liable to vary with circumstances, it was difficult for unionists to identify the methods used in any given case. There can remain little doubt, however, that such methods existed and were exercised, at least through the 1935–1950 period, and probably before and since.

A unanimous report of the Federal Communications Commission, based on an extensive investigation conducted from 1935 to 1937, found, despite AT&T and associated company attempts "to refute the fact," that "management control is concentrated in the parent company, the American Company [i.e., AT&T]. A description of most of the subsidiaries as autonomous corporations is only justified in the strict legal sense, for they function simply as parts of an integrated corporate system completely and directly controlled by the holding company officers."[1]

With respect to centralized coordination of telephone wage schedules, the National Telephone Panel—a subsidiary of the War Labor Board, composed of two industry members (including an Ohio Bell vice-president), two labor members, and two public members—unanimously reported to the WLB in February 1945 that "the overall wage structure of the Bell System reflects the centralized management policies of the A.T.&T. Co." It further noted that

all associated Bell companies are part of a single closely-woven system. This reflects itself in a wage policy extending beyond the local labor market areas in which the telephone exchanges are located. This policy has had a double focus: it has been concerned with keeping telephone wages in line with local community rates and, at the same time, with relating wage levels and wage changes in the different Associated Bell Companies. Any realistic application of wage policy [on the part of the WLB] to the telephone industry must take into account the existence of the Bell System itself.

This report was unanimously approved by the WLB.[2]

The most detailed treatment of the question of centralized control of Bell labor policies is contained in a 1951 report of the Senate Committee on Labor and Public Welfare, signed by a bipartisan majority of the committee and based on lengthy hearings before the Subcommittee on Labor-Management Relations. The report concluded that "the voluminous record demonstrates that control over the unified Bell System and its operation, including labor-management relations, is directly centered in A.T.&T." The report found that

This A.T.&.T. control flows from its stock ownership of most of the associated companies, from license contracts which it has with all the operating associated companies in the system, and from the long, continued control which A.T.&T. executives have exercised through the years over promotions and salary increases of administrative officers in the associated companies. This latter type of control has gradually built up within the Bell System a Nation-wide administrative staff which is highly responsive to the suggestions and advice on policies and practices emanating from the A.T.&T. management staff.

The report cited many instances where the "controlling influence of A.T.&T. had a direct effect upon the course of labor relations in the system"; it found that "personnel conferences are called by the personnel vice president of A.T.&T., at which representatives of all the associated companies and of A.T.&T. are present"; and if found that "bargaining sessions are often interrupted by the management at critical times to enable the management negotiators to have the company's position in the bargaining checked with A.T.&T.'s central staff." It further stated that a "striking example of the oneness of the Bell System and the controlling influence of A.T.&T. over its operation is to be found in the uniform treatment of pensions in the system."[3]

The only knowledgeable party to challenge the central conclusion of these various governmental studies was Bell management itself.[4] Even those unions whose interest seemed to lie in not conceding the existence of centralized control have in fact conceded it. At the 1950 hearings a spokesman for the unaffiliated, "independent unions" in the Bell companies testified that they "would like to have someone compel the different companies to bargain in good faith, without any A.T.&T. direction." But when asked "how that may be done, in view of the documentation that you have presented as to the financial control and the management control and the interlocking directorates," he was unable to offer an answer.[5]

A minority statement attached to the Senate report and signed by three Republican senators reached no conclusion regarding the question of AT&T control of labor policy. The evidence, it declared, "was directly conflicting," and since the majority had cited evidence supporting its conclusions the minority was justified in pointing out "some of the evidence to the contrary"—that offered, in other words, by Bell management. Yet even the minority recognized "that the power of the American Telephone & Telegraph Co. to control the labor policy of its affiliated companies does present a problem and some justification for requiring the company to bargain on a system-wide basis."[6]

Several independent scholars who have investigated labor relations in the telephone industry have confirmed the existence of centralized control. These include Melvin K. Bers, James Earl Williams, and Curry W. Gillmore. None, to the author's knowledge, has denied its existence. Gillmore qualifies his confirmation by saying,

> On these matters there is unified action, but it probably comes about less directly (or more subtly) than by *orders* from A.T.&T. In its dealings it [i.e., a Bell company] weights the effect of its action on other companies—and it does this with enlightened judgment based on the opinion of A.T.&T. specialists. This cooperative attitude springs from long drill in the virtues of such cooperation, and acute sensitivity to A.T.&T. suggestions. This sensitivity stems in the final analysis, from A.T.&T. ownership of the companies. Each company's management *is* responsible for its dealings with employees and unions, and this insures the flexibility and attention to details that is necessary for efficiency. But the company's management is responsible *to* the company's owner—A.T.&T.[7]

The veteran *New York Times* labor reporter A. H. Raskin remarked during Bell bargaining in 1950 that for years

> the various affiliates of the telephone company had a comfortable relation with hundreds of docile unions, each representing a segment of the work force in a particular Bell unit. Negotiations were carried on separately with each group. The American Telephone and Telegraph Company sat at the top of the corporate pyramid, aloof from direct contact with the union. The parent company maintained that each operating subsidiary set its own policies, even though there was an astonishing identity in these policies and changes had a way of happening at the same time and in the same way throughout the far-flung telephone system.[8]

E. Wight Bakke, in his study of the company and union in Connecticut, does not directly address the question of centralized control of labor policy. He does, however, remark that

> although the Southern New England Telephone Company is relatively independent of the Bell Telephone System [it being one of the two Bell companies in which A.T.&T. owns less than 50 percent of the stock], every manager is aware of the influence of the American Telephone and Telegraph Company upon his specific activities. Time after time management expressed to our interviewers the awareness of a certain restriction on their local freedom and inventiveness arising from the research activities of the A.T.&T. Fully aware of their freedom to challenge such suggestions and standards, and thoroughly appreciative of their value, they nevertheless sensed a compulsion to follow indicated patterns.[9]

Finally, John Brooks's *Telephone: The First Hundred Years* (1975) offers unqualified confirmation of the existence of centralized control. Brooks received extensive AT&T cooperation; he was given unprecedented access to AT&T files and personnel. Although his narrative usually verges toward neutrality when treating AT&T conflict with other organizations, it is, in general, an extremely friendly treatment of AT&T's history. Nonetheless, Brooks quotes Sanford B. Cousins, in 1947 the chief assistant to Cleo Craig, the AT&T vice-president for personnel, explicitly contradicting AT&T's protestations as to decentralized control. In discussing the aftermath of the 1947 nationwide telephone strike, Brooks writes: "As for A.T.&T., the nominal winner this time, both on wages and on the matter of nationwide bargaining—it was left with doubts about the continuing feasibility of holding out for local bargaining, and a new respect for Beirne. Cousins said much later, 'We were kidding ourselves that the operating companies did their own bargaining.'" Referring to 1950 bargaining and the subsequent 1950 Senate hearings discussed above, Brooks seems to say that AT&T attempted to mislead the Senate committee on the matter of centralized control in labor matters.

[AT&T President] Wilson's deputy in labor matters was Craig's successor as vice president for personnel—William C. Bolenius. . . . Early in 1950, negotiations began between Beirne, Bolenius, and their aides at the University Club in New York (of which, incidentally, Bolenius was a member and Beirne was not). Apart from wages and benefits, the basic issue was the same as in 1946 and 1947: Beirne wanted to force A.T.&T. into openly negotiating for the entire Bell System, and Bolenius wanted to maintain the appearance of local bargaining while he actually bargained nationally. Bolenius now says, "We negotiated what amounted to a national contract," although it was announced as being a series of local contracts. . . .

The settlement gave rise, later in 1950, to Senate Labor Committee hearings on Bell negotiating methods and telephone wages. . . . Bolenius, his tongue firmly planted in his cheek, affirmed that in labor matters A.T.&T. merely gave "advice and suggestions" to the associated companies, which the companies were not obliged to accept. He also, by his own account, negotiated behind the scenes with Beirne as to Beirne's testimony, pressing the union leader not to divulge the fact that earlier in the year Bolenius had for all practical purposes negotiated for the whole Bell System. "Joe," Bolenius says he said, "if you tell that, you'll never walk into my office again." Beirne, defying the threat, replied that he intended to testify to just that—and he did so.

Later, Brooks notes, "The CWA finally won its point on national bargaining, probably once and for all, in 1974, the year of Beirne's death."[10]

APPENDIX D

EARNINGS FIGURES,

SELECTED DATES

TABLE A.2. *Rank of Telephone Earnings among Other Industries*

	Rank of Telephone Hourly Earnings[a]	Rank of Telephone Weekly Earnings[a]	Rank of Telephone Straight-Time Hourly Earnings[b]	Rank of Telephone Weekly Earnings[b]
1939	16	22	—	—
Jan. 1941	—	—	12	20
March 1945	—	—	32	33
May 1945	75	86	—	—
Feb. 1946	91	88	—	—
Dec. 1947	—	—	34	38
May 1949	67	75	—	—

Sources: Cols. 1 and 2: *LMR*, 785; Subcommittee Exhibit K, 787–791; Subcommittee Exhibit L, 798–797, cols. 3 and 4: "How Do Your Wages Stack Up?" 26.

[a]The ranking is from among 123 industries on a standard list used by the Bureau of Labor Statistics (BLS).

[b]The ranking is from among 55 industries—a broad and inclusive list that was apparently selected without the intention of making any particular point about the telephone industry. Figures are based on BLS statistics.

TABLE A.3. *Average Telephone Carrier Earnings Compared to Earnings in Manufacturing*

	Average Gross Hourly Earnings, Telephone Carriers (cents)	Average Gross Weekly Earnings, Telephone Carriers (dollars)	Average Straight-Time Hourly Earnings, Telephone Carriers (cents)	Average Straight-Time Hourly Earnings, All Manu-facturing (cents)	Average Weekly Earnings, All Manu-facturing (dollars)
1939	82.2	31.94	—	62.3 (Jan. 1939)	23.86
Jan. 1941	82.4	32.52	80.4	66.4	26.64
Dec. 31, 1941	84.2	34.25	—	76.2 (Jan. 1942)	32.18
Jan. 1943	85.6	35.06	—	85.9	40.62
Mar. 1945	95.1	40.60	90.3	97.2	47.51
Dec. 1947	122.9	47.83	—	125.2	52.74

Sources: Cols. 1 and 2: *LMR*, AT&T Exhibit A-1, 478–500; col. 3: "How Do Your Wages Stack Up?" 26; cols. 4 and 5: pre-1945 figures are from Douty, "Review," 17–18, 22; figures for 1945 and 1947 are from "How Do Your Wages Stack Up?" 26.

Notes: Figures in cols. 1 and 2 are for all telephone carriers, including Long Lines. Figures for May 1945 and later are not strictly comparable to those for earlier dates. For an explanation of this, and for a summary of categories of employees included, see *LMR*, AT&T Exhibit A-1, 500.

Gillmore reports that "The Bell System is such a predominant influence on telephone wage statistics that even Bell management usually considers average earnings for the telephone industry as pretty representative of Bell average earnings" ("Bell," 21). For comparability of wages in Bell carriers and non-Bell class A telephone carriers, see FCCS, 1942, 15.

TABLE A.4. *Real Wages of Telephone Workers, 1939–1948*

Year of Annual Average	BLS Consumer Price Index	Actual Gross Hourly Earnings (dollars)	"Real Wages" (1935–39 dollars), Hourly Earnings (cents)	Actual Gross Weekly Earnings (dollars)	"Real Wages" (1935–39 dollars), Weekly Earnings (dollars)
1939	99.4	.82	82.5	31.94	32.14
1940	100.2	.83	82.8	32.44	32.40
1941	105.2	.82	77.9	32.74	31.12
1942	116.2	.84	72.1	33.97	29.16
1943	123.6	.87	70.4	36.30	29.37
1944	125.5	.91	70.6	38.39	30.59
1945	128.4	.95	74.0	40.01	31.16
1946	139.2	1.12	80.4	44.00	31.61
1947	159.2	1.20	75.4	44.77	28.12
1948	171.2	1.25	73.0	48.92	28.57

Source: *LMR*, Union Exhibit 0, 622.

Notes: Figures are for all telephone carriers and are drawn from BLS statistics. In all probability, the BLS grossly underestimated the wartime rise in actual consumer prices. Thus the 1941–1945 decline in telephone workers' average real wage was probably even greater than that indicated. See Seidman, *Defense*, 123–124.

ABBREVIATIONS

ATTA	American Telephone and Telegraph Archives
ATTR	American Telephone and Telegraph, *Annual Reports* (various dates)
CWA-NUTWP	Communications Workers of America–Northwestern Union of Telephone Workers Papers
CWAA	Communications Workers of America Archives
FB	*Federation Bulletin*
FCCS	U.S. Federal Communications Commission, *Statistics of the Communications Industry in the United States* (various dates)
JOEWAO	*Journal of Electrical Workers and Operators*
LDS	Pearce Davis and Henry J. Meyer, eds., *Labor Dispute Settlements in the Telephone Industry*
LMR	U.S. Congress, Senate, Committee on Labor and Public Welfare, *Labor-Management Relations in the Bell Telephone System, Hearings*
NFTWOP	National Federation of Telephone Workers, *Official Proceedings* (various dates)
OHP	Communications Workers of America–University of Iowa Oral History Project. Where OHP interviews are cited, the surname of the interviewee precedes the letters *OHP*; page numbers of the interview typescript follow. Full names and brief

descriptions of interviewees and the date and place of each interview may be found in the bibliography.

RL	"Repeaterman's Log"
TW	*The Telephone Worker*
UAT	Jack Barbash, *Unions and Telephones*
UTO	*Union Telephone Operator*
WTW	U.S. Department of Labor, Women's Bureau, *The Woman Telephone Operator*

NOTES

Introduction

1. For later periods, see *UAT*, 94–211, 224–228; Brooks, *Communications Workers*, 167–245.

2. Commons, "American Shoemakers," 53–59; John B. Andrews in Commons et al., *History of Labour*, 2:3. More recent observers have viewed the expansion of product markets to be a cause of centralization of power within established national unions. See Shister, "Locus," 520–522; Livernash, "New Developments," 244.

3. Ulman, *Rise*, 43, 49–152; Danielian, *A.T.&T.*, 235; Crull, OHP, 20–21.

4. Shister, "Locus," 523–525; Ulman, *Steel*, 4–14.

5. Lichtenstein, *Labor's War*, 178–180, 184–186, 190, 202. See also Freeman, "Delivering the Goods," 574–578; Weir, "American Labor on the Defensive," 168–169.

6. Selznick, "Theory of Bureaucracy," 51–54; Herberg, "Bureaucracy and Democracy," 407–408; Seidman, "Democracy in Labor Unions," 226–228; Lipset, "Political Process," 86–106. See also Lichtenstein, *Labor's War*, 2–3.

7. Langer, "Hospital Workers," 31.

8. Barbash, *Practice of Unionism*, 94. While the centralized character of management has often been acknowledged as a force producing centralization in unions, detailed treatment has been wanting. See Hoxie, *Trade Unionism*, 99; Cochrane, *Labor and Communism*, 336–337; France, *Union Decisions*, 12–13, 15, 17, 19, 25–26, 37, 47–48; Weber, *Structure*, xxv–xxvi; Craypo, "Impact," 287; Van Tine, *Labor Bureaucrat*, x, 66. Where union centralization has been considered an adaptation to the centralized character

of management, the adaptation has sometimes been viewed to have taken place after relations with management were firmly established, rather than as a prerequisite for building an effective union movement.See Lipset, "Political Process," 84–85; Lipset, Trow, and Coleman, *Union Democracy*, 9. In Great Britain, too, analysis in detail has been lacking while the impact of the force has often been acknowledged. See, for example, Webb and Webb, *Industrial Democracy*, 103.

Chapter 1. Prologue: The Failure of Outside Unionism, 1878–1920

1. Saposs, "Organizational and Procedural Changes," 803–805; Millis and Montgomery, *Organized Labor*, 862–864.

2. *UAT*, 2–3.

3. Ibid.; RL, Sept., Oct. 1961; Shapiro, "Workers of San Antonio," 265–271; Stimson, *Labor Movement in Los Angeles*, 240, 260–263; Knight, *San Francisco Bay Area*, 133–134, 191–192; George Y. Wallace, Rocky Mountain Bell president, to F. P. Fish, AT&T president, July 1, 1904, Box 1314, ATTA; W. T. Gentry, Southern Bell vice-president, to Fish, June 19, 1905, Box 11, ATTA; "The Reasons Why You Should Support the Telephone Girls' Strike" (flyer issued Mar. 12, 1907, in Helena, by the Montana Federation of Labor), Box 1314, ATTA; Wallace to F. A. Pickernell, assistant to the AT&T president, Mar. 21, 1907, Box 1314, ATTA. There is also mention of a 1906 walkout by Chicago operators in Foner, *Eve of World War I*, 316, and of a walkout by Des Moines operators, probably in 1908 or 1909, in U.S. Congress, Senate, *Investigation of Telephone Companies* (hereafter cited as Senate, *Investigation*), 78.

4. Manager of the New England district of the Manufacturers Information Bureau Co. (signature illegible) to Theodore N. Vail, AT&T president, May 25, 1907, Box 1365, ATTA; *UAT*, 3; F. J. McNulty, IBEW president, to Samuel Gompers, quoted in Gompers to Vail, June 25, Box 1365, ATTA.

5. O'Connor, "History," pt. 3 (Mar. 1921), 14–15; McNulty to officers and members of all local unions (IBEW flyer issued May 9, 1907), Box 1365, ATTA; *UAT*, 3; *UTO*, Apr. 1922, 12.

6. Torrence, "Case Study," 5; *JOEWAO*, Dec. 1914, 622, Dec. 1912, 680; O'Connor, "History," pt. 2 (Feb. 1921), 7. Among themselves, high Bell officials were explicit in their opposition to unions. Wallace, for example, in writing to Fish on April 8, 1907, mentioned that "I, like you, am opposed to contracts with labor agitators" (Box 1314, ATTA). On October 21, 1907, Wallace remarked in a letter to AT&T's new president, T. N. Vail: "I know it has always been the policy of the American Telephone & Telegraph Co. to decline to enter into contracts with labor organizations" (Box 1365,

ATTA). Fifteen years later, AT&T President Henry B. Thayer's thinking was much the same. See n. 22, and Thayer's quoted remarks in the text. A similar view was voiced by the president of AT&T's Western Electric subsidiary. See Montgomery, *Workers' Control*, 50.

7. Chicago Telephone management to "employees on strike" (flyer dated Mar. 1, 1911), Box 2108, ATTA; E. D. Nims, Southwestern Bell vice-president, to Thayer, AT&T vice-president, Aug. 23, 1913, Box 1363, ATTA; *JOEWAO*, Dec. 1916, 336.

8. IBEW, *Proceedings*, Sept. 1913, 68–69.

9. *JOEWAO*, Sept. 1912, 696; *UTO*, Apr. 1922, 12–14; O'Connor, "History," pt. 1 (Jan. 1921), 14–15; Mulcaire, *Electrical Workers*, 32. See also Foner, *Eve of World War I*, 252, 254.

10. O'Connor, "History," *passim;* Greenwald, *Women, War, and Work*, 204–205; *JOEWAO*, May 1913, 936–937, May 1914, 221–227, June 1914, 269; *UTO*, Jan. 1921, 23, May 1922, 9–10; Withington, "When the Telephone Girls Organized," 621–623. The Joint Adjustment Board, composed of three union and three management representatives, somehow avoided deadlocks. Its workings seem to have been satisfactory to both the union and local management. O'Connor, "Blight," 545–547.

11. Gentry, Southern Bell president, to U. N. Bethell, chairman of the board of Southern Bell, Sept. 10, 1918, Box 11, ATTA; O'Connor, "History," pt. 2 (Feb. 1921), 16–18, pt. 3 (Mar. 1921), 14; Julia O'Connor, president of the Telephone Operators' Department, in Telephone Operators' Department, IBEW, *Proceedings,* 1919 (hereafter cited as *Proceedings,* 1919), 14; Knight, *San Francisco Bay Area*, 355; Foner, *World War I to the Present*, 84–89.

12. Danielian, *A.T.&T.,* 243–270; Bing, *War-Time Strikes*, 108–110; O'Connor, "History," pt. 4 (May 1921), 15; *JOEWAO*, Mar. 1919, 385. For Burleson in his own defense, see his fifteen-page letter to William B. Wilson, secretary of labor, Mar. 15, 1919, Box 2, ATTA. Of the commission of inquiry's five members, two represented the government (supposedly neutral but in this case actually the employer), two represented company management, and one, Julia O'Connor, leader of the IBEW operators, represented labor. Greenwald, *Women, War, and Work*, 215; O'Connor, "History," pt. 4 (May 1921), 15–16, pt. 6 (July 1921), 14; Withington, "Telephone Strike," 146.

13. O'Connor, "History," pt. 4 (July 1921), 17; *Proceedings,* 1919, 12.

14. J. Epps Brown, Southern Bell president, to Thayer, AT&T president, June 19, 1919, Box 2, ATTA; *Proceedings,* 1919, 12; *NYT*, Apr. 7, p. 7, Apr. 16, p. 1, 1919; O'Connor, "History," pt. 4 (June 1921), 14–17; Greenwald, *Women, War, and Work*, 219–222.

15. *JOEWAO*, June 1919, 557; O'Connor, "History," pt. 6 (July 1921), 15–17.

16. *Proceedings*, 1919, 14–16, 98. For striking nonunion members, see O'Connor, "History," pt. 6 (July 1921), 15. The national office sent a strike cancellation order to locals in California, but it was ignored. Perry and Perry, *Los Angeles Labor Movement*, 143.

17. Like many unions with mere toeholds in a given industry, the IBEW did not reveal its telephone membership figures. The twenty-five thousand figure is a guess as to the highest possible number of dues-paying members, based mostly on unguarded statements that officers made from time to time as to the membership of regional, departmental, or local groupings, plus what sense I have gathered as to how large such union groups were relative to others whose membership was not revealed. It is clear that a substantial majority of the IBEW telephone members in 1919 were operators. See IBEW, *Proceedings*, Sept. 1919, 221; *JOEWAO*, Jan. 1921, 320–321; *Proceedings*, 1919, 5, 10, 26. At one point leaders of the overarching organization of operators within the IBEW, the Telephone Operators' Department, apparently told an early student of their movement, Edith Simpson, that their organization's membership *by itself* was twenty-five thousand. Since per capita dues that went to the Telephone Operators' Department amounted to forty cents per month, a dues-paying membership of twenty-five thousand should have produced a monthly income of ten thousand dollars. But the organization (which was never accused of dishonesty) never acted like it had an income anywhere near that sum. It was constantly importuning the IBEW general headquarters for a ten-thousand-dollar loan, and the largest number of staff members it could afford to pay—and that but briefly—was five. Using such expenditures as a very rough gauge, I would estimate the peak of the IBEW operators' dues-paying membership at between ten and fifteen thousand. (The twenty-five thousand figure given Simpson may actually have been an estimate of the total number of operators who struck in 1919, an estimate that seems reasonable.) Simpson, "Trade Union Organization among the Operators," pt. 2 (Nov. 1921), 14; *Proceedings*, 1919, 7; *UTO*, Mar. 1922, 16–17; IBEW, *Proceedings*, Sept. 1919, 218; *JOEWAO*, Oct. 1920, 515. See also Mulcaire, *Electrical Workers*, 37; Wolman, *Growth*, 98, 133, 143.

18. Brown to Thayer, June 19, 1919; *Proceedings*, 1919, 14, 97. O'Connor later summarized the outcome of the midwestern strikes: "All were settled on the basis of a quasi victory for the union, the settlement to be followed up by unremitting hostility on the part of the companies." "History," pt. 5 (June 1921), 20. See also 18–19.

19. O'Connor, "History," pt. 6 (July 1921), 17. See also *Proceedings*, 1919, 24–26.

20. Perry and Perry, *Los Angeles Labor Movement*, 142–145; O'Connor, "History," pt. 6 (July 1921), 16–18; RL, Jan.–Feb., 1962; *JOEWAO*, Apr. 1920, 518–519; *UAT*, 10–11.

21. Leiserson, "Employee Representation," 122.

22. Thayer to H. J. Wells, June 2, 1922, Box 1, ATTA.

23. Hall, "General Personnel Problems," 246.

24. McCowen, OHP, 4; Chisholm, OHP, 1; Wooding, OHP, 4.

25. O'Connor, "History," pt. 6 (July 1921), 18.

26. See notes 77 and 78, chap. 2.

27. Thayer to Wells, June 2, 1922.

28. Hall, "General Personnel Problems," 239.

29. Summary of the Aug. 8, 1918, meeting of the IBEW executive board in *JOEWAO*, Sept. 1918, 80, 82.

30. O'Connor, "History," pt. 3 (Mar. 1921), 15–19; Greenwald, *Women, War, and Work*, 226.

31. *JOEWAO*, May 1920, 579, Jan. 1920, 319–320, Jan. 1921, 322–324, Mar. 1927, 120; *NYT*, May 17, p. 21, July 26, p. 2, 1920; *UAT*, 10; *Boston Daily Globe*, July 3, 1923, p. 1.

32. *JOEWAO*, Jan. 1921, 322, Oct. 1923, 577; O'Connor, "Blight," 548. The seventy-five hundred estimate is based on the union's report of its strike vote. The company questioned the veracity of the strike vote figures. *NYT*, June 23, p. 15, June 27, p. 19, 1923; *Boston Daily Globe*, June 7, p. 1, June 9, p. 1, June 22, p. 1, 1923.

33. *NYT*, June 27, p. 19, July 2, p. 15, 1923; *Boston Daily Globe*, June 19, p. 1, June 22, p. 1, June 26, p. 1, June 27, p. 1, June 30, p. 2, July 4, p. 11, 1923; *Boston Evening Globe*, June 26, p. 1, July 6, p. 9, 1923; *JOEWAO*, Oct. 1923, 577.

34. *Boston Daily Globe*, June 29, p. 1, July 14, p. 1, July 27, p. 1, 1923; *NYT*, Oct. 19, p. 33, 1923; O'Connor, "Blight," 548.

35. *JOEWAO*, June 1927, 307; Herrington, OHP, 13–14; Newell, *Chicago*, 81. The IBEW also held onto at least one small group of non-Bell telephone workers. See "Telephone Operators: Bloomington, Ill., Labor Agreement," 104–106.

36. In his October 21, 1907 letter to Vail (see n. 6), Rocky Mountain Bell President Wallace—after noting Bell's policy of opposing contract signing with unions—reported that he too was "opposed to it everywhere excepting in Butte, Montana." Earlier, Wallace had explained that "In Butte, where all labor of every kind . . . is only done by union labor, it is absurd for any one institution to try to fight against it." Wallace to Vail, June 13, 1907, Box 1314, ATTA. See also Wallace to William S. Ford, AT&T, Apr. 1, 1907, with contracts attached, Box 1314, ATTA.

37. C. G. DuBois, comptroller, Mountain States Telephone and Telegraph (formerly Rocky Mountain Bell), to Vail, Aug. 30, 1917, Box 12, ATTA; telegram, Edward B. Field, vice-president and treasurer, Mountain States company, to U. N. Bethell, vice-president, AT&T, Dec. 30, 1918, Box 13,

ATTA; *JOEWAO*, Aug. 1947, 319. The live-and-let-live mood of Bell-IBEW relations in Montana in the 1920s is conveyed in Harry W. Bell, "'Inside Stuff,'" 116–117.

Chapter 2. The Problem of Union Organization, 1920–1935

1. *UAT*, 11. For continued use of repressive techniques, see RL, Apr. 1963; Stephens, OHP, 3; Gill, OHP, 1; Naughton, OHP, 3.

2. Loewenberg, "Effects," 1–3; U.S. Federal Communications Commission, *Proposed Report*, 2. The two Bell companies the majority of whose stock was not owned by AT&T were the comparatively small Cincinnati and Southern New England companies.

3. ATTR, 1930, 6; National Telephone Panel, "Report on Wage Stabilization Problems and Recommended Policy in the Telephone Industry, February 13, 1945" (hereafter cited as NTP, "Report"), in *LDS*, 7–8. Compare Bell employment data in U.S. Federal Communications Commission, *Proposed Report*, 49, with employment data for all class A carriers in FCCS, 1939, 16.

4. O'Connor, "Before and After Taking Unionism," 19; Livernash, "Relations of Power," 19. Selig Perlman remarked: "By abolishing competition among employers for labour and by giving the employer unlimited power to hold out against a strike, trustification destroyed every bargaining advantage which labour ever enjoyed." Commons et al., *History of Labour*, 2:526. On the other hand, monopoly conditions, by freeing the employer from competitive pricing in the market, might in some instances have served to reduce the intensity of the employer's antiunion motivation. Montgomery, *Workers' Control*, 157.

5. U.S. Works Progress Administration, *Production*, pt. 3, p. 160; Greenwald, *Women, War, and Work*, 201.

6. ATTR, 1937, 23; Page, *Bell*, 136.

7. Webb, OHP, 13; Beirne, OHP, 14; Patterson, OHP, 11. See also Daniel, OHP, 7; Gill, OHP, 6.

8. *Boston Daily Globe*, June 6, 1923, p. 1; *Boston Sunday Globe*, June 24, 1923, p. 1; *NYT*, Apr. 16, p. 1, Apr. 17, p. 1, June 11, p. 1, June 12, p. 1, 1919.

9. Leggett, "Uprootedness," 682–692. See also Dawley, *Class and Community*, 230–231.

10. Dunlop, "Structural Changes," 108; Wilensky, "Class," 37.

11. New York, Department of Labor, Bureau of Women in Industry, *Report* (hereafter cited as NY, *Report*), 17, 45; Ryan, OHP, 2–3; Pollock, OHP, 1; *WTW*, 8–9, 16; Shellabarger, "'Hurry,'" 367; Anderson, "Equal Opportunity," 181–185.

12. Telephone operators were 95.9 percent native-born white in 1920,

95.6 percent in 1930, and 97.2 percent in 1940. While figures for the other major telephone occupations are not so explicit, since in most cases they lump telephone and telegraph occupations, they suggest that the proportion ranged from a low of about 92 percent (linemen in 1920) to a high of about 95 percent (clerks in 1930). The major groups of white-collar wage earners were "clerks in stores" (86 percent native-born white in 1930), "salesmen and saleswomen" (87 percent), and "clerical occupations" (91 percent). U.S. Census Bureau (hereafter abbreviated USCB), *Fourteenth Census, 1920, Population, 4, Occupations* (hereafter cited as 14*th*, 1920, 4), 342, 352, 358; USCB, *Fifteenth Census, 1930, Population, 5, Occupations* (hereafter cited as 15*th*, 1930, 5), 76, 81, 85, 410, 554; USCB, *Sixteenth Census, 1940: Population, The Labor Force (Sample Statistics), Usual Occupations*, 37–38. The 10-to-10.5 years figure is an estimate based on the census' 10.2 figure, given for "Line and servicemen, telegraph, telephone, power." USCB, *Sixteenth Census, 1940: Population, The Labor Force (Sample Statistics), Occupational Characteristics*, 113–115. Although high nativity and education levels, in themselves, may have affected Bell workers' proneness to unionization, Ruth Kornhauser has outlined some of the pitfalls in gauging any such effect. Her own guarded conclusion is that "there appears to be only a tenuous relationship between union membership," on the one hand, and nativity and education on the other, at least among male manual workers. "Some Social Determinants," 41. Other studies, focusing on a variety of groups, have generally found level of education to have little effect on the propensity to join unions. Bain, Coates, and Ellis, *Social Stratification*, 34. The New York State Bureau of Women in Industry suggested in 1920 that Bell managers demanded lengthy schooling on the part of beginning operators not because they saw a real need for it on the job, but rather because they believed that young hirees whose years had been filled with schooling, as distinct from previous work experience, could better tolerate the schoollike discipline and paternalism they would encounter in their training and on the job. NY, *Report*, 17, 21–22. See also Pilgrim, "Pilgrim's Progress," 236.

13. Smith, "Prestige Status of Occupations," 186–188.

14. Alice Kessler-Harris suggests that unionization came easier among Russian Jewish women, "whose old world or American family norms encouraged more aggressive and worldly behavior" than was the case among other female workers. "Where Are the Organized Women Workers?" 95, 102. But see Dye, *As Equals and as Sisters*, 27. Many telephone workers have passed on to me their impression that few Jews worked in the telephone industry, particularly before World War II but also in the two decades following. See, for example, Patterson, OHP, 15. The only hard evidence or explanation I have been able to glean from the written record is a listing compiled by a Bell company about 1909, reproduced in a U.S Senate document in the course of a fed-

eral investigation of Bell, but without naming the company and indicating only that it came from "one of the largest cities." Listed are the reasons why 2,229 of the 6,152 women who applied for jobs as operators were rejected, along with tallies of the numbers rejected for each reason. Among the listings are: education, 519; accent, 90; colored, 7; Jewish, refused to work holidays, 11. Senate, *Investigation* (see chap. 1, n. 3), 19–20.

15. Friedlander, *Emergence of a UAW Local*, xii.

16. Gutman, "The Negro and the United Mine Workers," 184.

17. See, for example, Seidman et al., *Views*, 152–153; Mason, *To Win These Rights*, 87–88, 92.

18. Kornhauser, "Some Social Determinants," 37–38, 54; Kessler-Harris, "Where Are the Organized Women Workers?" 92–95, 102; Kessalow, "White Collar Unionism," 305, 338, 355–356, 359. See also, in n. 25 and n. 26, citations to the works of Kessler-Harris, Dye, Wolfson, Sangster, Strom, Tentler, and Tax.

19. Miller, OHP, 1; Massey, OHP, 3–4, 24; Dunne, OHP, 1; Novotny, OHP, 4, 12; DuVal, OHP, 6–9, 51–52; NFTWOP, 1939, 27; Schatz, *Electrical Workers*, 43–44.

20. Figures and calculations are drawn from charts labeled "Bell System Statistics" in ATTR, 1921–1940, and from Danielian, *A.T.&T.*, 204–206.

21. Gillmore, "Bell," 16; U.S. National War Labor Board, *Termination Report* (hereafter cited as *Termination Report*) 1:97, 1009; Seidman et al., *Views*, 142, 160; Benson, "Labor Turnover," 115; Mahady, OHP, 1; Gordon, OHP, 1; Loewenberg, "Effects," II–27; NTP, "Report," 16–21; Kuyek, *Phone Book*, 25, 34–35. Among its other effects, systematic hiring practices by the 1920s had driven itinerant "boomers" virtually out of Bell employment. These were men whose principal skill was climbing poles, whether telephone, telegraph, or light and power, who had drifted in and out of telephone employment in earlier decades, and who, according to legend at any rate, had helped spread the IBEW within the telephone industry. DiProspere, OHP, 5–6.

22. Patterson, OHP, 10; *WTW*, 8–10, 16–19; Gillmore, "Bell," 16; Seidman et al., *Views*, 142. Slightly mitigating the difficulties among accounting workers was their concentration in the headquarter cities of the operating companies, making them less geographically dispersed than the other departments' workers. Bers, "Unionism," 11; Patterson, OHP, 10, 11.

23. Gillmore, "Bell," 16.

24. Benson, "Labor Turnover," 115. The proportion of the female work force as a whole that was under twenty-five was 42 percent in 1920, 37 percent in 1930, and 28 percent in 1940. *14th, 1920*, 4: 378–379, 389; *15th, 1930*, 5: 119, 128; USCB, *Sixteenth Census, 1940, Population*, 3, *Labor Force* (hereafter cited as *16th, 1940*, 3), 111–114, 221–222; *WTW*, 17.

25. Riegel, "Caldwell Telephone Company," 312; Seidman et al., *Views*, 142; Kessler-Harris, *Out to Work*, 153, 159; Dye, *As Equals and as Sisters*, 27; Wolfson, "Trade Union Activities of Women," 123.

26. *15th, 1930*, 5: 278; *16th, 1940*, 3: 113–115; Shellabarger, "'Hurry,'" 367; Dilts, *Telephone in a Changing World*, 113; *WTW*, 2; Sangster, "1907 Bell Telephone Strike," 128; Strom, "Challenging 'Woman's Place,'" 360; Tentler, *Wage-Earning Women*, 61. See also Tax, *Rising of the Women*, 283. For proportions of women in various occupations living with parents, see USCB, *Women in Gainful Occupations*, 124.

27. *WTW*, 2, 33, 38; *Termination Report* 1: 1004; Senate, *Investigation*, 11, 74–83, 92, 99, 107. See also Davies, *Woman's Place*, 74–76. When women left traffic work to find nontelephone work, they gravitated toward white-collar occupations. U.S. Department of Labor, Women's Bureau, *Change from Manual to Dial* (hereafter cited as *Change from Manual*), 9; Seidman et al., *Views*, 143; Pilgrim, "Pilgrim's Progress," 237; NY, *Report*, 45, 47–51; Giles, OHP, 2; Moudy, OHP, 10–11; Miller, OHP, 5.

28. Kessler-Harris, *Out to Work*, 137–141; NY, *Report*, 12. See also Seidman et al., *Views*, 152–153; Langer, "Women of the Telephone Company," 17.

29. Pilgrim, "Pilgrim's Progress," 240.

30. *WTW*, 33–34; Senate, *Investigation*, 25, 33, 98; NY, *Report*, 24, 30–32; *Termination Report* 1: 1023; U.S. Department of Labor, Women's Bureau, *Women's Hours and Wages*, 40–41. Bell operators assigned to undesirable shifts were by 1920 compensated in part with varying packages of shortened hours combined with premium pay.

31. Nelle Wooding, untitled memoir, Dallas, n.d., typewritten, 1: 1, 3, Wooding Papers; *WTW*, 6–8, 14; U.S. Department of Labor, Women's Bureau, *Typical Women's Jobs*, 16–25.

32. Shellabarger, "'Hurry,'" 367; Miller, OHP, 5.

33. Michigan Telephone Traffic Employees Federation, Research Department, "Union Exhibit in NWLB Case Number 111–1132–D: Working Conditions and Job Requirements of the Telephone Operator," n.d., mimeographed, p. 5, Tierney Papers.

34. Wiencek, OHP, 27; Mahady, OHP, 11; Giles, OHP, 29; Franks, OHP, 28; Loewenberg, "Bell," II–17; O'Connor, "Blight," 547; Seidman et al, *Views*, 149. In larger offices there were also management positions called "evening chief operators" and "assistant chief operators." The latter position became widespread during the early 1940s. Loewenberg, "Bell," II–18. Traffic workers rarely dealt with authority figures who were male. Management authority, for them, was personified in the chief operator. Thus their everyday work experience was unlike that described by Tentler, in which authority was held by males, and "the sex-segregated work experience defined

the limits of female power in the world outside the home; it directed young women and young men toward the distinct and formally inegalitarian sex roles of working-class adulthood." Tentler, *Wage-Earning Women*, 27.

35. *WTW*, 4–5, 9; Senate, *Investigation*, 104–105; Moudy, OHP, 9; Mahady, OHP, 11; Seidman et al., *Views*, 141. An early designer of training for Bell defined the ideal: "The operator must now be made as nearly as possible a paragon of perfection, a kind of human machine." Katherine Schmitt, quoted in Maddox, "Women and the Switchboard," 270.

36. Senate, *Investigation*, 55; U.S. Congress, Senate, *Final Report*, 75; NY, *Report*, 27, 52, 54; *WTW*, 4–5; Patterson, OHP, 9–10; Seidman et al., *Views*, 154.

37. Moudy, OHP, 1–2; Berthelot, OHP, 1–2; NY, *Report*, 51. The quote is from O'Connor, "Blight," 545.

38. *Change from Manual*, 9–10; Kuyek, *Phone Book*, 69; Seidman et al., *Views*, 154.

39. Wooding, OHP, 3; Senate, *Investigation*, 107; *WTW*, 14. The quotes are from *Termination Report* 1: 1024; Berthelot, OHP, 5.

40. Berthelot, OHP, 5; Wooding, memoir, 2: 5. The quote is from DuVal, OHP, 37. The 1923 strike had been extended in the closing days by the operators' futile effort to secure a management guarantee that their striking supervisory comrades would not be demoted to operator once they returned to work. *Boston Daily Globe*, July 25, p. 1, July 27, p. 1, July 28, p. 1, 1923.

41. *UAT*, 19.

42. Atkinson, OHP, 2–3; Good, OHP, 2; Hubbard, OHP, 2; Wooding, OHP, 37; Beirne, OHP, 14; RL, Nov. 1961.

43. Hall, "General Personnel Problems," 239; John M. Shaw, "Our Employee Education Objectives" (mimeographed paper delivered at Apr. 1, 1936 Bell System conference entitled "Public Relations Program"), Box 2, Shaw Papers; National Industrial Conference Board, *Individual Bargaining*, 2–3. The quotes are from Wiebe, *Search for Order*, 294–295; Danielian, *A.T.&T.*, 281. See also 224–225, 271–333.

44. The quotes are from Hall, "To Get the Best," 374; Hall, "Executive Leadership," 566–567. See also Loewenberg, "Effects," 1–21; Page, *Bell*, 30.

45. Good, OHP, 1–2. Good's emphasis.

46. *WTW*, 35; Loewenberg, "Effects," 1–21, 22; RL, Nov. 1961, Jan.–Feb. 1962; Hall, "General Personnel Problems," 245.

47. Waterson, "Talk," 57: *WTW*, 36; Gilmore, "Bell," 93; Hanscom, OHP, 1; NFTW, Proceedings of the Pre-Assembly Traffic Session and Traffic Panel of the Sixth Annual Assembly, held at Omaha, June 16-19, 1941, mimeographed, p. 108, Box 1, CWAA; Loewenberg, "Effects," 1–21.

48. Douglas, *Real Wages,* 334, 392–93. The designation *utility worker* included telephone, telegraph, street railway, railroad, and gas and electric workers. It is doubtful that telephone workers' lower earnings can be explained by their having a shorter service with their employer. See employment flux rates of telephone workers, in both high and low flux periods, in Brissenden and Frankel, *Labor Turnover,* 52–53. In 1926 the average yearly earnings of a wage earner in manufacturing were $1,309, in telephone $1,117. So far as I have been able to determine, breakdowns of telephone workers' average wages or earnings by sex are unavailable. It may be helpful to note that in 1929, when average weekly earnings in a selection of twenty-five manufacturing industries were $17.62 for female wage earners, $24.36 for unskilled male wage earners, and $32.63 for skilled and semiskilled male wage earners (taken together), Bell's weekly wage rates in the largest cities averaged $13.43 for beginning operators, $22.24 for operators with fourteen or more years of experience, $18.00 for beginning central office repairmen, and $49.04 for central office repairmen with fourteen or more years of experience (the latter were craftsmen of considerable skill). The telephone wage rates in all but the largest cities were considerably less. For example, in Dallas the rate for operators with fourteen or more years of experience was $20.00, and in many small towns it was $15.00. Gillmore, "Bell," 101; National Industrial Conference Board, *Wages,* 75; Wooding, memoir, 2: 2, 10.

49. Wooding, memoir, 1: 3; McCowen, OHP, 3; Griffith, OHP, 7–8; Crull, OHP, 8.

50. ATTR, 1919, 29; Page, *Bell,* 56. For belief of this claim, see Loewenberg, "Effects," 1–26; Philip Taft, "Brief Review of Other Industries," in Twentieth Century Fund Labor Committee, *How Collective Bargaining Works,* 952. For a challenge to this claim, see *WTW,* 24–28.

51. Since there had been increases in outstanding stock in 1929–1930 to support large-scale capital improvements, total dividend payments, at the established $9 per share, grew from $116 million in 1929 to $168 million in 1935. A critic of AT&T remarked that "every dollar of dividends per share received during the depression was at the expense of leaving 18,000 people on the relief rolls." Danielian, *A.T.&T.,* 202–205, esp. 221. Meanwhile, the improvements meant that more jobs were being "automated." In the operating companies, the number of workers per thousand telephones in use fell from twenty-one in 1930 to fewer than eighteen in 1935. Page, *Bell,* 73.

52. Danielian, *A.T.&T.,* 205–206; Page, *Bell,* 73. WE employment declined disproportionately, falling from 84,848 in 1929 to 18,446 in 1933. Useful figures did not emerge from a subsequent CWA-Bell dispute over the total number of depression layoffs. The CWA claimed, incorrectly, that the decline in total employment, approximately 185,000, represented people who

were all "laid off due to lack of work." *LMR*, 122. In disputing this claim, Bell evaded giving a figure for layoffs. *LMR*, 933. See also Page, *Bell*, 71.

53. LeFevre, OHP, 1-2; Walsh, OHP, 2. The quote is from Naughton, OHP, 1.

54. *NYT*, Jan. 11, 1931, 2: 17; Wandersee, *Women's Work*, 99; Schatz, *Electrical Workers*, 21, 126; Smith, "Restrictions," 261-262; Strom, "Challenging 'Women's Place,'" 361; Wiencek, OHP, 23-24.

55. Page, *Bell*, 72; *LMR*, 993; William A. Mendenhall, "A History of the Illinois Bell Telephone Employees' Association," Chicago, 1939, mimeographed, 43-49, Griffith Papers; Ryan, OHP, 4; Wooding, memoir, 1: 4; Mahady, OHP, 2.

56. Page, *Bell*, 68; Edwards, OHP, 1; Crull, OHP, 8; Good, OHP, 1; Wooding, OHP, 6; Wiencek, OHP, 3.

57. Peil, OHP, 1; LeFevre, OHP, 1; Naughton, OHP, 2. For the West Coast account, see RL, Nov. 1962. For the New England account, see U.S. Department of Labor, Bureau of Labor Statistics, *Characteristics* (hereafter cited as *Characteristics*), 266. See also Kravif, *Telephone and Telegraph Workers*, 12, 25.

58. Levinson, *Labor on the March*, 245-246; Galenson, *CIO Challenge*, 248-250, 253-255, 265, 521, 628; Ulricksson, *Telegraphers*, 137-138, 143-147; *ACA News*, Apr. 16, 1938.

59. Between 1928 and 1933, due to layoffs, decreased hiring, and fewer resignations, the average length of service increased from five-and-a-half years to ten. Page, *Bell*, 72. The quotes are from Myerscough, OHP, 1; Chester I. Barnard, before an employee meeting in 1933, quoted in *LMR*, Appendix 10, Union Exhibit 24, p. 852. See also Barnard, "Some Principles," 17, 22.

60. Brody, *Workers*, 134. See also 76-77. For the breakdown of such systems elsewhere, see National Industrial Conference Board, *Effects*, 4, 6, 8, 10. For maintenance of the system and wage rates in Bell, see Loewenberg, "Effects," 1-21, 22; Page, *Bell*, 30; Danielian, *A.T.&T.*, 281; Bers, "Unionism," 228, 231-232. Bers suggests that general hourly wage cuts would have been impolitic, in view of Bell's relatively inflexible price structure—which owed much to Bell's position as a regulated monopoly. Bers further suggests that by maintaining the Bell wage rate in times of deflation (thus raising Bell workers' wage rate relative to other workers), the Bell companies "would build themselves a cushion against future inflation and the accompanying need to sue for rate increases."

61. Fine, *Automobile*, 15, 20; Gillmore, "Bell," 75; Stein, OHP, 1; Pollock, OHP, 1-2; Massey, OHP, 1; Walsh, OHP, 2-3; Gordon, OHP, 1; Beaver, OHP, 15-16.

62. Vail, AT&T president, to F. H. Bethell, Pennsylvania Bell president,

June 3, 1919; Vail to J. T. Moran, Southern New England Company president, June 3, 1919, with attached note: "Sent to all associated companies." Both in Box 2, ATTA; Bernstein, *Lean Years,* 168.

63. E. K. Hall was put in charge of the program. Thayer to H. J. Wells, June 2, 1922, Box 1, ATTA. For variations in structure, see Hall, "General Personnel Problems," 246. For the establishment of WE, accounting, and commercial units in the mid-1920s and later, see Mendenhal, "Employees' Association," 10; U.S. National Labor Relations Board (hereafter NLRB), PT&T 76:902 (1942); U.S. Congress, Senate, Committee on Education and Labor, *Violations* (hereafter cited as *Violations*), Supplementary Exhibits, Exhibit 7620, p. 16950.

64. *Characteristics,* 56; Griffith, OHP, 10; NLRB, Wisconsin Telephone 12: 381 (1939), Porter, "Technique," 138–140; Fitch, "Technique," 147–151; Riegel, "Caldwell Telephone Company," 310–311. There were two exceptions to the pattern of departmental separation within companies, Southern Bell and AT&T Long Lines, where all four departments were in single organizations. Even there most operations were on an intradepartmental basis. *UAT,* 13–14; NLRB, Southern Bell 35: 624–625 (1941).

65. *UAT,* 13; Griffith, OHP, 9, 14; Gordon, OHP, 1; NLRB, Southern Bell 35: 624–625 (1941); NLRB, Wisconsin Telephone 12: 381 (1939).

66. Porter, "Technique," 141. See also NLRB, Wisconsin Telephone 12: 381 (1939).

67. Hanscom, OHP, 1.

68. Orr, OHP, 1. See also Crull, OHP, 7; DiProspere, OHP, 5.

69. Hall, "Representation," 81; Lonergan, OHP, 2; DiProspere, OHP, 6.

70. The quotes are from Hall, "To Get the Best," 374; Good, OHP, 1. See also Hall, "Representation," 78–83; Hall, "Executive Leadership," 566–567; Porter, "Technique," 141.

71. Porter, "Technique," 139; Fitch, "Technique," 147; *UAT,* 12–13.

72. NLRB, Wisconsin Telephone 12: 396 (1939).

73. Illinois Bell Telephone Employees' Association, Proceedings of the 18th Annual Convention, Joint Plant Council, Oct. 29, 1936, mimeographed, p. 42, Griffith Papers. See also *Characteristics,* 50; Griffith, OHP, 9; Chisholm, OHP, 3.

74. J. J. Schacht, OHP, 8.

75. The quotes are from Hall, "Executive Leadership," 566–567; Hall, "To Get the Best," 374. See also Porter, "Technique," 143. In 1939 a New York telephone unionist was to note the "strange paradox" that, despite Bell's efforts to keep worker organizations separated, "Many years of job training, with the single purpose of furnishing telephone service to the public, has developed a unity among workers in the industry that bridges craft, departmental, and even company lines." *U.T.O. News,* quoted in *Pact News,* Jan. 1940.

76. Mendenhall, "History," 9–10, 43.

77. The quotes are from RL, Aug. 1962; Thomas Twigg in Bell System Employee Organizations, Official Minutes of the Second National Conference, Chicago, June 15–19, 1938, mimeographed (hereafter cited as Minutes, Chicago, 1938), p. 1, Box 1, CWAA; Mendenhall, "History," 26. See also Porter, "Technique," 141; Fitch, "Technique," 152.

78. Porter, "Technique," 143; Hall, "General Personnel Problems," 246. Barbash has written: "The company unions in the steel and telephone industries . . . provided a training ground for many of the local union leaders and, in the case of telephones, for the national leadership as well. . . . As it turned out, the leadership skills developed in the company unions were easily transferable to the free union environment." *Practice of Unionism,* 13. Telephone union leaders were inclined to view their association experience as helpful in this regard. Gill, OHP, 2, 4; DuVal, OHP, 58.

79. Chisholm, OHP, 3–4; RL, Sept.–Oct., Nov. 1962; Griffith, OHP, 11–12; *FB*, Apr. 1939.

80. NLRB, Wisconsin 12: 382 (1939); *Violations,* Supplementary Exhibits, Exhibit 7641, p. 16960, Exhibit 7620, p. 16950, and Exhibit 7623, p. 16951; NLRB, PT&T 76: 902 (1948); *FB,* Apr. 1939.

81. RL, Jan. 1964; Mendenhall, "History," 53, 58; Risser, OHP, 6.

Chapter 3. The Emergence of an Organizational Framework, 1935–1939

1. Illinois Bell Telephone Employees' Association, Minutes of the 17th Annual Convention, Joint Plant Council, [Oct. 1935], mimeographed, p. 4, Griffith Papers; NLRB, Southern Bell 35: 627 (1941). The quote is from a company notice of July 20, 1935, cited in this decision.

2. NLRB, WE 72: 759 (1947).

3. Ibid., 755, 758; NLRB, WE 57: 1183 (1944); NLRB, PT&T 76: 891 (1948).

4. Webb, OHP, 33. See also NLRB, WE 72: 755, 762–763 (1947); Mendenhall, "History" (see chap. 2, n. 55), 59.

5. Wooding, memoir (see chap. 2, n. 33), 2: 1; RL, Nov. 1964; NLRB, WE 57: 1189 (1944); NLRB, PT&T 76: 900, 902, 905 (1948); NLRB, WE 72: 764–765 (1947).

6. NLRB, Southern Bell 45: No. C–1911 (1941); NLRB, WE 57 : No. 5–C–1604 (1944); NLRB, WE 72: Nos. 2–C–4508 and 2–C–5069 (1947); NLRB, PT&T 76: Nos. 20–C–1287, 20–C–1291, 20–C–1309, 20–C–1370, and 20–C–1371 (1948); NLRB, Wisconsin Telephone 12: 391, 383 (1939). The quote is from Beirne, OHP, 3.

7. D. L. McCowen in *LMR*, p. 685.

8. Wooding, OHP, 5; Crull, OHP, 11–12. See also Webb, OHP, 3.

9. Saposs, "Organizational and Procedural Changes," 803. See also Troy, "The Course," 137.

10. *ACA News*, Apr. 16, 1938, Apr., Oct. 1942, July, Aug. 1946. The quote is from Beirne to Griffith, Sept. 23, 1941, Box 5, CWAA.

11. NLRB, Wisconsin Telephone 12: 388–400 (1939); *UAT*, 43–44; NLRB, WE 72: 775 (1947); NLRB, WE 57: 1191 (1944); Crull, OHP, 33–34. There was also a small, quickly abandoned 1937 UE organizing effort in Bell Telephone Laboratories. Report of the Bell Labs union in Maryland Federation of Telephone Workers, "Souvenir Program, Seventh National Assembly, NFTW" (Baltimore, June 1942), (hereafter cited as "Souvenir Program"), p. 11, Box 1, CWAA; *NYT*, Apr. 11, 1937, p. 1.

12. For these cases, with dates, see n. 6.

13. Chisholm, OHP, 3. For similar changes elsewhere, see Good, OHP, 3; Stephens, OHP, 4.

14. *LDS*, p. 95; *FB*, Dec. 1937; Griffith, OHP, 14, 17; Stein, OHP, 2–3; Beirne, OHP, 4; *TW*, May 1941; Crull, OHP, 8–9; J. J. Schacht, OHP, 1–2.

15. *FB*, Apr. 1939; LeFevre, OHP, 3–4; report of the Northwestern Bell commercial union in NFTW, Report Supplement to Official Proceedings of the Sixth National Assembly, Held at Omaha, June 16–21, 1941, mimeographed, (no pagination), (hereafter cited as Report Supplement, 1941), Box 1, CWAA; report of the Northwestern Union of Telephone Workers in NFTW, Annual Reports of the Member Organizations to the Seventh National Assembly, Held at Baltimore, Md., June 8–13, 1942, vol. 1, (no pagination), mimeographed, Box 1, CWAA; RL, Jan. 1965.

16. Mendenhall, "History" (no page number given), quoted in *UAT*, 22. See also Griffith, OHP, 15.

17. "Constitution of the Proposed National Federation of Telephone Workers, with Explanatory Notes," issued Feb. 1, 1939, by the NFTW ratification committee, mimeographed, pp. 1–3, Box 1, CWAA.

18. Ibid., pp. 2–3. See also Minutes, Chicago, 1938 (see chap. 2, n. 77), pp. 14–17.

19. *LMR*, 47–48; Gillmore, "Bell," 145–146.

20. Griffith, OHP, 14. Workers attempting to reach other groups within their own company sometimes encountered similar difficulties. DuVal, OHP, 66.

21. "Telephone Employees' Association, Plant Department, Northwestern Bell Telephone Territory," vol. 1, no. 1, Dec. 1937, mimeographed, (no pagination), Box 7, CWA-NUTWP.

22. Griffith, OHP, 15; Ernest Weaver, of the WE installation union, to Beirne, Dec. 20, 1944, Box 5, CWAA: *FB*, Jan. 1939; Twigg in Minutes, Chicago, 1938, pp. 14, 18. See also Pollock, OHP, 11.

23. *LMR*, 47–48. The quote is from *FB*, Jan. 1939.

24. Theresa Donahey, recorder, "Minutes of the First Meeting of the National Convention of Independent Telephone Workers Unions, St. Louis, Dec. 16–17, 1937," mimeographed, p. 1, Griffith Papers; representatives from Illinois, compilers, "Proceedings of the First National Conference of Bell Employee's Organizations, St. Louis, Dec. 16–17, 1937," mimeographed (hereafter cited as "Proceedings, St. Louis, 1937"), p. 1, Box 1, CWAA.

25. "Proceedings, St. Louis, 1937," pp. 1–6, 13. The quote is from Griffith, OHP, 15–16.

26. Donahey, "Minutes, St. Louis, 1937," 2–3. The quote is from "Proceedings, St. Louis, 1937," pp. 6, 10. See also Griffith, OHP, 15–16; Kendall T. Stevens, "National Convention" (report to the Telephone Employees Association, Plant Department, Northwestern Bell, Jan. 31, 1938), mimeographed, pp. 1–6, Box 7, CWA-NUTWP.

27. "Proceedings, St. Louis, 1937," pp. 6–7, 10–11. The quote is from Griffith, OHP, 17. See also Donahey, "Minutes, St. Louis, 1937," p. 3.

28. *FB*, July 1938. The quote is from Griffith, OHP, 19.

29. DuVal, OHP, 36–37.

30. Griffith, OHP, 18, 20, 29. See also Minutes, Chicago, 1938, pp. 10, 12–14, 25; *Pact News*, Sept. 1938; *The Pen*, July 1938.

31. Minutes, Chicago, 1938, 3, 10, 19. See also *The Pen*, July 1938.

32. Bell System Employee Organizations, Steno Transcriptions of the Third National Conference, New Orleans, Nov. 14–17, 1938, mimeographed, afternoon session of Nov. 14, p. 23, and morning session of Nov. 17, pp. 15–16, Box 1, CWAA; *FB*, Jan. 1939.

33. Steno Transcriptions, New Orleans, 1938, afternoon session of Nov. 14, pp. 11–12, morning session of Nov. 15, p. 1. Weil was probably acting with management's backing at New Orleans. Regarding his activities within his Southern Bell labor organization, at any rate, the NLRB later found that his employer "was responsible for his activities." NLRB, Southern Bell 35: No. C-1911 (1941), esp. p. 628n.

34. *FB*, June, Aug. 1939; NFTW, Proceedings of the Pre-Assembly Traffic Session and Traffic Panel of the Seventh Annual Assembly, held at Baltimore, June 8–14, 1942, mimeographed, p. 171, Box 1, CWAA.

35. NFTWOP, 1939, 5–7; *UAT*, 28 ; ATTR, 1939, 33, 1940, 33, 1941, 37, 1942, 39, 1943, 39, 1944, 39, 1945, 39.

36. "Constitution with Explanatory Notes," 1–5, 9–12; NFTWOP, 1939, 28; Central Region Conference of Independent Telephone Unions, Official Minutes, Chicago, Sept. 15–17, 1939, mimeographed, minutes of the general session of Sept. 15, p. 1, Box 1, CWAA. See also *UAT*, 27.

37. "Constitution with Explanatory Notes," 2, 7; NFTWOP, 1939, 14–15.

38. "Constitution with Explanatory Notes," 5–6; *UAT*, 38.

39. "Constitution with Explanatory Notes," 6–8, 10; NFTWOP, 1939, 14–16, 27–28; NFTW, "Constitution and Bylaws of the NFTW, as Revised by the Seventh National Assembly, Baltimore, Md., June 8–14, 1942," mimeographed, pp. 111–114, Box 1, CWAA; Pre-Assembly Traffic Panel, 1941 (see chap. 2, n. 47), pp. 135–138.

40. Griffith, OHP, 21; NFTWOP, 1939, 28, 1940, 16.

41. For other points of possible comparison, see Schacht, "Toward Industrial Unionism," 35. Comparisons seem apt, in light of the fact that employees of large chemical and oil-refining firms resembled Bell employees not only in having experienced company unionism and having largely accepted the employer-inspired successors, but also in having faced roughly similar obstacles to unionization. All three groups were geographically and "functionally" dispersed, and they faced generally prosperous large employers whose labor policies could be centrally controlled. Large oil and chemical firms did not employ the proportions of young female and white-collar workers that Bell did, but offsetting this in some degree was an antiunion advantage not held by Bell: their labor costs constituted a small proportion of total costs, making it relatively inexpensive to use "a store of indulgences with which [they could] win and maintain the workers' loyalty." See Weber, "Relations in the Chemical Industry," 664–667; and the appendix by Herbert Werner in Williamson et al., *Age of Energy*, 828–830. For descriptions of the linking together of employer-inspired organizations (or the lack of it) in chemical, oil-refining, and other nontelephone industries—links that in all cases seem to have been forged belatedly and on a small scale—see, in addition, Weber, "Competitive Unionism," 19; Brandt, "Unionism in the Oil Refining Industry," 33–37; Shostak, *Forgotten Labor Organizations*, 87–107; Troy, "The Course," vi–vii, 145–146; Troy, "Local Independent and National Unions," 503–504.

Chapter 4. Development of the Bell Labor Organizations, 1938–1941

1. Central Region Minutes, 1939 (see chap. 3, n. 36), minutes of the accounting and commercial panel conference of Sept. 17, p. 13; McCowen, OHP, 9; Crull, OHP, 12; Hanscom, OHP, 12; DuVal, OHP, 54; Atkinson, OHP, 3.

2. Welsh, OHP, 2–3. See also Crull, OHP, 12. Inclusion of company practices in the contract was, nonetheless, not an insignificant step. As David Brody has pointed out, inclusion meant that these practices could become bargainable issues in subsequent negotiations. *Workers*, 179.

3. DiProspere, OHP, 11.

4. J. J. Schacht, OHP, 6.

5. Page, *Bell,* 72, 74. In WE the average term was undoubtedly shorter. See chap. 2, n. 52; ATTR, 1936, 23, 1937, 23, 1938, 33, 1939, 33.

6. Norma Naughton in Pre-Assembly Traffic Panel, 1941 (see chap. 2, n. 47), 32, 34. See also Mann, OHP, 17. When dial conversion came to an area, it of course reduced the traffic workload, but in normal economic periods the displacing effect on operators was eased by not replacing resigned or retired operators for several years preceding conversion and by the general increase in demand for telephone service. During the 1930s, however, resignations were much reduced, and growth in demand for service was slow or nil. In the late 1930s the problem was aggravated by Bell's acceleration of dial conversion. The proportion of dial phones to total phones in Bell increased from 42.7 percent in 1932 to 49 .8 in 1937; then it jumped to 59.9 percent by 1940 and to 63.3 percent in 1941. Loewenberg, "Effects," III–38; *Change from Manual* (see chap. 2, n. 27); Baker, *Technology and Women's Work,* 239–241; Seidman et al., *Views,* 144.

7. *LMR,* Subcommittee Exhibit K, pp. 786–790. WE formed the bulk of an "industry" that the BLS labeled "communication equipment." Average weekly earnings here were $28.74, ranking twenty-sixth among the 123. For telephone wages being exceptionally high relative to other industries in this period as compared to other periods, see Bers, OHP, 5–6. Some workers did suffer a two-dollar weekly wage cut when the work week was reduced from six days to five. Wooding, memoir (see chap. 2, n. 33), 1:4. See also Page, *Bell,* 73.

8. Hubbard, OHP, 3. See also Good, OHP, 2; Atkinson, OHP, 3–4; Di-Prospere, OHP, 7–8.

9. Central Region Minutes, Sept. 1939, minutes of the plant panel conference of Sept. 17, p. 23. Participants were reviewing the New York meeting.

10. Ibid. See also Central Region Minutes, Sept. 1939, minutes of the accounting and commercial panel conference of Sept. 17, p. 14.

11. Naughton in Pre-Assembly Traffic Panel, 1941, p. 34; Wiencek, OHP, 3.

12. NFTWOP, 1939, 27; Green, "Fighting on Two Fronts," 12; *TW,* Aug. 1942. The downstate New York plant union did briefly picket a construction site in December 1940, during a jurisdictional dispute with the IBEW. See n. 19.

13. *FB,* Jan. 1939.

14. Griffith, OHP, 8–9. Griffith is paraphrasing the remarks of Illinois Bell's general plant manager.

15. Wooding, OHP, 6. Wooding is quoting her own remarks in a meeting with a Southwestern Bell traffic area director. Actually, there is some reason to suspect that management, in implementing the lack-of-work-days system, was moved less by the desire for efficiency than by benevolent motives and,

perhaps, considerations arising from AT&T President Walter Gifford's chairmanship of the President's Organization on Unemployment Relief, which endorsed the share-the-work concept. See Brody, *Workers*, 68–69; Bernstein, *Lean Years*, 460–462, 476–479.

16. Beaver, OHP, 16–17; Pollock, OHP, 2; Gordon, OHP, 1.

17. *FB*, Mar. 1938; Walsh, OHP, 2; Gillmore, "Bell," 266. A former Ohio Bell worker recalled that in the late 1930s there was "a desire for some kind of security because during the Depression years the company was laying off people without regard for seniority. For many years in bargaining contracts with the Bell System, we concerned ourselves more with security than we did with money. And this was at the request of the people. They wanted seniority in layoffs. They wanted seniority in promotions. They wanted seniority in choice of hours." Welsh, OHP, 3. See also n. 16; Central Region Conference of Independent Telephone Unions, Official Minutes, Chicago, Jan. 29–30, 1940, minutes of the plant panel conference, mimeographed, p. 11, Box 1, CWAA. For the movement outside telephone, see Schatz, *Electrical Workers*, 107, 111.

18. *UAT*, 43; *LDS*, 107, 115, 208.

19. *LDS*, 107–108; Hubbard, OHP, 2; Dunn, OHP, 6–7; report of the Mountain States union and the Indiana and Wisconsin plant unions in *TW*, June 1942. During construction of a New York airlines terminal, the downstate New York plant union actually picketed the site, with threats of expanded picketing, before the New York company backed the plant workers' claim. *NYT*, Dec. 29, 1940, p. 23; *TW*, June 1942; *LDS*, 144, 151, 209; *UAT*, 43–44.

20. Dunn, OHP, 6–7. Dunn's emphasis.

21. Ibid., 4. See also the report of the Michigan traffic union in "Souvenir Program," (see chap. 3, n. 11), 3.

22. Everett Cotter, Southwestern Union general counsel, to Arthur Fortner, union president, Apr. 13, 1938, Griffith Papers. See also Palmer, OHP, 2.

23. *FB*, Feb. 1940; RL, Feb. 1965; "Souvenir Program," 4; Pre-Assembly Traffic Panel, 1941, 30–31; Walsh, *Connecticut Pioneers*, 285; *Pact News*, Feb., Dec. 1941; Minutes, Chicago, 1938, pp. 10, 19; Crull, OHP, 17–18; McCowen, OHP, 32–33; Cotter to Fortner, Apr. 13, 1938; NFTW, Summary of the Sixth National Assembly, June 1941, typewritten, p. 171, Box 1, CWAA.

24. *FB*, May 1940; Gillmore, "Bell," 143–144.

25. *FB*, May 1940; DiProspere, OHP, 13; Mann, OHP, 14–15.

26. Bruce, OHP, 3; Mann, OHP, 15.

27. Pollock, OHP, 2–4; NFTWOP, 1940, 23; RL, Oct. 1965; *LDS*, 43–44, 64, 67; Loewenberg, "Effects," I-38–39.

28. Wooding, memoir, 2: 2, 6; Wooding, OHP, 9–10.

29. A Southwestern Union leader of this period says, "In fairness to the company, the many skirmishes, disagreements—some very bitter—in which they had to make good, I've never found them taking revenge on anyone." DiProspere, OHP, 12. See also Dunn, OHP, 7. No evidence of reprisals during this period has come to the author's attention.

30. Atkinson, OHP, 2–3. See also Wooding, OHP, 9; Walsh, OHP, 5.

31. With respect to Bell's motives, a leader of the Cincinnati union says, "I think one of the reasons they were reluctant to move and stop what we were doing was the fear that if they stopped *us,* we might move differently. But I don't think they knew which way we would move. They feared, I think, CIO more than AF of L." Dunn, OHP, 7 (Dunn's emphasis).

32. Wooding, memoir, 2: 6; McCowen, OHP, 12.

33. Quotes are from McCowen, OHP, 41; J. J. Schacht, OHP, 10.

34. *UAT,* 50. Quotes are from Webb, OHP, 4; Naughton in Pre-Assembly Traffic Panel, 1941, p. 33.

35. Wiencek, OHP, 4. See also NFTW, Proceedings of the Plant Panel of the Sixth Annual Assembly, Omaha, June 16–21, 1941, mimeographed, pp. 58–59, Box 1, CWAA.

36. McCowen, OHP, 12–13. The date was "maybe '39 or '40." It should be noted that bargaining was taking place in St. Louis, far from the union negotiators' homes, and, as McCowen recalls, "I don't know what we would have done because we didn't have money to stay there even if we'd have known to call [the Conciliation Service] in ourselves."

37. DuVal, OHP, 3, 31, 39; Koons, OHP, 2.

38. Ken Blount to J. A. Mead, chairman, "Washington Legal Representation Committee," Jan. 17, 1939, printed in *FB,* Feb. 1939. See also L. A. Palabykian, Report of Proceedings at Baltimore Conference, Jan. 7 and 8, 1939, mimeographed, p. 2, Box 1, CWAA; "Minutes of Special Conference Called by Mutual Consent of Employee Associations of the Bell System Operating in this Region, Baltimore, Jan. 7 and 8, 1939," mimeographed, Box 1, CWAA. In a separate episode, when six NFTW unions disaffiliated in 1943, onlookers in the Northwestern Telephone union found it "significant that the four Illinois independent unions which withdrew from the NFTW all had the same legal counsel." *Pact News*, Sept. 1943.

39. Torrence, "Case Study," 139; DiProspere, OHP, 12.

40. *FB,* Feb. 1940; Wiencek, OHP, 2, 4; Hanscom, OHP; Pre-Assembly Traffic Panel, 1941, pp. 31, 35; report of the Wisconsin plant union in *TW,* June 1942; report of the WE distributing house union in Report Supplement, 1941 (see chap. 3, n. 15); *UAT,* 45–46; Report of the Plant Model Contract Committee of the Central-Southern Region, June 7, 1941, (no pagination), in Report Supplement, 1941; *WTW,* 24–28.

41. Central Region Minutes, Sept. 1939, minutes of the general session of

Sept. 15, p. 6; Good, OHP, 12; McCowen, OHP, 52; Atkinson, OHP, 11. High turnover rates among male local officers, abetted by promotions to supervisory positions, have continued to create problems (as well as certain benefits) for telephone unionism. Carroll, OHP, 6, 18; Hackler, OHP, 27; McCowen, OHP, 52, 59; Walsh, OHP, 6; Griffith in NFTW, Minutes of the Western Regional Conference, San Francisco, Apr. 17-19, 1942, mimeographed, p. 40, Box 1, CWAA.

42. Wooding, memoir, 2: 5; Hanscom, OHP, 15; Mann, OHP, 16.

43. Berthelot, OHP, 29; DuVal, OHP, 37; Miller, OHP, 4. In 1940 33 percent of all operators were married, 28 percent were under 25, 60 percent were 25 to 44, and 12 percent were over 44. *16th, 1940*, 3: 113-115 (see chap. 2, n. 24). See also Wertheimer and Nelson, *Trade Union Women*, viii, 92, 153; Abicht, "Women's Leadership," 28, 84; Hartman, *Home Front*, 87. The quote is from Naughton in Pre-Assembly Traffic Panel, 1941, p. 4.

44. Patterson, OHP, 13; Gill, OHP, 7-8; Moudy, OHP, 7. But with the advent of mixed, "industrial" locals in most CWA units in the 1950s, the participation of traffic women in top local leadership plummeted, and it has stayed proportionally low ever since, apparently largely as a result of those two factors: female reluctance and male resistance. Cooney, OHP, 14; Berthelot, OHP, 29; Brown, OHP, 20-21; Burch, "The Rebel in Me," 6-7, 9, 13. On reluctance and resistance in unions generally, see Hillman, "Gifted Women in the Trade Unions," 101; Wertheimer and Nelson, "American Women at Work," 40; "Women Workers," 106.

45. Wooding, memoir, 2: 5-6 (emphasis mine). See also Berthelot, OHP, 29; Miller, OHP, 4; Seidman et al., *Views*, 144.

46. NFTW, Minutes of the Central-Southern Regional Conference, Cleveland, Oct. 18-20, 1940, mimeographed, p. 14, Box 1, CWAA; NFTW, Verbatim Typed Transcript, Proceedings, Sixth National Assembly, Omaha, June 16-21, 1941, typewritten, Box 1, CWAA. The quote is from Griffith in Western Region Minutes, 1942, p. 40.

47. Wiencek, OHP, 4. See also the report of the Michigan traffic union in Reports of Organizations, 1942 (see chap. 3, n. 15), vol. 1.

48. Western Region Minutes, 1942, p. 33; report of the Southwestern Union in Reports of Organizations, 1942, vol. 1; NFTWOP, 1940, 22-23.

49. Frances Smith, of Michigan, in Pre-Assembly Traffic Panel, 1941, p. 148.

50. Wayne Gray, "History of Western Electric Installation Bargaining" ("Report based on materials in the CWA research department and the CWA installation bargaining unit national office, Sept. 29, 1962"), mimeographed, Gray Papers; NFTWOP, 1939, 27; report of the WE distributing house union in Report Supplement, 1941; NFTW, Minutes, Eastern Regional Conference, Huntington, W. Va., Oct. 31-Nov. 2, 1941, mimeographed, Box 1, CWAA.

51. NFTWOP, 1939, 27; Novotny, OHP, 4.

52. Stein, OHP, 3; Massey, OHP, 3; Dunne, OHP, 3.

53. Pre-Assembly Traffic Panel, 1941, pp. 31–34. The quote is from Frances Smith.

54. McCowen, OHP, 32–33; *Pact News,* Dec. 1941; reports of the Illinois plant and Wisconsin plant unions in "Souvenir Program," pp. 3–4; Pre-Assembly Traffic Panel, 1941, p. 154; reports of the Illinois and Chicago traffic unions in Reports of Organizations, 1942, vol. 1; *TW,* June 1941, Apr. 1942; LeFevre, OHP, 3.

55. Park, "Strike," 11. As late as June 1941, CIO unions held very few contracts with union shop provisions. Freeman, "Delivering the Goods," 574.

56. John J. Moran, of the Long Lines union, in NFTW, Minutes, Eastern Regional Conference, New York, Mar. 26–29, 1942, mimeographed, p. 27, Box 1, CWAA. See also Park, "Strike," 12; RL, Dec. 1966; *FB,* Oct. 1941; report of the Long Lines union in Reports of Organizations, 1942, vol. 1.

57. *FB,* Oct., Nov., Dec. 1941. For strike threats, see n. 60.

58. Wooding, memoir, 1: 7–8; *TW,* May, June 1941, Apr. 1942; *FB,* Oct. 1941; Eastern Region Minutes, Oct.–Nov. 1941, p. 9; Park, "Strike," 12; NFTW, Minutes of the Central-Southern Regional Conference, Chicago, Apr. 18–20, 1941, mimeographed, p. 16, Box 1, CWAA.

59. McCowen in Plant Panel, 1941, p. 43; Moran in Eastern region Minutes, Oct.–Nov. 1941, p. 43.

60. Conclusions regarding strike threats and strike votes are based on records concerning about half of the seventy-five-odd non-WE telephone unions of 1940–1941: yearly proceedings and reports concerning NFTW affiliates (twenty-nine unions in 1940 and thirty-four in 1941), as well as historical summaries of two non-NFTW unions (RL and Southern Bell 35: No. C-1911 [1941])—which, it may be safely assumed, reported most strike threats and strike votes undertaken by those unions. The records reveal seven strike threats and, in connection with each of these threats, seven strike votes (in which an affirmative result would authorize leaders to call a strike but not require them to do so). Six of the strike votes polled the membership of small subunits of unions. The results of five of these votes were not revealed, but in each of these five cases, leaders claimed a majority had voted to authorize strike action. Plant Panel, 1941, p. 87; *FB,* Oct. 1941. Here, as elsewhere, no strike action was taken. In the sixth subunit strike vote—involving a division of the Order of Repeatermen and Toll Testboardmen (a non-NFTW union of plant workers in PT&T engaged largely in servicing long distance equipment)—the affirmative vote was 186 to 101, but this fell short of the 75 percent required by the union's constitution for strike authorization. RL, Jan. 1966. The remaining strike vote involved the entire membership of the Long Lines union (between ten and eleven thousand at the time of the vote). Full

voting returns were not revealed, but the union president at one point remarked that "We have probably close to 6,000 ballots counted up to now and the strike vote is running around five to one in favor of strike." However, several months after the vote, he said, "We got some pretty good support even if we didn't get the support that would enable us to carry out the strike. We weren't kidding ourselves too much at the time we threatened a strike." Moran in Eastern Region Minutes, Oct.–Nov. 1941, p. 43, and in Western Region Minutes, 1942, p. 6.

61. William R. Dawson, of the Ohio union, and Frances Smith in Verbatim Transcript, 1941, p. 404; Moran in Eastern Regional Minutes, Oct.–Nov. 1941, p. 43.

62. The average length of service was eleven years in 1941, as compared to thirteen years in 1939. ATTR, 1941, 23. Bureau of Labor Statistics figures illustrating a decline in non-WE telephone workers' relative wage position are in *LMR*, Union Exhibit S, p. 628. But average (non-WE) telephone wages of $32.52 weekly and 80.4 cents hourly in January 1941 still compared favorably with average wages of $29.64 weekly and 66.9 cents hourly in the manufacturing work force as a whole, and ranked twentieth and twelfth, respectively, in a standard BLS list of fifty-five industries (including nonmanufacturing industries). *LMR*, Union Exhibit Q, pp. 625–626. The quote is from Moran in Eastern Region Minutes, 1942, p. 27.

63. Pre-Assembly Traffic Panel, 1941, p. 34; Plant Panel, 1941, p. 88. The quotes are from Beirne, OHP, 17; George W. Hunter, of the Virginia union, in Eastern Region Minutes, 1942, p. 29. See also pp. 27–28.

64. See Appendix B.

65. Paul Boyce, of the Connecticut union, and Moran in Eastern Region Minutes, 1942, p. 27.

Chapter 5. The NFTW and the Problem of Centralization, 1939–1941

1. Webb, OHP, 8. Of the twenty-eight union presidents who attended the November 1938 New Orleans meeting, twelve were presidents of NFTW affiliates in April 1941. Bell System Employee Organizations, Roster of the Third National Conference, New Orleans, La., Nov. 14–16, 1939, mimeographed, (no pagination), Box 1, CWAA; *TW*, May 1941. See also Appendix B.

2. Beirne, OHP, 14–15. See also Kendall T. Stevens, "National Convention" (report to the Telephone Employees Association, Plant Department, Northwestern Bell, Jan. 31, 1938), mimeographed, pp. 2, 5, Box 7, CWA-NUTWP.

3. Purdy, OHP, p. 5.

4. Selig Perlman and Philip Taft, "Labor Movements," in Commons et al., *History of Labour,* 4: 356; *FB,* Aug. 1939.

5. Or so their leaders claimed. These unions included those in Connecticut, Chicago traffic, and Illinois traffic. NFTWOP, June 1943, 34, and appended Exhibit 7. At least two unions even refused to join the NFTW for allegedly similar reasons. These were the New England plant union and the Order of Repeatermen and Toll Testboardmen. Pre-Assembly Traffic Panel, 1941 (see chap. 2, n. 47), p. 172; RL, Jan. 1965.

6. DuVal, OHP, 41. DuVal is paraphrasing the remarks of J. B. Broderick, president of the New York downstate plant union. See also Charles Parsons, of that union, in Eastern Region Minutes, 1942 (see chap. 4, n. 56), p. 52.

7. Lena Trimble, of the Southwestern Union, in Pre-Assembly Traffic Panel, 1941, p. 139. See also DuVal, OHP, 41; Wooding, OHP, 11; McCowen, OHP, 13–14.

8. Pre-Assembly Traffic Panel, 1942 (see chap. 3, n. 34), pp. 88–89, 191; NFTWOP, June 1943, 43, 45.

9. Pre-Assembly Traffic Panel, 1941, pp. 7, 131–132, 135, 219; Berthelot, OHP, 7; Wooding, OHP, 30. The quote is from Theresa Donahey, of the Ohio union, in Pre-Assembly Traffic Panel, 1942, p. 158.

10. The quotes are from Griffith, OHP, 19; Wiencek, OHP, 19; DuVal, OHP, 38.

11. Wertheimer and Nelson, "American Women at Work," 40; Wertheimer and Nelson, *Trade Union Women,* 26. See also Burch, "The Rebel in Me," 13.

12. Wooding, OHP, 12. See also Berthelot, OHP, 29; Miller, OHP, 4; Wooding, memoir, 2: 5–6. There were, of course, exceptions. But the exceptional telephone union women of the 1940s seemed ill starred in terms of their union careers. The three women most prominent in the early and mid-1940s—who were apparently quite able and ambitious as well—were Patricia Harris of southern California traffic, Frances Smith, of Michigan traffic, and Mary Gannon of Washington, D.C., traffic. But by the end of the decade Harris had long since left the union movement for marriage and a move to Florida with her serviceman husband, and Smith and Gannon had become victims of disabling illnesses. Harris interview; Berthelot, OHP, 7–8; Gannon interview.

13. Berthelot, OHP, 29. See also McCowen, OHP, 61–62.

14. Eighteen accounting and commercial union presidents, representing a total of seven different unions, appeared at NFTW assemblies from 1938 to 1946. Of the eighteen, sixteen were male, one was female, and the sex of the last I was unable to discover. For this, and the sex of amalgamated union pres-

idents, see the sources cited in Appendix B, n. 1. Most of the later amalgamations included traffic segments that had once been separate unions. That the female presidents of those traffic unions unselfishly concurred in amalgamations that in all cases stripped them of the title of president also speaks for their lack of concern for office bearing.

15. Telegram, Cleo Craig, AT&T vice-president, to Griffith, Apr. 11, 1941, printed in *League News,* May 1941.

16. ATTR, 1946, 36; Loewenberg, "Effects," III-38.

17. Al Herrington et al. in Plant Panel, 1941 (see chap. 4, n. 35), pp. 58–59.

18. For antiscabbing resolutions and pledges, see n. 36.

19. The quote is from Ernest Weaver's summary of the proposal. See Eastern Region Minutes, Oct.–Nov. 1941 (see chap. 4, n. 50), pp. 6, 45–46; also Moran in Western Region Minutes, 1942 (see chap. 4, n. 43), p. 41.

20. See, for example, Plant Panel, 1941, p. 36.

21. Remarks of a "Mr. Seeber" in Plant Panel, 1941, p. 87.

22. NFTWOP, 1939, 1940; Verbatim Transcript, 1941 (see chap. 4, n. 46).

23. Report of the Executive Board to the Sixth National Assembly, 1941, p. 2 in Report Supplement, 1941 (see chap. 3, n. 15); Griffith, OHP, 36–37.

24. DuVal, OHP, 17; Beirne, OHP, 17; Dunn, OHP, 16.

25. Beirne, OHP, 17; Griffith, OHP, 13, 48, 50, 52.

26. Dunn, OHP, 4; Griffith, OHP, 41–42.

27. Naughton in Pre-Assembly Traffic Panel, 1941, p. 34; Boyce in Eastern Region Minutes, 1942, p. 29; Griffith, OHP, 13, 48, and esp. 52.

28. Craig in *TW,* June 1941; E. R. McLaughlin, New York Telephone vice-president, in *LMR,* 435, 437, 440; Page, *Bell,* 55–56; *LDS,* 13. See also the report of the Connecticut union in NFTW, Annual Reports of Member Organizations to the Ninth National Assembly, held at Cleveland, Ohio, June 7–12, 1943, mimeographed, vol. 2, (no pagination), Box 1, CWAA.

29. NFTWOP, 1939, 8. WE distributing houses were generally located in large cities, and while Long Lines workers were spread across forty-two states, a majority worked in fourteen of the nation's largest cities. Naughton, OHP, 7–8; *UAT,* 48; DuVall, OHP, 5; report of the Long Lines union in "Souvenir Program" (see chap. 3, n. 11), 11.

30. Bers, "Unionism," 5–9. The quote is from Beirne, OHP, 5–6.

31. Lonergan, OHP, 5; Griffith, OHP, 25.

32. U.S. Federal Communications Commission, *Proposed Report,* 12; Pre-Assembly Traffic Panel, 1941, pp. 55, 71; Plant Panel, 1941, p. 11; Eastern Region Minutes, Oct.–Nov. 1941, p. 36.

33. Central-Southern Regional Minutes, 1941 (see chap. 4, n. 58), p. 16.

34. "Resume of Talk Given by Paul E. Griffith," 1, appended to Eastern

Region Minutes, 1942. See also *LDS*, 11, 38; Eastern Region Minutes, Oct–Nov. 1941, p. 36; *TW*, June 1941.

35. NFTW, "Report of Statistical and Research Director and 'A Brief Study of Job Evaluation' by J. A. Beirne," Baltimore, 1942, mimeographed, p. 2, Box 1, CWAA; Pre-Assembly Traffic Panel, 1941, p. 31; *UAT*, 45; Eastern Region Minutes, Oct.–Nov. 1941, p. 10; report of the southern California traffic union in *TW*, June 1942; "Resume of Talk by Griffith," 2.

36. Report of the Plant Model Contract Committee of the Central-Southern Region, June 7, 1941, (no pagination), in Report Supplement, 1941; NFTW, Proceedings of the Commercial and Accounting Panel of the Sixth Annual Assembly, held at Omaha, June 16–21, 1941, mimeographed, pp. 39–40, Box 1, CWAA; Eastern Region Minutes, 1942, pp. 28–30.

37. Report of the Executive Board, 1941, pp. 24, 26–27; NFTWOP, 1939, 27, 1940, 23–24; NFTW, "Strike Manual," 1945, typewritten, pt. D, p. 1, Box 1, CWAA.

38. Robert Pollock in NFTW, Verbatim Record of Constitutional Matters as Discussed at the Tenth National Assembly, Denver, June 12–17, 1944, typewritten, p. 11, Box 1, CWAA; NFTW, Verbatim Transcript, 1941, p. 404; Griffith, OHP, 45.

39. NFTWOP, 1940, 22, 1942, 18; NFTW, Information Supplement, issue 4, May 11, 1940, mimeographed, Griffith Papers; DuVal, OHP, 21.

40. NFTWOP, 1939, 23, 1940, 77, 1942, 15–16.

41. Gillmore, "Bell," 149; ATTR, 1939, 21; NFTW, "Copy: Statement by Charles P. Cooper before the Sub-Committee on Finance of the U.S. Senate, Tuesday, December 13, 1938," mimeographed, p. 3, Griffith Papers.

42. NFTWOP, 1939, 19, 1940, 22–26, 1944, 19, 37–38; NFTW, "Data Supplied 7th National Assembly on the Bell System Pension Plan and Industrial Pension Plans Generally, Baltimore, Md., June 8–13, 1942 (Arthur Stedry Hansen, Consulting Actuary)," mimeographed, p. 1, Box 1, CWAA; Dunn, OHP, 16–17. For Bell pension plan provisions as of 1941, see Page, *Bell*, 223–224, 242.

43. NFTW, Minutes, Eastern Region Conference, New York, May 23–25, 1941, mimeographed, p. 36, Box 1, CWAA; reports of the Cincinnati and southern California traffic unions in *TW*, June 1942; Dunn, OHP, 4; *TW*, May 1941; NLRB, Lincoln Telephone and Telegraph 30: 949–955, 962–963 (1941).

44. By mid-1942, NFTW affiliates included non-Bell telephone unions based in Tampa, Fl.; Lexington, Ky.; Long Beach, Calif.; and Lincoln, Neb. Eastern Region Minutes, Oct.–Nov. 1941, p. 4; NFTWOP, 1942, 4, 9–10, 24; Minutes, Chicago, 1938 (see chap. 2, n. 77), p. 4.

45. Griffith, OHP, 68–69; *FB*, Oct. 1941; *NYT*, Oct. 9, p. 14, Oct. 10,

p. 12, 1941; *TW*, Feb., June 1942; "Resume of Talk by Griffith," pp. 3–4; *LDM*, 144, 158, 204; *UAT*, 43–44.

46. Report of the Executive Board, 1941, pp. 20–21; Eastern Region Minutes, Oct.–Nov. 1941, p. 5; NFTWOP, 1942, 21–22; *UAT*, 31; *TW*, Apr. 1942; Eastern Region Minutes, 1942, p. 10; Griffith, OHP, 61–62.

47. *NYT*, Aug. 10, 1939, p. 2, Apr. 9, 1940, p. 43; Central Region Minutes, 1940 (see chap. 4, n. 17), p. 3; Report of the Executive Board to the Eleventh National Assembly, 1945, p. 10, in NFTW, Report of the Executive Board and Certain Other Reports to the Eleventh National Assembly, held at Chicago, Ill., June 11–16, 1945, mimeographed, (no pagination), (hereafter cited as Report of the Executive Board and Other Reports, 1945), Box 2, CWAA; *WTW*, 1, 24–28; Eastern Region Minutes, May 1941, pp. 16–17; ATTR, 1941, 12–13; *TW*, June 1941, June 1942; *UAT*, 32.

48. *UAT*, 29; ATTR, 1943, 17; Report of the General Counsel on Washington Activities, June 1942–June 1944, p. 1, in NFTW, Report of the Executive Board and Certain Other Reports to the Tenth National Assembly, held at Denver, Colo., June 12–17, 1944, mimeographed, (no pagination), (hereafter cited as Report of the Executive Board and other Reports, 1944), Box 1, CWAA. For the reasoning behind the NFTW's opposition to the FCC order, see NFTWOP, 1942, 13–14. See also *TW*, May, June 1942; Gillmore, "Bell," 154. The actuary hired by the NFTW to study Bell's pension plan agreed with AT&T's estimate that a 150 percent increase in pension funds would be needed to meet the proposed standards. *TW*, Apr. 1942.

49. *UAT*, 51. Beirne later recalled that in 1944, when he was the NFTW president, "I had the feeling then that our problems were only handled by government officials like second cousin problems: 'Here comes the old company-dominated union,' which we had to fight out from under. . . . 'It really is not a dispute' is the way I felt that the people on the War Labor Board were looking at our [conflicts with management]." Beirne, OHP, 19–20.

50. Report of the Executive Board, 1941, pp. 2, 7; NFTW, Minutes, Central Regional Conference, Chicago, Nov. 20–22, 1942, mimeographed, p. 7, Box 1, CWAA.

51. NFTWOP, 1940, 17–18, 1942, 18; Report of the Executive Board, 1941, pp. 2–8; Eastern Region Minutes, Oct.–Nov. 1941, p. 4; Griffith, OHP, 36–37; *UAT*, 28.

52. Moran and Beirne in NFTWOP, Feb. 1943, 17, 20.

53. "Text of President Griffith's Address," (no pagination), appended to Western Region Minutes, 1942; Report of the Executive Board, 1941, Exhibit A, "Report of Hilmer J. Gengler, CPA," (no pagination); Eastern Region Minutes, Oct.–Nov. 1941, p. 4.

54. Report of Leonard B. Rowles, CPA, to the NFTW Executive Board,

June 1, 1943, typewritten, p. 4, Box 4, CWAA; DuVal, OHP, 67. On Horth's many burdensome tasks, see Dunn, OHP, 4; *TW*, May 1941; NFTW, Verbatim Typed Transcript, Proceedings, Eighth National Assembly, Cincinnati, February 1–6, 1943, Tuesday Evening, typewritten, p. 4, Box 1, CWAA.

55. Pre-Assembly Traffic Panel, 1941, p. 69; Eastern Region Minutes, Oct.–Nov. 1941, p. 4; Central Region Minutes, 1942, p. 3.

56. Wiencek, OHP, 3.

Chapter 6. Deprivation, Militancy, and National Unionism, 1942–1944

1. Griffith, OHP, 7–8.

2. FCCS, 1944, 13; 1943, 8; 1944, 13, 38.

3. ATTR, 1941, 3; 1942, 12; 1943, 7–8; 1944, 2, 12–13. Figures do not include the Bell companies in Cincinnati and Connecticut.

4. The FCC in 1941 reported employment figures by job category for all class A carriers, and not for Bell carriers separately. The 1941 Bell employment figures are therefore estimates, obtained by multiplying class A employment in each category by .942, which was the proportion of total Bell employment to total class A employment in 1941. FCCS, 1941, 15, 1944, 21; report of the WE installation union in Reports of Organizations, 1943 (see chap. 5, n. 28), vol. 2; report of the WE installation union in NFTW, Annual Reports of Member Organizations to the Tenth National Assembly, held at Denver, June 12–17, 1944, mimeographed, (no pagination), Box 1, CWAA; Novotny, OHP, 3–4; ATTR, 1941, 9, 14, 37, 1944, 12.

5. FCCS, 1939, 19, 1941, 15, 1944, 21; Page, *Bell*, 72, 74; *WTW*, 10; *LMR*, Subcommittee Exhibit K, p. 787.

6. *WTW*, 2, 18; ATTR, 1944, 9. The quote is from the report of the Washington–northern Idaho accounting union in Reports of Organizations, 1942 (see chap. 3, n. 15).

7. ATTR, 1945, 11; *WTW*, 32; FCCS, 1944, 10, 11. The 61,500 figure does not include employees of the Bell companies in Connecticut and Cincinnati.

8. The figures exclude employees of the Bell companies in Cincinnati and Connecticut. ATTR, 1941, 15, 1942, 16, 1943, 15, 1944, 8–9; Williams, "Labor Relations," 196; Bers, "Unionism," 19.

9. *LMR*, AT&T Exhibit A-5, p. 504; ATTR, 1941, 15, 1942, 16, 1943, 15. The figures exclude employees of the Bell companies in Cincinnati and Connecticut.

10. ATTR, 1944, 19.

11. Moudy, OHP, 10; Armstrong, OHP, 16; *WTW*, 5, 35. The quote is from Iva Kokensparger, of the Ohio union, in Pre-Assembly Traffic Panel, 1941 (see chap. 2, n. 47), p. 50.

12. *TW*, Feb. 1942; *Federation of Women Telephone Workers of Southern California News*, July 1942; Beirne in *LMR*, 115. The quote is from Dunn, OHP, 21.

13. *WTW*, 30–31. See also *Termination Report* (see chap. 2, n. 21) 1: 971, 1027.

14. Figures are for the operating sector of the industry, including Long Lines. (See Appendix D, table A.4.) For the telephone operating sector's wages being "representative" of the *Bell* operating sector's wages, see Appendix D, notes to table A.3. See also *LMR*, Union Exhibit S-1, p. 630.

15. *Telephone wages* here means those in the operating sector, including Long Lines. See Appendix D; *LMR*, Subcommittee Exhibit K, p. 498; Douty, "Review," 19. Nor was the brunt of the losses borne by any one small segment of the work force. In 1944, as in 1941, about two-thirds of the Bell operating sector's work force earned less than $36.00 per week (66.9 percent in 1941; 64.2 percent in 1944). It is true, however, that the low wages and small average wage gains were borne, to an extraordinary degree, by the industry's female majority. The median female wage increased from $23.25 per week in 1941 to only $26.50 in 1944, while the male median wage increased from $49.55 to over $60.00. The disparity is explained in part, of course, by the entrance of many young female workers and the simultaneous departure of many of the younger, lesser-paid male workers to the armed services. FCCS, 1941, 19, 1944, 21; *WTW*, 21; Gillmore, "Bell," 258.

16. According to one labor economist, it is difficult and perhaps impossible to determine how much of the decline was attributable to each cause. Williams, "Labor Relations," 261–263. See also Central-Southern Regional Minutes, 1941 (see chap. 4, n. 58), p. 9; Wooding, memoir (see chap. 2, n. 33), 2: 10–11; Dunn, OHP, 20; *FB*, Oct. 1942; "Henry Mayer's Monthly Report," Sept. 30, 1971, p. 33; NTP, "Report" (see chap. 2, n. 3), 12, 14; Gray, "Installation Bargaining" (see chap. 4, n. 50), attachment 2; Gillmore, "Bell," 93, 263, 272. Operators' schedules were reduced from 13 years or more in 1939 to 10 or 11 years at the end of 1944, while plant workers' schedules were reduced from 10 or 11 years in 1939 to an average of 9 years in late 1944. Bers, "Wage Structure in the Telephone Industry," 32.

17. Dunn, OHP, 20. Lichtenstein's most detailed analysis of generally unfair treatment is in his "Industrial Unionism under the No-Strike Pledge," 189–192, 220, 240, 280–281, 288–293, 305, 318–319, 326, 340–341. See also Cochran, *Labor and Communism*, 197, 201; Koistinen, "Mobilizing the World War II Economy," 450–451, 468–469; Seidman, *Defense*, 122–126; Howe and Widick, *UAW*, 116.

18. Seidman, *Defense,* 80–81, 84, 109–117.

19. Dunn, OHP, 20; *LDS,* xii; *Tel-U,* Dec. 1944. Griffith had asked for an invitation to the White House conference but was denied it. *Pact News,* Jan. 1942.

20. Wiencek, OHP, 3; Beirne, OHP, 19.

21. Gillmore, "Bell," 267; *LDS,* 67, 144, 158, 209.

22. Gillmore, "Bell," 267. In practice, few workers left their unions during the escape periods at the termination of contracts. Seidman, *Defense,* 100, 104, 107.

23. *LDS,* xiii; Gillmore, "Bell," 151, 254. Established in the Little Steel case of July 1942, the 15 percent figure was based on the estimated 15 percent rise in the cost of living between January 1941 and May 1, 1942, at which date it was rather arbitrarily assumed that the rise in living costs had ceased. Seidman, *Defense,* 113–116.

24. *Tel-U,* Mar. 1943; *FB,* Oct., Nov. 1942; "Henry Mayer's Monthly Report," Feb. 28, pp. 27–28, Apr. 30, pp. 36–37, 1971; Gillmore, "Bell," 262–263; *LMR,* 765; *TW,* Aug. 1942.

25. Seidman, *Defense,* 90; ATTR, 1944, 2; Brooks, *Telephone,* 214. In addition, it could of course be argued that the unusually high standing of telephone wages as of 1939–1940—partly a result of Bell maintenance of basic wage rates during the depression, when other employers were cutting wages—was harmful and in need of correction through the withholding of increases during the war. On this point, see chap. 2, n. 6; chap. 4, n. 7.

26. ATTR, 1941, 6; 1942, 5; 1943, 4; 1944, 6. Perhaps more important than the slightness of the decline was that the public relations effects of the decline were slight enough to be viewed with equanimity. See John M. Shaw, untitled report, May 14, 1944, typewritten, p. 1, Box 3, Shaw Papers.

27. *LDS,* xii; Park, "Strike," 15; Edelman, "Interest Representation," 221. The quotes are from *Tel-U,* Mar. 1943; *FB,* Oct. 1942.

28. *UAT,* 33; *NYT,* Apr. 11, 1943, p. 33; NTP "REPORT," 12–13; NFTWOP, Feb. 1943, 49–51; *ACA News,* Jan. 1943.

29. *ACA News,* Nov. 1942, Aug., Oct., Nov., Dec. 1943, Jan. 1944; *UAT,* 34; *LDS,* 126. The quote is from Moran, then NFTW vice-president, in *Tel-U,* Oct. 1943. The ORTT was unique in that its jurisdiction was confined to plant toll maintenance workers, and the group's history was somewhat unusual in that it extended back through the company union experience into a pre-1920 period of militancy. RL, Jan.–Feb., Sept.–Oct., Nov. 1962, Mar.–Apr. 1966, Apr. 1967. Joe Selly, president of the ACA from 1941 until its absorption by the Teamsters in 1966, remarked in 1972 that the ACA's "reputation as a left-wing union was always a barrier to its organizing telephone workers." Selly interview.

30. *LDS,* 126; *Tel-U,* May 1944; RL, Nov. 1967.

31. Under pressure from two midwestern Long Lines locals, the executive council of the Long Lines union met with Haywood in January 1943 to explore the possibility of CIO affiliation. According to a report by Long Lines union president Moran, Haywood "first said that they were not at present interested in organizing telephone workers, that they had made no real attempt to do so. But if there was a large group of telephone workers that were interested in joining the CIO, he indicated that they would take them in. . . . He advised that if we decided to join, that we join as a unit and under no circumstances let ourselves be split up, whether we join the AFL, or CIO, or whether we stay independent. He suggested we do it on a system-wide basis. He also made it very clear that the only way in which the CIO would attempt to establish an organization would be on a Bell System basis. Any large group of telephone workers could be taken in as a nucleus of the main organization. Mr. Haywood explained that he did not think it would be mandatory that the ACA have jurisdiction over all communications workers." NFTWOP, Feb. 1943, 17. Selly then wrote CIO president Philip Murray, objecting to Haywood's "undercutting A.C.A." RL, Aug.–Sept. 1966. With regard to CIO telephone organizing strategy later, in 1947–1948, Albert Kanagy, long an ORTT officer and at one time a vice-president of ACA, has written: "I had nothing but cooperation from Murray and Haywood until they saw a chance to get a big block of telephone people. I do not think they were particularly opposed to ACA. . . . It was just a case of working both sides of the street in order to organize. The telephone workers were very conservative so they opposed ORTT-ACA and to a lesser extent the Long Lines and W.E. groups. CWA-NFTW represented the largest but most conservative group so I believe Murray and Haywood were just grabbing the biggest group." Kanagy to the author, July 28, 1972.

32. Seidman, *Defense*, 121; *LDS*, xii-xiii; Gillmore, "Bell," 255.

33. NTP, "Report," 15.

34. Ibid., 15–16; George W. Taylor, "Foreword," in *LDS*, iv; *Termination Report* 1: 1002–1003.

35. *LDS*, xii; McLaughlin and William Dunn in *LMR*, 459, 665; Seidman, *Defense*, 120–123; Howe and Widick, *UAW*, 116; NFTWOP, 1942, 25, 1944, 21–22, 45–46; Park, "Strike," 16.

36. Bernstein, "Growth of American Unions," 318; Beirne in *LMR*, 31.

37. Bers, "Unionism," 30. For expressions of this reluctance, see *FB*, Jan. 1942; *TW*, Apr. 1942; *NYT*, Apr. 12, 1943, p. 31.

38. *LDS*, xii.

39. *FB*, Jan. 1942; NFTW, Proceedings, Plant Panel of the Seventh Annual Assembly, held at Baltimore, Md., June 5–6, 1942, mimeographed, p. 9, Box 1, CWAA; *Tel-U*, Mar. 1943; report of the WE distributing house union in NFTW, Annual Reports of Member Organizations to the Eleventh

National Assembly, held at Chicago, June 11-16, 1945, mimeographed, (no pagination), Box 2, CWAA; J. J. Moran, "The Menace of the Non-Member," in NFTW, Text of Lectures Presented at Educational Conference, Denver, June 12-17, 1944, mimeographed, p. 6, Box 1, CWAA.

40. *TW*, Apr., May, Aug. 1942; *NYT*, Dec. 3, p. 50, Dec. 20, p. 24, Dec. 21, p. 19, 1944; *UAT*, 41-42; report of the WE installation union in Reports of Organizations, 1943, vol. 2; I. R. Hudson, Strike Director's Report, pp. 1-3, in Report of the Executive Board and Other Reports, 1944 (see chap. 5, n. 48); *Pact News*, Oct. 1944; report of the WE installation union in Reports of Organizations, 1945. Four of the NFTW union strike votes were conducted under procedures set forth in the War Labor Disputes Act. With regard to such procedures, Seidman has written that workers in many industries, "joining cheerfully in the game, voted overwhelmingly for strikes in which they had no intention of participating in order to strengthen their leaders' hands in bargaining." *Defense*, 189-190.

41. *NYT*, Aug. 6, p. 14, Aug. 7, p. 2, 1942; *FB*, Aug. 1942; *TW*, Aug. 1942; Park, "Strike," 18.

42. Park, "Strike," 18. The longer quote is from Walsh, OHP, 5.

43. Pollock, OHP, 6 (Pollock's emphasis). See also *UAT*, 41.

44. *TW*, Aug. 1942.

45. *Pact News*, Sept. 1944.

46. *NYT*, July 15, p. 3, July 16, p. 6, 1942, Dec. 22, 1944, p. 8; Report of J. J. Schacht, Field Organizer, NFTW, p. 5, in Report of the Executive Board and Other Reports, 1944. The Illinois plant strike vote was the one wartime telephone strike vote where a majority did not vote in the affirmative. The membership of non-NFTW telephone unions was slightly less than the NFTW unions' 120,000-to-140,000 members during these years. Estimated from figures in *UAT*, 28.

47. An NLRB "intermediate report" of September 1943 found evidence of company domination, which may have affected the decision to strike. NLRB, Western Electric 57: No. 5-C-1604 (1944); *NYT*, Dec. 14, p. 20, Dec. 20, pp. 1, 17, 1943; Foner, *Organized Labor and the Black Worker*, 265.

48. Herrington, OHP, 14-16; Wiencek, OHP, 20-21; Bruce, OHP, 5-6; Hanscom, OHP, 12-15; Anderson, "Equal Opportunity," 179, 182-83, 198. See also Anderson, "Last Hired, First Fired," 89.

49. Report of the Executive Board, 1944, p. 12, in Report of the Executive Board and Other Reports, 1944.

50. Beirne, then president of the NFTW, quoted in *ACA News*, Feb. 1944.

51. Koons in NFTWOP, Feb. 1943, 50-51.

52. The quotes are from, respectively, McCowen, OHP, 23; Mary Gannon in Pre-Assembly Traffic Panel, 1942 (see chap. 3, n. 34), p. 95; and an unidentified delegate, Weaver, and Moran in NFTWOP, Feb. 1943, 61, 21, 17.

53. NFTWOP, Feb. 1943, 89.

54. In a report of June 1944, the NFTW executive board declared: "According to our rules and regulations, it is impossible for the Federation to step in and regulate contemplated or actual strike activity on the part of the member organizations." Report of the Executive Board, 1944, p. 12.

55. Hudson, Strike Director's Report, pp. 2–3.

56. NFTWOP, 1944, 15, 37; Report of the Executive Board, 1945, p. 16, in Report of the Executive Board and Other Reports, 1945 (see chap. 5, n. 47). Here the report was reviewing an executive board meeting of January 8–13, 1943.

57. "Strike Manual," pt. D, p. 1.

58. Hudson, Strike Director's Report, p. 3; Report of the Executive Board, 1945, p. 16.

59. NFTW constitutional committee to the NFTW executive board and the executive heads of all member organizations, Sept. 12, 1942, p. 3, Box 1, CWAA. See also NFTW, Summary of Assembly, 1941 (see chap. 4, n. 23), p. 41; NFTW, Report of the National Strike Director Committee, Cleveland, June 7–12, 1943, mimeographed, p. 1, Box 1, CWAA. Only two affiliates established permanent strike funds of their own during the war. Report of the WE distributing house union in Reports of Organizations, 1945; *TW*, June 1942.

60. *NFTW* constitutional committee, "Proposed Constitution of the International Federation of Communication Workers," Sept. 1942, mimeographed, p. 14, Box 1, CWAA. The quote is from Report of the National Strike Director Committee, p. 1.

61. *NYT*, Apr. 11, 1943, p. 33.

62. Quotes are from NFTWOP, Feb. 1943, 70, 89; *NYT*, Apr. 12, 1943, p. 31.

63. Report of the Plant Model Contract Committee of the Central-Southern Region, June 7, 1941, (no pagination), in Report Supplement, 1941 (see chap. 3, n. 15); Beirne to delegates of NFTW traffic organizations, May 22, 1943, Box 1, CWAA; NFTWOP, June 1943, 35–36.

64. Elmer Reinker, of the Ohio union, in NFTW, Verbatim Typed Transcript, Proceedings, Ninth National Assembly, Cleveland, June 7–12, 1943, Thursday P.M. session, typewritten, pp. 10–11, Box 1, CWAA.

65. Beirne to delegates, May 22, 1943; NFTW, Panel Committee Report to the Tenth National Assembly, Denver, June 12–17, 1944, mimeographed, (no pagination), Box 1, CWAA.

66. Report of the Plant Model Contract Committee; Commercial and Accounting Panel, 1941 (see chap. 5, n. 36), p. 39; Beirne to delegates, May 22, 1943. Quotes are from Hanscom, OHP, 3; Good, OHP, 2.

67. Constitutional committee to executive board and heads, Sept. 12, 1943.

68. Anne Benscoter, of the Illinois traffic union, and Naughton in Pre-Assembly Traffic Panel, 1942, pp. 95, 168; Cecil Risk, of the Indiana plant union, in NFTWOP, Feb. 1943, 16; report of the Long Lines union in Reports of Organizations, 1942, vol. 1.

69. Among NFTW unions that were represented on both a roster of April 1941 and a roster of February 1943, fourteen presidencies changed hands and twelve did not. *TW,* May 1941; NFTWOP, Feb. 1943, 3–4. See also Appendix B.

70. McCowen, OHP, 2, 7–15; Griffith, OHP, 33; Herrington, OHP, 21; Pollock, OHP, 1–6; Gannon interview.

71. Dunn, OHP, 9; roll call votes in Verbatim Transcript, Feb. 1943 (see chap. 5, n. 54), Thursday afternoon session, adding machine tape stapled between pp. 8 and 9, Box 1, CWAA, and in NFTWOP, June 1943, 58–59; DuVal, OHP, 58; *FB,* Oct. 1942; *TW,* Aug. 1942; NFTWOP, Feb. 1943, 9.

72. NFTW, Minutes, Central-Southern Regional Conference, Chicago, May 15–16, 1942, mimeographed, p. 11, Box 1, CWAA; Dunn, OHP, 15–16; "Constitution and Bylaws as Revised, 1942" (see chap. 3, n. 39), pp. 113–114; Pre-Assembly Traffic Panel, 1942, p. 69; NFTWOP, 1942, 19, 24.

73. Dunn, OHP, 15–16; Pre-Assembly Traffic Panel, 1942, p. 191; Griffith, OHP, 38–39.

74. Griffith, OHP, 36–37.

75. DuVal, OHP, 17, 67; Report of Leonard B. Rowles (see chap. 5, n. 50), p. 3; NFTW, Uniform Report, Minutes of Executive Board Meeting held at Cincinnati, Jan. 29–Feb. 8, 1943, mimeographed, p. 3, Box 4, CWAA; Beirne in NFTWOP, Feb. 1943, 19.

76. Central Region Minutes (see chap. 5, n. 50), p. 3; NFTW, Uniform Report, Minutes of Executive Board Meeting held at Cincinnati, Ohio, Jan. 29–Feb. 8, 1943, mimeographed, p. 3, Box 4, CWAA; Beirne in NFTWOP, Feb. 1943, 19.

77. Moran and an unidentified delegate in NFTWOP, Feb. 1943, 19, 24; Beirne, OHP, 18.

78. Central Region Minutes, 1942, pp. 2–4, 6; NFTWOP, Feb. 1943, 18–20.

79. Griffith, OHP, 32–34, 38–41. On Beirne's and McCowen's reluctance, see Beirne, OHP, 18; McCowen, OHP, 22; Crull, OHP, 24; Dunn, OHP, 10; DuVal, OHP, 99.

80. Griffith has remarked that notice of his departure did "create quite a bombshell. Even in retrospect, however, I think it did enable the organization to maintain itself as an entity, even though I'm sure there were a lot of bitter feelings." Griffith, OHP, 42.

81. Executive Board Minutes, Jan. 29–Feb. 8, 1943, p. 3.

82. Beirne, OHP, 22; NFTWOP, Feb. 1943, 3–5, 24; *UAT,* 85. On

Horth's absence, see also Executive Board Meeting, Jan. 29–Feb. 8, 1943, p. 3; NFTWOP, Feb. 1943, 39.

83. Dunn, OHP, 16; NFTWOP, Feb. 1943, 24, 45–46, 64.

84. NFTWOP, Feb. 1943, 7; Beirne, OHP, 22–23.

85. Verbatim Transcript, Feb. 1943, Tuesday Evening, pp. 4–16; NFTWOP, Feb. 1943, 33–39, 46, 63, 68–71; Beirne, OHP, 23.

86. NFTWOP, Feb. 1943, 25; NFTW constitutional committee to executive board and heads, Sept. 12, 1943, pp. 1, 3; "Proposed Constitution of the International Federation of Communication Workers," pp. 1–4. Members of the committee were Beirne, McCowen, Frances Smith, and Edwin Hackett, a lawyer and officer in the Illinois commercial union.

87. NFTWOP, Feb. 1943, 25–27; Verbatim Transcript, Feb. 1943, Tuesday Evening, p. 13; UAT, 85.

88. NFTWOP, Feb. 1943, 60, 82.

89. An unidentified delegate and Beirne in NFTWOP, Feb. 1943, 61–62. See also 60, 82.

90. Verbatim Transcript, Feb. 1943, Thursday Afternoon, adding machine tape stapled between pp. 8 and 9 and between pp. 17 and 18.

91. Al Philip Kane, NFTW general counsel, to the executive heads of all member organizations, Mar. 1943, printed in part in Federation of Women Telephone Workers of Southern California News, Aug. 1943; Gravem, OHP, 2.

92. Unidentified delegate in NFTWOP, June 1943, 23.

93. NFTWOP, Feb. 1943, 62, June 1943, 23, 58–59.

94. Dunn, OHP, 71; Beirne, OHP, 24.

95. Verbatim Transcript, Feb. 1943, Thursday Afternoon, p. 16.

Chapter 7. Toward One National Union, 1943–1946

1. Dunn, OHP, 13; UAT, 231; NFTWOP, June 1943, 42–45; Pollock, OHP, 9; DuVal, OHP, 18.

2. Dunn, OHP, 13. See also Wooding, memoir (see chap. 2, n. 33), 2: 3.

3. NFTWOP, June 1943, 21, 34; UAT, 86; Federation of Women Telephone Workers of Southern California News, Aug. 1943; Beirne, OHP, 24.

4. Dunn, OHP, 13; NFTW, Minutes, Eastern Regional Conference, Wilmington, Del., Nov. 2, 1940, mimeographed, pp. 3–4, Box 1, CWAA; Eastern Region Minutes (see chap. 4, n. 56), pp. 10–13; DuVal, OHP, 40–42; Griffith, OHP, 24.

5. Beirne, OHP, 4, 18, 25, 35 (Beirne's emphasis); Griffith, OHP, 30–31, 39; Novotny, OHP, 1. Beirne's foremost allies were Frances Smith, Dunn, Weaver, DuVal, McCowen, and Moran. DuVal, OHP, 69; Dunne, OHP, 8; Massey, OHP, 4.

6. Perhaps a stronger factor in Beirne's reluctance was his desire to remain in the New York area. There he had a young family to support, a full-time WE union post that was more secure than anything the NFTW could then offer, and a budding political career as a Fairview, New Jersey, city councilman. See NFTWOP, June 1943, 42; Dunn, OHP, 10–11; DuVal, OHP, 66; Pollock, OHP, 9.

7. Beirne, OHP, 16–17, 35.

8. McCowen, OHP, 10, 13–15, 24; DiProspere, OHP, 5; Griffith, OHP, 33; Crull, OHP, 24–25; Herrington, OHP, 21.

9. NFTW, Report of the Executive Board to the Ninth National Assembly, Cleveland, Ohio, June 7–12, 1943, typewritten, p. 4, Box 1, CWAA; Report of the Executive Board, 1944, p. 14, in Report of the Executive Board and Other Reports, 1944 (see chap. 5, n. 48); Dunn, OHP, 13; NFTWOP, 1944, 44–45, 52.

10. Of the total NFTW expenses of June 1944 to June 1945, amounting to $83,506.50, the three largest items were organizing ($10,828), clerical salaries ($9,963), and the *Telephone Worker* ($6,996). Cost of the education program was $2,855, up from $1,200 the previous year. The move to the storefront office in Washington came in April 1945; in May 1946 headquarters was moved to a three-story house in the capital. From June 1945 to June 1946, with the $1.20 dues rate in force through the whole year, the NFTW was able to spend $204,048, with organizing, the *Telephone Worker*, and building expenses the largest costs. Report of the Educational Department to the Tenth National Assembly, p. 2, in Report of the Executive Board and Other Reports, 1944; NFTWOP, 1945, 40–43; Report of the Executive Board to the Twelfth National Assembly, 1946, pp. 6, 11, in NFTW, Report of the Executive Board and Certain Other Reports to the Galveston Assembly, June 3–8, 1946, mimeographed, (no pagination), Box 2, CWAA; Dunn, OHP, p. 30. For other details, see "Conclusion," including n. 7.

11. NFTWOP, June 1943, 25–27, 31–32; NFTW, Constitutional Committee Report, Ninth National Assembly, Cleveland, June 7–12, 1943, mimeographed, p. 3, Box 1, CWAA; Crull, OHP, 26. Quotes are from Beirne and McCowen in NFTW, Verbatim Record, Constitutional Matters, 1944 (see chap. 5, n. 38), pp. 20–21, 43, 51. See also NFTW, Report of the Executive Board, 1945 (see chap. 5, n. 47), p. 22.

12. Report of the WE distributing house union in Reports of Organizations, 1945 (see chap. 6, n. 39); Crull, OHP, 33; Waldeck, OHP, 5; *TW*, Dec. 1945; Report of the Executive Board, 1944, p. 9; Eastern Regional Board Member Report on Organizing Activities, May 23, 1944, (no pagination), and Annual Report of the National Organizer to the Tenth National Assembly, pp. 3–4, in Report of the Executive Board and other Reports, 1944; Report

of Central Regional Director, 1945, (no pagination), in Report of the Executive Board and Other Reports, 1945.

13. *UAT*, 37; Report of J. J. Schacht (see chap. 6, n. 46), pp. 1–7; J. J. Schacht, OHP, 10–11.

14. Sims, OHP, 1–3; Gill, OHP, 4; Brown, OHP, 2–3; Bradbury interview. The quote is from Mahady, OHP, 16 (Mahady's emphasis).

15. Mahady, OHP, 13–14; Daniel, OHP, 2; Report of the Executive Board, 1944, p. 7; Report of J. J. Schacht, p. 3; Gill, OHP, 11; Beaver, OHP, 15–16.

16. Annual Report of the National Organizer, 1944, pp. 2–3; Bradbury interview. The quote is from Brown, OHP, 2.

17. Gill, OHP, 4–11, 29; Mason, *To Win These Rights*, 87–92; Dunn, OHP, 20. The seventy-two-day Southern Bell strike of 1955 involved some fifty thousand workers in all four departments and resulted in the largest set of discharge arbitration hearings—involving 238 people, each accused of acts of violence—ever held in the United States. Arbitrators upheld the discharges of 39. The company counted 4,261 acts of sabotage. Derby, "Common Law Principles," 1, 47, 54, 95, 110, 134, 160, 170, 187; Bradbury interview.

18. NFTWOP, 1944, 21–22; Gillmore, "Bell," 152; Report of the General Counsel, 1942–1944 (see chap. 5, n. 48), p. 4; John J. Moran, "NFTW Activities on Independent Representation," pp. 1–5, in Report of the Executive Board and Other Reports, 1944. The quote is from McCowen, OHP, 24.

19. Report of the General Counsel, 1942–1944, pp. 1–2; Koons in NFTWOP, Feb. 1943, 54; NFTWOP, 1944, 25.

20. Park, "Strike," 18; Pollock, OHP, 6–7; *LDS*, xii; *NYT*, Nov. 23, 1944, p. 1.

21. Pollock, OHP, 6–7.

22. Ibid. On November 19 the WLB chairman estimated the number of strikers at four thousand. *NYT*, Nov. 20, p. 17, Nov. 22, p. 1, 1944.

23. Pollock, OHP, 7; *NYT*, Nov. 21, p. 17, Nov. 22, p. 1, 1944. Pollock's refusal to share control may have been due to an unwillingness to place such a burden on the NFTW. This is suggested by remarks in the 1945 Report of the Executive Board (p. 15): "The president of the Ohio federation stated later in a speech at the Central Region meeting that no formal request was made of the NFTW because the strike was spontaneous and had not been called under the rules of the War Labor Disputes Act [i.e., the Smith-Connally Act], therefore NFTW established procedures were not followed." But another possibility is that Pollock doubted whether the NFTW leadership shared his boldness. In a 1970 interview Pollock, without actually saying so, conveyed to the author an impression that this was his belief at the time. Pollock, OHP, 7. It is possible

that NFTW officers faintheartedly *asked* Kane to advise Pollock as he did. Kane later reported: "At 12:30 A.M. on November 22, Mr. Moran telephoned counsel who thereupon met with Mr. Moran, Mr. Werkau, Mr. Hudson [of the Ohio union], Mr. Weaver, Mr. Pollock, and Miss Reedy, from 1:00 A.M. to 3:30 A.M. Counsel recommended that the Ohio Federation return to work because it was in a bad position because of its non-compliance with the Smith-Connally Act and it could not hope to gain anything by staying out on strike." NFTW, Uniform Report, Minutes of Executive Board Meeting Held at Baltimore, Jan. 8-13, 1945, Exhibit 10, Report of General Counsel on Washington Activities, Second Half of Year, 1944, mimeographed, p. 4, Box 4, CWAA. The executive board's version of the incident, in its 1945 report (p. 15), is that the WLB "attempted to prevail upon the vice-president and the secretary of the NFTW to order the strikers to return to work but were informed that the NFTW did not have such authority. A meeting was held with the Ohio officers, NFTW vice-president, secretary, Central Region Director [Weaver], and legal counsel, at which time the Ohio officers decided to appeal directly to the member organizations rather than to the NFTW for support."

24. Beirne, OHP, 20.

25. Report of the Executive Board, 1945, pp. 15-16; Executive Board Minutes, Jan. 8-13, 1945, Exhibit 10, p. 4. Jeannette Reedy, after meeting with NFTW officers, was convinced she had their support. Reedy interview.

26. *NYT*, Nov. 21, p. 17, Nov. 23, p. 1, 1944; Pollock, OHP, 7-8. The three groups initiating strike votes were Long Lines traffic in New York City, the Cincinnati union, and New York City traffic (non-NFTW). Dunn, OHP, 21; *NYT*, Nov. 24, 1944, p. 1; Report of the Executive Board, 1945, p. 15; *UAT*, 42. The executive board's estimate of the number on strike was twelve thousand, Barbash's ten thousand.

27. Pollock, OHP, 8-9; *NYT*, Nov. 24, 1944, p. 1.

28. *NYT*, Nov. 25, 1944, p. 11; *LDS*, 63-64; Beirne, OHP, 21; "Henry Mayer's Monthly Report," Apr. 30, 1971; Report of the Executive Board, 1945, p. 22.

29. *LDS*, 3-4; "Henry Mayer's Monthly Report," Apr. 30, 1971.

30. *LDS*, xi, xiii; NTP, "Report" (see chap. 2, n. 3), 16-21. See also Gillmore, "Bell," 259-260; *Termination Report* (see chap. 2, n. 21) 1: 1003-1009.

31. *LDS*, xv, 3-4, 36, 44-45, 51, 63, 70-72; Park, "Strike," 20; Report of the Executive Board, 1946, p. 12; Gillmore, "Bell," 264; *Termination Report* 1:1013-1015, 1026-1027, 1036, 1044. Quotes are from the language of the report of the two public members of the panel in *Termination Report*. The panel also wiped out the one vestige of discrimination against *married* women to come to light, in July 1945 in the Upstate Telephone Company of Johnstown, New York, where married women had been offered only tempo-

rary employee status, thus denying them the fringe benefits due regular employees. U.S. National War Labor Board, *War Labor Reports* 27:129; Dickason, "Women in Labor Unions," 74.

32. See Appendix D, tables A.2 and A.4. See also *LMR*, Union Exhibit 41, p. 757. The only other walkout was by "a small number of telephone operators employed by the Warren Telephone Company at Warren, Ohio . . . for about 10 days in August 1945." *Termination Report* 1:1043.

33. *NYT*, Nov. 23, 1944, p. 1; Loewenberg, "Effects," I-40; LeFevre, OHP, 1–2; Gillmore, "Bell," 265, 267; Bers, "Unionism," 29.

34. Dunn, OHP, 21.

35. Ibid., 23. Dunn's salary was paid by the NFTW; his NFTW title was "assistant to the president." Moran, still the NFTW vice-president and Long Lines union president, appears to have been carried on the Long Lines union payroll. For Dunn's and Moran's scant bureaucratic support at NFTW headquarters during 1945, see "Conclusion," especially n. 7.

36. For Lichtenstein and the other scholars, see "Introduction," nn. 5 and 6.

37. *UAT*, 28, 38; Report of the Executive Board, 1946, p. 10; NFTWOP, 1944, 47–51; NFTW, *Report of Assembly*, June 1946, 5–6.

38. Report of Central Regional Director, 1945; General Pension Committee Report covering June 1944–May 1945, Chicago, June 11–16, 1945, mimeographed, p. 1, Box 2, CWAA; reports of the Indiana accounting union, the Michigan traffic-accounting union, and the southern California commercial union in Reports of Organizations, 1945; NFTW, *Report of Assembly*, June 1946, 5–6; Report of the Executive Board, 1946, p. 13; *TW*, Mar. 1946; Mann, OHP, 2. The Wisconsin traffic and Michigan accounting unions "affiliated" by amalgamating with NFTW unions in their areas.

39. Some 394,000 were union eligible in late 1945. ATTR, 1945, 37.

40. Report of Central Regional Director, 1945; Beirne, OHP, 18.

41. Dunn, OHP, 22.

42. NTP, "Report," 8.

43. NFTWOP, 1945, 24–25, 31; Report of the Executive Board, 1945, p. 21.

44. NFTWOP, 1945, 33–36. In other action, the assembly adopted a resolution calling for the elimination of sex distinctions in all the contracts of NFTW unions. *Termination Report* 2:971.

45. Seidman, *Defense*, 90; Brooks, *Telephone*, 218; Welsh, OHP, 4.

46. Brooks, *Telephone*, 214–215; ATTR, 1943, 39, 1944, 37, 1945, 9, 1946, 10, 13, 21; John M. Shaw, "Digest of Talk to Michigan Bell Personnel Seminar, Feb. 19, 1947," typewritten, Box 3, Shaw Papers; Bers, "Wage Structure in the Telephone Industry," 36; Loewenberg, "Effects," V-60–61.

47. Douty, "Review," 123; FCCS, 1945, 22–23.

48. Quotes are from Welsh, OHP, 4. See also *WTW*, 18.

49. Report of the Illinois traffic union in NFTW, General Reports of Member Organizations to the Twelfth National Assembly, Galveston, June 3-8, 1946, mineographed, (no pagination), Box 2, CWAA; *TW*, Dec. 1945; Park, "Strike," 19.

50. Dunn, OHP, 25; Crull, OHP, 29; NFTW, Uniform Report, Minutes of Executive Board Meeting, Baltimore, Sept. 17-22, 1945, mimeographed, pp. 1-7, Box 4, CWAA; *TW*, Jan. 1946.

51. *Tel-U*, Dec. 1945; NFTW, Uniform Report, Minutes of Executive Board Meeting, Milwaukee, Dec. 3-7, 1945, mimeographed, p. 11, Box 4, CWAA; *TW*, Dec. 1945.

52. McCowen, OHP, 18; NFTW, "Speech by Joe Beirne, President of NFTW, at Labor Temple," [Detroit, Aug. 24, 1946], typewritten, Box 5, CWAA.

53. *TW*, Jan. 1946; NFTW, Uniform Report, Minutes of Executive Board Meeting, Washington, Jan. 12-13, 1946, mimeographed, pp. 13-15, Box 4, CWAA.

54. *NYT*, Jan. 12, 1946, 3. See also Park, "Strike," 23-24; Segal, "Communications," 433; Executive Board Minutes, Jan. 12-13, 1946, pp. 13-18.

55. Chisholm, OHP, 15. See also Minnesota State Board Bulletin, vol. 5, no. 2, Jan. 8, 1946, mimeographed, (no pagination), Box 7, CWA-NUTWP.

56. Executive Board Minutes, Jan. 12-13, 1946, p. 18; *TW*, Jan. 1946.

57. Park, "Strike," 22; Segal, "Communications," 432; Report of the Executive Board, 1946, p. 6; DuVal, OHP, 14-15; report of the WE Kearny union in Reports of Organizations, 1946. For alleged AT&T sympathy with the demonstration, see DiProspere, OHP, p. 13; Wooding, OHP, 13; Webb, OHP, 42.

58. Report of the WE Kearny union in Reports of Organizations, 1946; DuVal, OHP, 44. The picket-legitimizing issue was pertinent because the Kearny union had considered picketing central offices (a move of questionable legality). See Executive Board Minutes, Jan. 12-13, 1946, pp. 8-13; Park, "Strike," 23.

59. Beirne, OHP, 25. See also Report of the Executive Board, 1946, Appendix K, "Report on Wage Negotiations during March, 1946, by J. A. Beirne, May 25, 1946" (hereafter cited as App. K), pp. 1-2; Beirne in *LMR*, 126.

60. "Speech by Joe Beirne," 28; Beirne, OHP, 25.

61. App. K, p. 1; *LMR*, 581.

62. Beirne, OHP, 25; App. K, pp. 2, 7; *UAT*, 60; Dunn, OHP, 28.

63. App. K, pp. 3-4; *LMR*, 582; *NYT*, Feb. 24, p. 7, Mar. 1, p. 3, 1946; Bers, "Unionism," 82.

64. Craig in *LMR*, 583. See also App. K, p. 4.

65. *LMR*, Union Exhibit 22, p. 130. See also *LMR*, 583; App. K, pp.

4–5. Craig's 1950 description of his acceptance of the proposal is: "I asked the Conciliation Service if they would arrange for me to have a meeting with Mr. Beirne. At this meeting I advised him that the companies were willing to try to bargain out agreements on the basis of the tentative long-lines agreement." *LMR*, 584. There is no NFTW-AT&T disagreement concerning the incidents in post-Memphis bargaining as they are presented in the text. However, union versions of the incidents in 1946 bargaining imply that the Bell companies were responding to the wishes of AT&T, while AT&T versions imply that AT&T was responding to the wishes of the Bell companies. For a discussion of whose "implications" are closer to the truth, see Appendix C. It may be noted here that Craig, some thirty years later, said: "I suppose you could say that the paper Beirne and I initialed committed the whole Bell System. The operating companies could have reneged on it, but they never did, and I would have been disappointed if they had done so. To a degree, Beirne did force us to negotiate nationally." Brooks, *Telephone*, 220.

66. App. K, pp. 5–7; *LMR*, 130–132, 400–401, 586–588, 683–686; Crull, OHP, 30–31; n. 65.

67. App. K, p. 5; *TW*, Mar., Apr. 1946; Beirne, OHP, 27; *LMR*, 31, 364–366, 461–462; Gillmore, "Bell," 158.

68. FCCS, 1946, 22–23; Dunlop, "Decontrol," 21; Park, "Strike," 25. For comparisons with wage gains elsewhere, see Seidman, *Defense*, 240.

69. See n. 65; Appendix C; Brooks, *Telephone*, 220.

70. McCowen, OHP, 16; Dunn, OHP, 28; Brooks, *Telephone*, 219; *UAT*, 74; Park, "Strike," 26; Gillmore, "Bell," 155.

71. Beirne, OHP, 29.

72. Bers, "Unionism," 31; report of the Southern Bell union in Reports of Organizations, 1946. The quote is from Schaar, OHP, 8.

73. Beirne, OHP, 26. The sign-off unions included Maryland and Washington State plant, Illinois accounting, and Oregon, Virginia, and Mountain States. These unions, along with Wisconsin and the Northwestern Union (as well as the departed southern California traffic and Illinois plant unions, and the Connecticut union, which disaffiliated March 1, 1946), had been the vocal autonomist unions in 1943. Some of these probably moved away from the autonomist camp after 1943; since the issue was not openly fought at the assemblies, it is hard to tell which ones, and I have been unable to do so. For sign-offs, see *TW*, Mar., Apr. 1946.

74. Beirne, OHP, 27; *TW*, Mar. 1946; Dunn, OHP, 28; Frances Smith, "One National Union of Telephone Workers," Apr. 1946, mimeographed, p. 2, Box 2, CWAA. See also Dunn, OHP, 28; Beirne, OHP, 27.

75. Dunn, OHP, 28; Smith, "One National Union," p. 1.

76. Beirne, OHP, 30.

77. Ibid., 29–30; *TW*, Mar. 1946.

Chapter 8. National Strike, National Union, 1947

1. Gifford, "Responsibility of Management," 70-71. See also *UAT*, 52.

2. Remarks of an anonymous Bell official, quoted in Park, "Strike," 54.

3. McCowen, OHP, 16; Beirne, OHP, 27; Webb, OHP, 9.

4. *TW*, Dec. 1945, Jan., May 1946; Report of the Executive Board, 1945 (see chap. 7, n. 10), pp. 12-13.

5. Dunn, OHP, 25-26; Beirne, OHP, 13-15; *TW*, May 1946; NFTW, Report of Assembly, June 1946, 13-17, 21-22; Crull, OHP, 8.

6. Verbatim Minutes, Sixth [Minnesota] State Assembly, Northwestern Union of Telephone Workers, Minneapolis, Nov. 11-13, 1946, typewritten carbon copy, p. 12, Box 7, CWA-NUTWP; NFTW, "Proposed Constitution, Communications Workers of America," [Summer 1946] with subheading: "To the executive heads of all member unions and chairmen of locals," Box 2, CWAA; Webb, OHP, 9. The quote is from "Speech by Joe Beirne" (see chap. 7, n. 52), 37, 40. See also *TW*, June, Oct. 1946.

7. For the initial belief, held by the Galveston delegates, that the entire changeover could take place in the fall of 1946, see "Speech by Joe Beirne," 45-46. For subsequent legal and constitutional difficulties, see Dunn, OHP, 25; Park, "Strike," 26; *TW*, Nov. 1946; NFTW, *Summarized Report of Assembly*, Nov. 1946 (hereafter cited as *SR*), 14.

8. Report of Field Organizer J. J. Schacht, May 9, 1946, pp. 1-4, in Report of the Executive Board and Other Reports, 1946 (see chap. 7, n. 10); J. J. Schacht, OHP, 17-18; *TW*, Sept., Nov. 1946; RL, Nov. 1967; *ACA News*, Apr. 1947. Northern California traffic leaders had come to admire the ACA's organizing and bargaining abilities, particularly its feat in securing a better than average settlement for its ORTT affiliate in the aftermath of the Beirne-Craig agreement. Kanagy to the author, July 28, 1972; Bruce, OHP, 3-4.

9. *UAT*, 41; CWA, *Summary of Proceedings*, June 1947 (hereafter cited as *SOP*), 14.

10. *TW*, Mar., Aug., Nov., Dec. 1946, Mar. 1, 1947; Report of the National Strike Director, C. W. Werkau, p. 3, in Report of the Executive Board and other Reports, 1946; *Michigan Federation News*, Apr.-May 1946. The upstate New York plant group had affiliated only very recently; the WE Hawthorne group had been dropping in and out of the NFTW since its inception; and the WE Kearny group was prompted less by the national union issue than by bitterness arising from the sixty-five-day strike earlier in the year. *SR*, 14, 25; DuVal, OHP, 44.

11. *TW*, Dec. 1946; *SR*, 13-15, 25; NFTW, Thirteenth National Assembly, Motions, Nov. 1946, mimeographed, pp. 1-5, Box 2, CWAA.

12. WE installation, WE distributing houses, WE manufacturing, and Bell

Laboratories were placed in the manufacturing-research group. NFTW constitution committee, Report—October 17, 1946, mimeographed, pp. 1–3, Box 2, CWAA.

13. NFTW, constitution committee, "Proposed Constitution, Communications Workers of America," [Oct. 1946], mimeographed, pp. 1–3, Box 2, CWAA; Thirteenth National Assembly, Motions, pp. 3–4; Beirne, OHP, 30–31; Crull, OHP, 27–28.

14. "Proposed Constitution," [Oct. 1946], pp. 2, 5, 8–10.

15. Ibid., pp. 4–9; *TW*, May, Nov., Dec. 1946; *CWA News*, July 1950; Verbatim Minutes, Minneapolis, Nov. 11–13, 1946, p. 12; Minnesota State Board Bulletin (see chap. 7, n. 55), vol. 7, no. 2, Dec. 8, 1946, p. 2.

16. Thirteenth National Assembly, Motions, pp. 3–4.

17. Crull, OHP, 27–28. It was believed that a June transition would accommodate the 180 days deemed necessary for referenda and other legal action. And it would allow the NFTW unions to conduct 1947 bargaining (expected to last through February and March) unimpeded by legal and administrative difficulties arising from the transition. *TW*, Dec. 1946; Park, "Strike," 26; *SR*, 17–18.

18. *TW*, Dec. 1946; Crull, OHP, 28–29.

19. *TW*, Feb. 15, Mar. 1, 1947.

20. For abandonment of the April 1 date, see *TW*, June 1947. Dangers to the unions' legal status included the possibility that Bell would withdraw recognition on grounds that the CWA divisions were "new" organizations needing to prove their majority status. This the Bell companies in fact did upon the CWA's establishment in June 1947. Gillmore, "Bell," 166–167; Bers, "Unionism," 78.

21. Bernstein, *Lean Years*, 36–40; Bernstein, *Turbulent Years*, 548–551, 597–600.

22. The average number of hours worked weekly was 37.9 in telephone, 40.0 in all manufacturing. *NYT*, Dec. 20, 1947, p. 5; Douty, "Review," 118–120; *LMR*, AT&T Exhibit A-1, p. 500; Seidman, *Defense*, 341.

23. *NYT*, Mar. 2, 1947, p. 1; Park, "Strike," 28, 33; J. G. Bradbury, *A Talk by J. G. Bradbury to Some 4,500 Supervisory Employees between May 21 and June 25, 1947* (pamphlet published by Southern Bell, Atlanta, 1947), 5–6, Bradbury Papers.

24. NFTW, Policy Committee Minutes, Meeting held in Washington, D.C., March 24–May 6, 1947, session of Apr. 24, typewritten, p. 6, Box 3, CWAA (hereafter cited as PC Minutes); Gillmore, "Bell," 160; Brooks, *Telephone*, 226–230, 238.

25. Bers, "Unionism," 96–97; Park, "Strike," 5; *LMR*, 385, 395.

26. *Sr*, 18–28; *TW*, Dec. 1946, Feb. 15, 1947.

27. Park, "Strike," 35; McCowen, OHP, 17, 51; Schaar, OHP, 9; Gray OHP, 11; Pollock, OHP, 9; Good, OHP, 2; Wooding, OHP, 37; Gwin, OHP, 3.

28. PC Minutes, Apr. 15 session, p. 7, May 6 session, p. 21; Schaar, OHP, 9; Bers, "Unionism," 114.

29. *TW*, Mar. 1, 1947; Bers, "Unionism," 92; Bradbury, *A Talk*, 8; *NYT*, Mar. 2, 1947, p. 42; anonymous Bell officials, quoted in Park, "Strike," 54.

30. Gillmore, "Bell," 163; McCowen, OHP, 18; Beaver, OHP, 11. But management denied the allegations then and since. Bradbury interview. FCC yearly reports, covering October employment data, do not show a significant increase. It is possible that yearly reports covering October data would not reflect a prestrike increase even if one had occurred, particularly since continuous large-scale hiring offered management the opportunity to reduce the proportion of management employees once the strike was over. See FCCS, 1945, 22; 1946, 22; 1947, 24. For unionist allegations that many local officers were offered management positions shortly before the strike, see Moye, OHP, 3; Gwin, OHP, 6.

31. *TW*, Mar. 1, Mar. 15, 1947; Gillmore, "Bell," 161–162; *NYT*, Mar. 24, p. 13, Mar. 26, p. 19, 1947; *LMR*, 134.

32. Beirne, OHP, 32–33; McCowen, OHP, 31; "Henry Mayer's Monthly Report," June 30, 1971, p. 2; PC Minutes, session of Mar. 24, p. 16.

33. *TW*, June 1947; Gillmore, "Bell," 162; *NYT*, Mar. 28, 1947, p. 17.

34. *TW*, June 1947.

35. *NYT*, Apr. 8, p. 1, Apr. 9, p. 1, 1947; Vincent, "Labor Under Review, 1947," 859; *TW*, June 1947. There have since been nationwide telephone strikes, but dialization and centralization of exchanges have reduced the number of communities and women involved.

36. Bers, "Unionism," 92; LeFevre, OHP, 15; *TW*, June 1947; *UAT*, 68. In New Jersey unionists continued their strike despite a utility antistrike law that was hurriedly enacted April 8. Traffic leaders were arrested April 11, but on April 15, as a result of a union-obtained federal injunction, all penalties were stayed until the law's constitutionality could be tested. Mayer and Weiner, "New Jersey Case," 492–499; Hanscom, OHP, 5. All state utility antistrike laws, including those passed by other states soon after the 1947 strike, were eliminated or greatly weakened following a 1951 Supreme Court decision invalidating such a law in Wisconsin. Gillmore, "Bell," 193–194.

37. Webb, OHP, 17–18; Beaver, OHP, 12; Park, "Strike," 35; Johnson, "Union Organization," 81; Wooding, OHP, 14; Seidman et al., *Views*, 150. For the strike period as a whole, the volume of long distance calls was about 44 percent of normal. Figures are based on union analyses, which were drawn from FCC reports and were consistent with management statements. Melvin D. Bers, "Effect of 1947 Telephone Strike on Bell System Operations," CWA

Research and Statistics Department, July 16, 1947, mimeographed, (no pagination), Box 4, CWAA; Bers, "Unionism," 145; ATTR, 1947, 9; Brooks, *Telephone*, 221; *TW*, June 1947.

38. Brooks, *Telephone*, 221; Koons, OHP, 4; Wooding, OHP, 16; Palmer, OHP, 18; Walsh, OHP, 21; *NYT*, Apr. 9, p. 18, Apr. 26, p. 3, 1947; *UAT*, 69; Bradbury, *A Talk*, 11–12.

39. *UAT*, 73; Armstrong, OHP, 16; Walsh, OHP, 19–20; Webb, OHP, 19; Wooding, OHP, 16; Gwin, OHP, 5; Moye, OHP, 5–6; Gill, OHP, 13; Giles, OHP, 8.

40. *Chicago Daily News*, Apr. 29, 1947, p. 20; PC Minutes, session of Apr. 23, p. 34; Gill, OHP, 27; Gray, OHP, 6; Gwin, OHP, 5. Unionists later detected some slippage in sympathy. Schaar, OHP, 9.

41. Bers, "Unionism" 145; *NYT*, Apr. 30, 1947, p. 19; Bers, "Effect of Strike"; ATTR, 1947, 3. The quote is from Dunne, OHP, 3.

42. *NYT*, Apr. 18, p. 4, Apr. 20, p. 1, Apr. 24, p. 1, Apr. 25, p. 1, 1947; *UAT*, 70; Beirne to Truman, Apr. 18, 1947; Gillmore, "Bell," 164; Park, "Strike," 38; PC Minutes, session of Apr. 15, p. 1. George W. Taylor later spoke persuasively on behalf of federal nonintervention: "Some industry-wide strikes have compelling public emergency characteristics; others do not. On the other hand, some local stoppages may be of vital importance. It would appear, from past experience, that a rather extensive shut-down of telephone service, for example, is not nearly as crucial as a stoppage in a local plant making gas for domestic use, which creates almost immediate peril. As a matter of public policy, it should be made clear that, wherever possible and to the fullest feasible extent, a strike called will be permitted to run its course. Nor should government intervention be undertaken to avoid more public inconvenience. That is one of the costs of maintaining collective bargaining." "Arbitration," 67.

43. *TW*, June 1947; Beirne to Haywood, Apr. 15, 1947, Box 4, CWAA.

44. LeFevre, OHP, 5–6; Brown, OHP, 5; Hubbard, OHP, 4; Wooding, OHP, 15; Bers, "Unionism," 114; Good, OHP, 6; Armstrong, OHP, 5; Gray, OHP, 5, 7; NFTW, "Telephone Workers Defense Committee, Outline, April 27, 1947," typewritten, (no pagination), Box 4, CWAA; *TW*, June 1947; Follis, OHP, 14; Gill, OHP, 14.

45. *TW*, June 1947; Johnson, "Union Organization," 79. For morale-killing effects of the halving of the wage demand in some areas, see Chisholm, OHP, 6.

46. Edwards, OHP, 2, 14; LeFevre, OHP, 7; Chisholm, OHP, 6; PC Minutes, Apr. 26 session, pp. 1–2, May 5 session, p. 2; *NYT*, Apr. 29, 1947, p. 1; Gillmore, "Bell," 164. The quote is from Pollock, OHP, 10.

47. In Northwestern Bell, the union signed a company proposal that stated: "It is understood that if the union produces a telegram from J. A. Beirne,

President of the N.F.T.W., stating in effect that the Northwestern Union of Telephone Workers has final authority to negotiate a contract for the five state area, the Northwestern Bell Company through its bargaining board who are authorized to negotiate in said area will submit written proposal to Governor Luther Youngdahl, containing an increase in the basic wages of employees represented by said Union over present wages. And upon acceptance by said Union, of the proposal or such other proposal as may be agreed upon the strike will be settled." Quoted in Minnesota State Board, NUTW, "Confidential Resume" (July 21, 1947, Minneapolis), (no pagination), mimeographed, in the author's possession. In southern California plant, the offer of a wage increase was contingent upon the union's withdrawing from the policy committee. PC Minutes, session of Apr. 23, p. 2. See also PC Minutes, session of Apr. 22, p. 2; *NYT*, Apr. 23, 1947, p. 18; *LMR*, 136–137; *TW*, June 1947; Brooks, *Telephone*, 221.

48. PC Minutes, sessions of Apr. 22, p. 2, Apr. 23, p. 2, Apr. 24, pp. 3–5, Apr. 26, pp. 1–2, May 5 (afternoon), pp. 2–5, May 6, pp. 8–30; *UAT*, 71.

49. "Confidential Resume"; *LMR*, 139; *NYT*, May 1, p. 1, May 3, p. 1, May 19, p. 1, May 21, p. 1, 1947; *TW*, June 1947; *UAT*, 73.

50. McCowen, OHP, 18; Schaar, OHP, 9.

51. Beirne, OHP, 31; *UAT*, 78; Gray, OHP, 4–5; Welsh, OHP, 2. The quote is from Henry Mayer in PC Minutes, session of Apr. 24, p. 3.

52. Bers, "Unionism," 114. But it should be added that building an adequate strike fund was virtually impossible in the years preceding the strike.

53. June McDonald, untitled diary-notebook (written when traveling as an TWOC-CIO organizer), entry for Sept. 24, 1947, handwritten, June McDonald Papers. See also Edwards, OHP, 2; Giles, OHP, 12; *CWA News*, Aug. 1947; Wooding, OHP, 19.

54. Quoted in Wooding, OHP, 19.

55. Bers, "Unionism," 78; Gillmore, "Bell," 166–167.

56. Park, "Strike," 61; PC minutes, session of May 6, p. 35; Pollock, OHP, 12–13; *UAT*, 79; Gillmore, "Bell," 166–167. The quote is from Follis, OHP, 2 (Follis's emphasis).

57. Stein, OHP, 10. See also Gillmore, "Bell," 167.

58. Brown, OHP, 5; Chisholm, OHP, 7; Patterson, OHP, 5.

59. Gill, OHP, 11; Daniel, OHP, 7.

60. *NYT*, May 25, p. 48, May 27, p. 23, 1947. The quote is from a TWOC-CIO organizing pamphlet, quoted in *UAT*, 95.

61. Executive Board Minutes, Dec. 3–7, 1945 (see chap. 7, n. 51), p. 11; Dunn, OHP, 8–9; Beirne, OHP, 9–10; *UAT*, 101–102.

62. NFTW, "Report of the Committee to Investigate Affiliation as Authorized by the Presidents' Convention at Milwaukee, Dec., 1945," Apr. 25,

1946, typewritten, pp. 2–6, Box 5, CWAA. A class B member was one failing to meet "certain age and physical qualifications." He or she paid one-sixth of the dues and held a hundredth of the voting power of a class A member. NFTW, Assembly Addresses: Talks Made by Representatives of the AFL and the CIO at the Memphis Presidents' Conference, Peabody Hotel, Memphis, Feb. 20, 1946, mimeographed, pp. 25–35, Box 5, CWAA; *UAT*, 101–102. Like the IBEW, the ACA and the UE (which would be the WE workers' vehicle for piecemeal CIO affiliation) had recently fought bitter organizing battles against NFTW unions and had initiated company-domination suits against some of them. And by 1947 their reputation as Communist-dominated unions was a larger liability than ever. Selly interview.

63. *UAT*, 96–98; Gray, OHP, 8; Dunn, OHP, 34; Gill, OHP, 11, 14, 28; Mahady, OHP, 13; Moye, OHP, 12; Edwards, OHP, 2; Schaar, OHP, 6–7; *Telephone Talk*, Jan.–Feb. 1948. On 1947 Southern Bell negotiations, see Henry Mayer, "The C.I.O. or A.F.L.: Which Shall It Be for Telephone Workers?" June 2, 1947, typewritten, p. 5, Box 4, CWAA; Bradbury, *A Talk*, 12–13.

64. *NYT*, May 25, p. 48, May 27, p. 23, July 11, p. 4, 1947; Gray, OHP, 8; *UAT*, 79, 96; Schaar, OHP, 6–7; Edwards, OHP, 2; *CWA News*, Feb. 1948.

65. Beirne, OHP, 10, 33–34; Palmer, OHP, 4–5; Giles, OHP, 9; Mayer, "The C.I.O. or A.F.L.," p. 2; Schaar, OHP, 13; Stephens, OHP, 6; Purdy, OHP, 10.

66. Beirne, OHP, 33–34; Purdy, OHP, 9; Watts, OHP, 8; "Wrong Number?" 25.

67. Gill, OHP, 10, 29. See also Mahady, OHP, 17; Beaver, OHP, 13.

68. Quotes are from Edwards, OHP, 3; Schaar, OHP, 11.

69. The Southwestern Union leaders were besieged with questions from leaders of other unions as to their intentions concerning the CWA. Lonergan, OHP, 2.

70. Good, OHP, 6; Watts, OHP, 19.

71. *SP*, 40; Schaar, OHP, 6–7; *UAT*, 79; Beirne, OHP, 33–34. For an explanation of the "nearly three-fourths" estimate, see n. 81.

72. *CWA News*, July 1947. The number of dues-paying members in March was, however, undoubtedly greater than the number in June. See n. 81.

73. Dunn, OHP, 34. See also *UAT*, 79.

74. Schaar, OHP, 6–7, 11; *CWA News*, Aug. 1947.

75. *SOP*, 3; Schaar, OHP, 12; Berthelot, OHP, 7–8. Beirne's annual salary was set at $13,200, Werkau's and Crull's at $10,200. The group representatives on the executive board were not, for the time being, to serve full time, but the regional representatives were; their salaries were set at $9,000. *SOP*, 29, 33–34.

76. Bell companies quickly demanded that the CWA divisions provide proof of their majority status. See n. 20. See also Myers, *Economics*, 252; Bers, "Unionism," 102–103.

77. *JOEWAO*, Aug. 1947, 319.

78. *SOP*, 33; CWA, *Proceedings*, June 1948, 30; *CWA News*, Mar. 1948.

79. *CWA News*, July 1947; *SOP*, 51–52.

80. *CWA News*, July 1947; *SOP*, 47–49.

81. Because of the telephone unions' policy of not revealing membership figures during the poststrike months, the actual membership of the CWA in the summer of 1947 cannot be ascertained precisely. The figure used at the June convention was 161,669, but that figure was based on dues paid the enrolled unions in March. (This reporting procedure was in accordance with the CWA constitution.) The March membership of the Michigan plant union, which joined the CWA in July, was some 5,300 (estimated on the basis of a 5,070 membership reported in November 1946). The sum of these figures, 166,969, amounted to 73 percent of the 228,677 total NFTW membership for March 1947. It is reasonable to suppose that losses due to the strike were roughly proportional; that is, the percentage loss in those NFTW unions that went into the CWA was about equal to the percentage loss in those NFTW unions that did not. Thus the 73 percent figure seems a reasonable estimate of total CWA membership, as compared to total former NFTW union membership in the summer of 1947. Actually, the loss in membership was probably about 20 percent in the group that went into the CWA and in the group that did not. Thus CWA membership in the summer of 1947 was probably between 130,000 and 140,000. For hard figures used above, see *SOP*, 40; *SR*, 5–6; Park, "Strike," 51; see also sources cited in n. 57. In the summer of 1947 the CWA did not represent workers in Maine, Vermont, New Hampshire, Rhode Island, Delaware, Montana. In six other states it represented small groups (such as distributing house, accounting, commercial, or non-Bell workers) but did not represent the large traffic or plant groups in the local Bell operating company; these were Massachusetts, Connecticut, New York, Pennsylvania, Maryland, and Oregon. Of the three largest WE manufacturing plants, the CWA represented workers at Point Breeze but not Kearny or Hawthorne. In all, the CWA was the bargaining representative for about 220,000 workers. *SOP*, 40; *CWA News*, Mar. 1948. For the CWA's representation in Bell during the 1947–1950 period, see Johnson, "Union Organization," 92–97; *LMR*, Union Exhibit 1, p. 4

82. The CWA in 1947 was not thoroughly industrial in structure: at the divisional and especially the local level, workers in the various operating company departments in many cases remained in separate units. However, a series of structural changes—particularly the institution of a "two-level" structure in 1951 (which eliminated the "divisions" and redistributed their responsibilities

down to the locals and up to the "national")—had the effect of greatly augmenting the industrial character of the CWA's structure. Beirne, OHP, 37–42; Gill, OHP, 7–8.

Conclusion

1. Bers, "Unionism," 120–128, 201–202; Gillmore, "Bell," 166–170.

2. Bers, "Unionism," 116–124.

3. Beirne, OHP, 48–51; CWA, *Daily Proceedings*, June 1959, 17–18; discussions with AT&T and Bell company officials in New York, Omaha, and Jackson, Miss., 1970–1972; *CWA News*, Jan., Feb. 1959, Nov. 1962, June 1968, Aug. 1971; *NYT*, Sept. 4, 1974, p. 19, Aug. 7, 1977, p. 1, Aug. 10, 1980, p. 19. For changes in telephone industry economics that also have pushed Bell toward acceptance of the CWA, see Knappen, "Wage Rate Increases," 59–67. As with most other large unions, the CWA's success in raising wages and benefits has not been matched by gains in working conditions or workplace control. Commenting in 1981 upon continuing management-induced job pressures and the resulting, frequently severe stress felt by Bell workers, Stanley Aronowitz remarked that "because the Bell System pay is good and the benefits are good, people stay around a long time. The result is that they go bananas." Quoted in Howard, "Strung Out at the Phone Company," 44. On continuing Bell pressures and other workplace conditions, see also Goulden, *Monopoly*, 282, 291; Kuyek, *Phone Book*, 15–28, 37, 69; Howard, "Brave New Workplace," 21–31; von Auw, *Heritage*, 242, 247.

4. *NYT*, Sept. 27, 1970, p. 13, Aug. 6, 1974, p. 29; Bers, "Unionism," 222; Gill, OHP, 34–36.

5. *CWA News*, July, Oct. 1949, Jan. 1950, July 1961, May 1963, July 1974.

6. CWA, *Summary of Proceedings*, June 1947, 39; Bers, "Unionism," 79–80; *CWA News*, July 1960; U.S. Census Bureau, *Statistical Abstract*, 482.

7. NFTW headquarters in March 1946 was a one-story, storefront office in Washington. The research analyst was Ann Herlihy, who was replaced by Sylvia Gottlieb in June 1946; Gottlieb had assisted Herlihy early in 1946. Al Herrington was the editor, Ruth Wiencek the education director. NFTW, *Report of Assembly*, June 1946, 40–43; Report of the Executive Board, 1946 (see chap. 7, n. 10), 6–11. For information on the budget and a later move to a larger headquarters, see chap. 7, n. 10.

8. Wiencek, OHP, 9–10. Wiencek, who on a part-time basis had directed the education program of the Michigan traffic union since 1940 and the NFTW since 1943, joined the TWOC in 1947 and left the telephone union movement by 1954.

9. Lipset, Trow, and Coleman, *Union Democracy*, 365. See also "Introduction," n. 8.

10. Evan, *Organization Theory*, 120. See also Kochan, "Determinants," 434, 436; Cuff, " 'Organizational Factor,' " 21.

11. Records of F.L.U. 18386, Jan. 17, 1934, Wayne State University Archives, quoted in Fine, *Automobile*, 294.

12. Brooks, *As Steel Goes*, 6, 84. See also Millis and Montgomery, *Organized Labor*, 887.

13. Green, *World of the Worker*, xii.

14. Wiebe, *Search for Order*, 181, 296–297.

Appendix B

1. Bell System Employee Organizations, Roster of the Second National Conference, Chicago, June 15–17, 1938, mimeographed, (no pagination), Box 1, CWAA; *TW*, May 1941; NFTWOP, 1939, 5–7, 1940, 5–7, 1942, 6–9, June 1943, 3–5, 1944, 47–51, 1945, 4–6; NFTW, *Report of Assembly*, June 1946, 5–6.

Appendix C

1. U.S. Congress, House, *Report*, 107, 122.

2. NTP, "Report" (see chap. 2, n. 3), 16, 22.

3. U.S. Congress, Senate, Committee on Labor and Public Welfare, *Labor-Management Relations*, 1951 S. Rept. 139 (hereafter cited as S. Rept. 139), 1:3–4, 11–30.

4. See *LMR*, 329–330, 332, 334, 345.

5. Colloquy between Senator Hubert H. Humphrey and Edward J. Moynihan, of the Alliance of Independent Telephone Unions, in *LMR,* 304.

6. S. Rept. 139, 39, 45–46.

7. Gillmore, "Bell," 219 (Gillmore's emphasis). See also Bers, "Unionism," 15; Williams, "Labor Relations," 187–190.

8. Raskin, "Trends in Collective Bargaining," 32.

9. Bakke, *Bonds of Organization*, 42–43.

10. Brooks, *Telephone*, 221, 239–241.

BIBLIOGRAPHY

Oral History Project Interviews

The following interviews were conducted by the author for the Communications Workers of America–University of Iowa Oral History Project. Transcripts and tapes of the interviews are located at CWA national headquarters, Washington, D.C. Transcripts are also located in the University of Iowa Libraries, Special Collections Department.

Armstrong, Roy. Former Southern Bell plant worker and in 1970 retired CWA north Florida director, district 3; Lake Okeechobee, Fla., Feb. 20, 1970.

Atkinson, Al. Former C&P Telephone Co. of Virginia plant worker and in 1969 CWA legislative director; Washington, D.C., Apr. 25, 1969.

Beaver, Farrell. Former Southern Bell plant worker and in 1969 a CWA special representative at national headquarters; Washington, D.C., Apr. 22, 1969.

Beirne, Joseph. Former WE distributing house worker and in 1971 CWA president; Washington, D.C., July 9, 1969, and Aug. 30, 1971.

Bers, Melvin K. Former research analyst, NFTW and CWA, and in 1970 with the State University of New York at Albany; Albany, N.Y., July 9, 1970.

Berthelot, Helen. Former Michigan Bell traffic worker and in 1969 a CWA legislative representative; Washington, D.C., May 6, 1969.

Brown, Willard. Former Southern Bell plant worker and in 1970 assistant to the vice-president, district 3, CWA; Birmingham, Ala., Feb. 13, 1970.

Bruce, Marie DeMartini. Former PT&T traffic worker and in 1971 a former CWA special representative, district 9; San Francisco, Feb. 21, 1971.

Carmody, Helen. Former New Jersey Bell worker and in 1970 a CWA representative, district 1; Hamilton Township, N.J., May 11, 1970.

Carroll, John C. Former PT&T plant worker and in 1971 CWA vice-president, district 8; Denver, Jan. 12, 1971.

Chisholm, Douglas. Former PT&T plant worker and in 1971 a retired CWA area director, district 9; Seattle, Feb. 18, 1971.

Cooney, Mabel. Former president of the CWA local in Louisville, Ky., and in 1970 with the South Central Bell Telephone Company; Louisville, Mar. 4, 1970.

Crull, John. Former Southwestern Bell plant worker and in 1970 a retired CWA executive vice-president; Washington, D.C., Apr. 30, 1969, and Jan. 26, 1970.

Daniel, Lonnie. Former Southern Bell plant worker and in 1970 a CWA area director, district 3; Nashville, Mar. 3, 1970.

DiProspere, Al. Former Southwestern Bell plant worker and in 1970 a retired CWA area director, district 6; Florissant, Mo., July 14, 1970.

Dunn, William. Former Cincinnati and Suburban Telephone Co. plant worker and in 1969 an assistant to the secretary-treasurer, CWA; Washington, D.C., May 7, 1969.

Dunne, Joe. Former WE installation worker and in 1970 assistant to the national director, Long Lines bargaining unit, CWA; New York, May 19 and May 21, 1970.

DuVal, George. Former WE Kearny, N.J., manufacturing worker and in 1970 a retired assistant to the president, CWA; Washington, D.C., Apr. 24, 1969, and Falls Church, Va., Jan. 22, 1970.

Edwards, Muriel. Former Illinois Bell traffic worker and in 1971 a CWA representative, district 5; Iowa City, Iowa, Oct. 12, 1971.

Follis, E. J. Former PT&T plant worker and in 1970 assistant to the vice-president, district 7, CWA; Omaha, Neb., Apr. 1, 1970.

Franks, Nancy. Retired Southwestern Bell traffic worker and former officer of the Southwestern Telephone Workers Union; St. Joseph, Mo., Mar. 27, 1970.

Giles, Madge. Former C&P Telephone Co. of the District of Columbia traffic worker and in 1970 president of Local 2300, CWA; Washington, D.C., Feb. 6, 1970.

Gill, George. Former Southern Bell plant worker and in 1970 a CWA executive vice-president; Washington, D.C., Apr. 28, 1969, and May 7, 1970.

Good, Clarence. Former PT&T plant worker and in 1971 a retired CWA area director, district 9; Jamestown, Calif., Feb. 22, 1971.

Gordon, D. K. Former Northwestern Bell plant worker and in 1970 CWA vice-president, district 7; Omaha, Neb., Apr. 2, 1970.

Gravem, Arne. Former WE distributing house worker and in 1971 a CWA representative, district 9; Seattle, Feb. 17, 1971.

Gray, Wayne. Former WE installation worker and in 1970 a CWA area director, district 3; Greensboro, N.C., Feb. 9, 1970.

Griffith, Paul. Former Illinois Bell plant worker and former NFTW president; Denver, Jan. 13–15, 1971.

Gwin, Claude W. Former CWA South Carolina state director, district 3, and in 1970 a South Central Bell plant worker; Nashville, Mar. 2, 1970.

Hackler, Richard. Former WE installation worker and in 1971 an assistant to the president, CWA; Washington, D.C., Oct. 4, 1971.

Hanscom, Mary. Former New Jersey Bell traffic worker and in 1970 a retired CWA district director, district 1; Nutley, N.J., July 13, 1970.

Herrington, Al. Former Illinois Bell plant worker and in 1970 retired CWA public relations director; Washington, D.C., Jan. 27, 1970.

Hubbard, Stanley. Former Southwestern Bell plant worker and in 1970 a CWA area director, district 6; Kansas City, Mo., Mar. 30, 1970.

Koons, Charles V. In 1970 general counsel, CWA; Washington, D.C., Jan. 27, 1970.

LeFevre, Arthur B. Former Wisconsin Telephone Co. plant worker and in 1971 CWA vice-president, district 5; Chicago, Mar. 13, 1971.

Lonergan, Frank. Former Southwestern Bell plant worker and in 1970 retired assistant to the vice-president, district 6, CWA; St. Louis, Mar. 20, 1970.

McCowen, D. L. Former Southwestern Bell plant worker and in 1970 CWA vice-president, district 6; St. Louis, Mar. 19, 1970.

Mahady, James. Former Southern Bell plant worker and in 1970 CWA Louisiana director, district 3; New Orleans, Feb. 26, 1970.

Mann, Mae. Former Indiana traffic worker and in 1970 CWA Indiana state director, district 5; Indianapolis, June 1, 1970.

Massey, James. Former WE installation worker and in 1969 a CWA executive vice-president; Washington, D.C., May 5, 1969.

Miller, George. Former Southern Bell plant worker and in 1970 an assistant to the president, CWA; Washington, D.C., Aug. 6, 1969, and July 7, 1970.

Moudy, Martha. Former Southern Bell traffic worker and in 1970 a CWA representative, district 3; Atlanta, Feb. 17, 1970.

Moye, Earl. Former Southern Bell plant worker and in 1970 a CWA area director, district 3; Atlanta, Feb. 16, 1970.

Myerscough, George. Former AT&T Long Lines plant worker and in 1971 national director, Long Lines bargaining unit, CWA; New York, Oct. 1, 1971.

Naughton, Norma. Former AT&T Long Lines traffic worker and in 1970 former chairman, branch 127, Federation of Long Lines Telephone Workers; Bergen County, N.J., Mar. 24, 1970.

Novotny, Frank. Former WE distributing house worker and in 1970 national director, WE Sales bargaining unit, CWA; New York, July 11, 1970.

Orr, James. Former Indiana Bell plant worker and in 1971 a CWA representative, district 5; West Allis, Wis., Mar. 15, 1971.

Palmer, Eleanor. Former C&P Telephone Co. of the District of Columbia traffic worker and in 1970 a CWA representative, district 2; Washington, D.C., Jan. 23, 1970.

Patterson, Audrey Smid. Former president, Division 16, CWA (Maryland commercial and accounting workers) and in 1970 with the C&P Telephone Co. of Maryland; Baltimore, May 4, 1970.

Peil, Ed V. Former Wisconsin Telephone Co. plant worker and in 1971 CWA Wisconsin state director, district 5; interview in West Allis, Wis., Mar. 15, 1971.

Pollock, Robert. Former Ohio Bell plant worker and in 1970 a CWA special representative, district 6; St. Louis, Mar. 17, 1970.

Purdy, LaRoy. Former Mountain States Telephone plant worker and in 1969 an assistant to the president, CWA; Washington, D.C., Apr. 22, 1969.

Risser, John. Former Northwestern Bell plant worker and in 1969 retired CWA Iowa state director, district 7; Des Moines, Feb. 17, 1969.

Ryan, Thomas C. Former Ohio Bell plant worker and in 1970 CWA Ohio state director, district 4; Cleveland, July 28, 1970.

Schaar, Walter. Former Michigan Bell plant worker and in 1971 CWA vice-president, district 4; Lansing, Mich., Aug. 17, 1971.

Schacht, J. J. Retired Southwestern Bell plant worker and former Southern Regional Director, NFTW; University City, Mo., Mar. 16, 1970.

Sims, Sam. Former Southern Bell plant worker and in 1970 a CWA special representative, district 3, CWA; Birmingham, Ala. Feb. 12, 1970.

Stein, Anthony W. Former national vice-president, Association of Communications Equipment Workers and in 1971 with the WE installation division; interview in Bloomington, Minn., Feb. 15, 1971.

Stephens, Scott. Former Indiana Bell plant worker and in 1970 a retired CWA representative, district 5; Santa Maria, Fla., Feb. 23, 1970.

Waldeck, Fred. Former WE distributing house and WE manufacturing worker, and in 1969 assistant to an executive vice-president, CWA; Washington, D.C., Apr. 18, 1969.

Walsh, William B. Former Ohio Bell plant worker and in 1969 CWA community relations director; Washington, D.C., Apr. 6, 1969.

Watts, Glenn. Former C&P Telephone Co. of the District of Columbia plant and commerical worker and in 1970 CWA secretary-treasurer; Washington, D.C., July 8, 1970.

Webb, T. E. Former Southwestern Bell plant worker and in 1970 a retired CWA area director, district 6; Gilmer, Tex., Mar. 23, 1970.

Welsh, Philip. Former Ohio Bell plant worker and in 1970 a retired CWA representative, district 4; Cleveland, July 28, 1970.

Wiencek, Ruth. Former Michigan Bell traffic worker and former NFTW and CWA education director; Drum Point, Md., Apr. 30, 1970.

Wooding, Nelle. Former Southwestern Bell traffic worker and in 1970 a retired CWA representative, district 6; Dallas, Mar. 24, 1970.

Archives, Manuscript Collections, Personal Papers, Interviews, and Correspondence

American Telephone and Telegraph Archives. American Telephone and Telegraph Headquarters, New York.

Bradbury, Jack G. Papers. Atlanta. Bradbury was the operating vice-president of Southern Bell in the 1940s.

————. Tape-recorded interview with the author. Atlanta, Sept. 15, 1970.

Communications Workers of America Archives. Communications Workers of America National Headquarters, Washington, D.C.

Communications Workers of America–Northwestern Union of Telephone Workers Papers. Archives/Manuscripts Division of the Minnesota Historical Society, St. Paul.

Gannon, Mary. Interview with the author. Norfolk, Va. May 2, 1970.

Gray, Wayne. Papers. Greensboro, N.C.

Griffith, Paul. Papers. Drake, Colo.

Harris, Patricia. Interview with the author. Los Angeles, Feb. 23–24, 1971.

Kanagy, Albert. Letter to the author, July 28, 1972.

McDonald, June. Papers. Des Moines, Iowa. McDonald was an Illinois traffic unionist, a TWOC organizer in the late 1940s, and later a CWA representative.

Mayer, Henry. "Henry Mayer's Monthly Report." Feb. 22, 1971; Apr. 30, 1971; Sept. 30, 1971. Mimeographed. This series was syndicated to newspapers of unions and union locals engaging Mayer as their attorney; in the author's possession.

Minnesota State Board, Northwestern Union of Telephone Workers. "Confidential Resume." Minneapolis, July 21, 1947. Mimeographed. In the author's possession.

Pollock, Robert. Papers. St. Louis.

Reedy, Jeannette. Telephone interview with the author. Nov. 16, 1974.

Selly, Joe. Interview with the author. New York, May 16, 1972. Selly was president of the ACA-CIO in the 1940s.

Shaw, John M. Papers. State Historical Society of Wisconsin, Madison. Shaw was an assistant vice-president with AT&T in the 1940s.

Tierney, Ann. Papers. Toledo, Ohio. Tierney was an Ohio traffic unionist in the 1940s and later a CWA representative.

Wooding, Nelle. Papers. Dallas.

Dissertations, Theses, Published Works, and Periodicals

ACA News. Apr. 10, 1937–May 1951. New York, American Communications Association; entitled *People's Press, ACA Edition* to Aug. 19, 1938.

Abicht, Monika. "Women's Leadership Roles in Two Selected Labor Unions in the United States and Belgium: A Comparative and Descriptive Study." D.Ed. diss., University of Cincinnati, 1976.

Anderson, Bernard E. "Equal Opportunity and Black Employment in the Telephone Industry." In *Equal Employment Opportunity and the AT&T Case*, edited by Phyllis Wallace, 179–200. Cambridge: MIT Press, 1976.

Anderson, Karen Tucker. "Last Hired, First Fired: Black Women Workers during World War II." *Journal of American History* 69 (June 1982): 82–97.

Annual Reports, 1919-1947. New York: American Telephone and Telegraph, 1920–1948.

Bain, George Sayers; Coates, David; and Ellis, Valerie. *Social Stratification and Trade Unionism: A Critique*. London: Henneman Educational Books, 1973.

Baker, Elizabeth Faulkner. *Technology and Women's Work*. New York: Columbia University Press, 1964.

Bakke, E. Wight. *Bonds of Organization: An Appraisal of Corporate Human Relations*. New York: Harper and Brothers, 1950.

Barbash, Jack. *Unions and Telephones: The Story of the Communications Workers of America*. New York: Harper and Brothers, 1952.

———. *The Practice of Unionism*. New York: Harper and Brothers, 1956.

Barnard, Chester. "Some Principles and Basic Considerations in Personnel Relations" (an address given at Princeton University, Sept. 20, 1935). In *Organization and Management: Selected Papers*, edited by Chester I. Barnard, 3–13. Cambridge: Harvard University Press, 1948.

Bell, Harry W. "'Inside Stuff' on Erecting the Northwest Toll Line." *Journal of Electrical Workers and Operators* 26 (Feb. 1927): 116–117.

Benson, Marguerite. "Labor Turnover of Working Women." *Annals of the American Academy of Political and Social Science* 143 (May 1929): 109–119.

Bernstein, Irving. "The Growth of American Unions." *American Economic Review* 44 (June 1954): 301–318.

———. *The Lean Years: A History of the American Worker, 1920–1933*. Boston: Houghton Mifflin. 1960.

———. *Turbulent Years: A History of the American Worker, 1933–1941*. Boston: Houghton Mifflin, 1969.

Bers, Melvin K. "Wage Structure in the Telephone Industry." M. A. thesis, George Washington University, 1948.

———. "Unionism and Collective Bargaining in the Telephone Industry." Ph.D. diss., University of California, Berkeley, 1956.

Bing, Alexander M. *War-Time Strikes and Their Adjustment*. New York: E. P. Dutton, 1921.

Boston Globe. June–July, 1923 (daily, evening, and Sunday editions).

Brandt, Floyd S. "Independent and National Unionism in the Oil Refining Industry: A Study of Work Assignment, Subcontracting, and Seniority Practices." Ph.D. diss., Harvard Graduate School of Business Administration, 1960.

Brissenden, Paul E., and Frankel, Emil. *Labor Turnover in Industry: A Statistical Analysis*. New York: Macmillan, 1922.

Brody, David. *Workers in Industrial America: Essays on the Twentieth Century Struggle*. New York: Oxford University Press, 1980.

Brooks, John. *Telephone: The First Hundred Years*. New York: Harper and Row, 1975.

Brooks, Robert R. R. *As Steel Goes: Unionism in a Basic Industry*. New Haven: Yale University Press, 1940.

Brooks, Thomas R. *Communications Workers of America: The Story of a Union*. New York: Mason/Charter, 1977.

Burch, Selina. "The Rebel in Me." *Southern Exposure* 4, nos. 1–2 (1976): 4–15.

Cochran, Bert. *Labor and Communism: The Conflict That Shaped American Unions*. Princeton: Princeton University Press, 1977.

Commons, John R. "American Shoemakers, 1648–1895." *Quarterly Journal of Economics* 24 (Nov. 1909): 39–84.

Commons, John R.; Saposs, David J.; Sumner, Helen L.; Mittelman, E. E.; Hoagland, H. E.; Andrews, John B.; Perlman, Selig; Lescohier, Don D.; Brandeis, Elizabeth; and Taft, Philip. *History of Labour in the United States*. 4 vols. New York: Macmillan, 1918–1935.

Communications Workers of America. *Summary of Proceedings of the First Annual Convention*. Miami Beach, June 9–12, 1947.

———. *Proceedings of the Second Annual Convention of the Communications Workers of America*. Spokane, June 7–12, 1948.

———. *Summary of Proceedings of the Third Annual Convention of the Communications Workers of America*. Chicago, June 13–17, 1949.

———. *Daily Proceedings and Reports of the 21st Annual Convention of the Communications Workers of America*. Cleveland, June 22–26, 1959.

Craypo, Charles. "The Impact of Changing Corporate Structure and Technology on Telegraph Labor, 1870–1978." *Labor Studies Journal* 3 (Winter 1979): 283–305.

Cuff, Robert D. "American Historians and the 'Organizational Factor.'" *Canadian Review of American Studies* 4 (Spring 1973): 19–31.

CWA News. July 1947–Aug. 1980. Washington, D.C., Communications Workers of America.

Danielian, N. R. *A.T.&T.: The Story of Industrial Conquest*. New York: Vanguard Press, 1939.

Davis, Margery W. *Woman's Place Is at the Typewriter: Office Work and Office Workers, 1870–1930*. Philadelphia: Temple University Press, 1982.

Davis, Pearce, and Meyer, Henry J., eds. *Labor Dispute Settlements in the Telephone Industry, 1942–1945*. Washington, D.C.: Bureau of National Affairs, 1946.

Dawley, Alan. *Class and Community: The Industrial Revolution in Lynn*. Cambridge: Harvard University Press, 1976.

Derby, Robert J. "Common Law Principles Developed from the Arbitration of Strike Discharge Cases: Southern Bell Telephone Company vs. CWA-CIO (1955)." M.A. thesis, University of Illinois, 1963.

Dickason, Gladys. "Women in Labor Unions." *Annals of the American Academy of Political and Social Science* 251 (May 1947): 70–78.

Dilts, Marion May. *The Telephone in a Changing World*. New York: Longmans, Green, 1941.

Douglas, Paul. *Real Wages in the United States, 1890–1926*. Boston: Houghton Mifflin, 1930.

Douty, H. M. "Review of Basic American Labor Conditions." In *War Labor Policies*, edited by Colston E. Warne, Warren Catlin, S. Raymond Walsh, Dorothy Douglas, Constance Williams, and Katherine Lumpkin, 7–50. New York: Philosophical Library, 1945.

Dunlop, John T. "The Decontrol of Wages and Prices." In *Labor in Postwar America*, edited by Colston E. Warne, Dorothy W. Douglas, Everett C. Hawkins, Lois MacDonald, Emmanuel Stein, and Katherine Lumpkin, 3–24. New York: Remsen Press, 1947.

————. "Structural Changes in the American Labor Movement and Industrial Relations System." In *Labor and Trade Unionism: An Interdisciplinary Reader*, edited by Walter Galenson and Seymour Martin Lipset, 102–116. New York: John Wiley, 1960.

Dye, Nancy Schrom. *As Equals and as Sisters: Feminism, the Labor Movement, and the Women's Trade Union League of New York*. Columbia: University of Missouri Press, 1980.

Edelman, Murray. "Interest Representation and Policy Choice in Labor Law Administration." *Labor Law Journal* 9 (Mar. 1958): 218–226.

Evan, William M. *Organization Theory: Structure, Systems, and Environment*. New York: Wiley, 1976.

Federation Bulletin. Dec. 1937–Jan. 1943. Cleveland, Ohio Federation of Telephone Workers.

Federation of Women Telephone Workers of Southern California News. July 1942–Aug.–Sept. 1944. Los Angeles, Federation of Women Telephone Workers of Southern California.

Fine, Sidney. *The Automobile under the Blue Eagle*. Ann Arbor: University of Michigan Press, 1963.

Fitch, H. L. "Technique of Holding Employee Representation Council or Committee Meetings: Where Female and Often Young Workers Predominate." *Personnel* 4 (Feb. 1928): 147–152.

Foner, Philip S. *Organized Labor and the Black Worker, 1619–1973.* New York: Praeger, 1974.

———. *Women and the American Labor Movement, From Colonial Times to the Eve of World War I.* New York: Free Press, 1979.

———. *Women and the American Labor Movement: From World War I to the Present.* New York: Free Press, 1980.

France, Robert R. *Union Decisions in Collective Bargaining.* Princeton: Princeton University Press, 1955.

Freeman, Joshua. "Delivering the Goods: Industrial Unionism During World War II." *Labor History* 19 (Fall 1978): 570–593.

Friedlander, Peter. *The Emergence of a UAW Local, 1936–1939: A Study in Class and Culture.* Pittsburgh: University of Pittsburgh Press, 1975.

Galenson, Walter. *The CIO Challenge to the AFL.* Cambridge: Harvard University Press, 1960.

Gifford, Walter. "The Responsibility of Management in the Bell System." *Bell Telephone Magazine* 26 (Spring 1947): 70–72.

Gillmore, Curry W. "Bell Telephone Labor Economics." Ph.D. diss., Columbia University, 1952.

Goulden, Joseph C. *Monopoly.* New York: G. P. Putnam's Sons, 1968.

Green, James. "Fighting on Two Fronts: Working Class Militancy in the 1940s." *Radical America* 9 (July–Aug. 1975): 7–48.

———. *The World of the Worker: Labor in Twentieth Century America.* New York: Hill and Wang, 1980.

Greenwald, Maurine Weiner. *Women, War, and Work: The Impact of World War I on Women Workers in the United States.* Westport, Conn.: Greenwood, 1980.

Gutman, Herbert. "The Negro and the United Mine Workers of America: The Career and Letters of Richard L. Davis and Something of their Meaning, 1890–1900." In *Work, Culture, and Society in American Working Class and Social History,* by Herbert Gutman, 121–208. New York: Random House, 1976.

Hall, E. K. "Executive Leadership and Personnel Work in Public Service Corporations." *Proceedings of the Academy of Political Science* 9 (Jan. 1922): 563–568.

———. "General Personnel Problems and Policies." In *Proceedings of the Bell System Educational Conference, 1926,* 238–248. New York: American Telephone and Telegraph, 1926.

———. "What is Employee Representation?" *Personnel* 4 (Feb. 1928): 71–84.

————. "To Get the Best from Each." *System* 57 (Apr. 1930): 205–207, 374–375.

Hartman, Susan. *The Home Front and Beyond: American Women in the 1940s.* Boston: Twayne, 1982.

Herberg, Will. "Bureaucracy and Democracy in Labor Unions." *Antioch Review* 3 (Fall 1943): 407–408.

Hillman, Bessie. "Gifted Women in the Trade Unions." In *American Women: The Changing Image*, edited by Beverly Benner Cassara, 99–115. Boston: Beacon, 1962.

"How Do Your Wages Stack Up?" *Business Week*, Apr. 17, 1948, 26.

Howard, Robert. "Brave New Workplace." *Working Papers for a New Society* 7 (Nov.–Dec. 1980): 21–31.

————. "Strung Out at the Phone Company: How AT&T's Workers are Drugged, Bugged, and Coming Unplugged." *Mother Jones*, Aug. 1981, 39–45, 54, 59.

Howe, Irving, and Widick, B. J. *The UAW and Walter Reuther*. New York: Random House, 1949.

Hoxie, Robert F. *Trade Unionism in the United States*. New York: Appleton, 1923.

International Brotherhood of Electrical Workers. *Minutes of the Seventh Bi-Annual Convention*. St. Louis, Oct. 21–27, 1901.

————. *Proceedings of the International Brotherhood of Electrical Workers at their Tenth Convention*. Chicago, Sept. 20–Oct. 2, 1909.

————. *Proceedings of the International Brotherhood of Electrical Workers at their Tenth Convention*. Chicago, Sept. 20–Oct. 2, 1909.

————. *Proceedings, 12th Convention*. Boston, Sept. 15–Oct. 2, 1913.

————. *Proceedings of the 13th Convention*. St. Paul, Sept. 20–Oct. 7, 1915.

————. *Proceedings of the 14th Convention*. Atlantic City, Sept. 17–28, 1917.

————. *Proceedings of the 15th Convention*. New Orleans, Sept. 15–25, 1919.

————. *Proceedings of the 17th Convention*. Quebec, Aug. 20–25, 1923.

————. *Proceedings of the 19th Biennial Convention*. Detroit, Aug. 15–20, 1927.

————. *Proceedings of the 20th Biennial Convention*. Miami, Sept. 9–13, 1929.

————. *Proceedings of the 21st Convention*. St. Louis, Oct. 27–Nov. 1, 1941.

————. *Proceedings of the 22nd Convention*. San Francisco, Sept. 2–10, 1946.

―――. *Proceedings of the 23rd Convention*. Atlantic City, Sept. 13–17, 1948.

―――. Telephone Operators' Department. *Proceedings of the First Regular Convention*. New Orleans, Oct. 1, 1919.

Jennings, Ed. "Wildcat! The Wartime Strike Wave in Auto." *Radical America* 9 (July–Aug. 1975): 77–105.

Johnson, Howard Wesley. "Union Organization in the Telephone Industry: A Study in White Collar Unionism." M.A. thesis, University of Chicago, 1947.

Journal of Electrical Workers and Operators. Sept. 1896–Nov. 1897, Sept. 1900–Oct. 1902, Dec. 1902–Dec. 1947. Springfield, Ill. and Washington, D.C., International Brotherhood of Electrical Workers. Entitled *The Electrical Worker* to Aug. 1914. Signed articles in this journal are listed individually under authors' names.

Kassalow, Everett M. "White Collar Unionism in the United States." In *White-Collar Trade Unionism: Contemporary Developments in Industrialized Societies*, edited by Adolf Sturmthal, 305–364. Urbana: University of Illinois Press, 1966.

Kessler-Harris, Alice. "Where Are the Organized Women Workers?" *Feminist Studies* 3 (Fall 1975): 92–110.

―――. *Out to Work: A History of Wage-Earning Women in the United States*. New York: Oxford University Press, 1982.

Knappen, Laurence S. "Wage Rate Increases Versus Telephone Rate Increases." *Land Economics* 37 (Feb. 1961): 59–67.

Knight, Robert Edward Lee. *Industrial Relations in the San Francisco Bay Area, 1900–1918*. Berkeley: University of California Press, 1960.

Kochan, Thomas. "Determinants of the Power of Boundary Units in an Interorganizational Bargaining Relation." *Administrative Science Quarterly* 20 (Sept. 1975): 434–452.

Koistinen, Paul A. C. "Mobilizing the World War II Economy: Labor and the Industrial-Military Alliance." *Pacific Historical Review* 42 (Nov. 1973): 443–478.

Kornhauser, Ruth. "Some Social Determinants and Consequences of Union Membership." *Labor History* 2 (Winter 1961): 30–61.

Kravif, H. *The Telephone and Telegraph Workers*. Pamphlet no. 44. New York: International Pamphlets, 1935.

Kuyek, Joan Newman. *The Phone Book: Working at the Bell*. Kitchener, Ont.: Between the Lines, 1979.

Langer, Elinor. "The Women of the Telephone Company." *New York Review of Books*, Mar. 26, 1970, 14–22.

―――. "The Hospital Workers: 'The Best Contract Anywhere'?" *New York Review of Books*, June 30, 1971, 30–37.

League News. May 1941. Los Angeles, Telephone Traffic Employees' League of Southern California.

Leggett, John D. "Uprootedness and Working-Class Consciousness." *American Journal of Sociology* 68 (May 1962): 682–692.

Leiserson, William A. "The Accomplishments and Significance of Employee Representation." *Personnel* 4 (Feb. 1923): 119–135.

Lester, Richard. *As Unions Mature*. Princeton: Princeton University Press, 1957.

Levinson, Edward. *Labor on the March*. New York: Harper and Brothers, 1938.

Lichtenstein, Nelson. "Industrial Unionism Under the No-Strike Pledge: A Study of the CIO during the Second World War." Ph.D. diss. University of California, Berkeley, 1974.

————. *Labor's War at Home: The CIO in World War II*. New York: Cambridge University Press, 1982.

Lipset, Seymour Martin. "The Political Process in Trade Unions: A Theoretical Statement." In *Freedom and Control in Modern Society*, edited by Monroe Berger, Theodore Abel, and Charles H. Page, 86–106. New York: D. Van Nostrand, 1954.

Lipset, Seymour Martin; Trow, Martin A.; and Coleman, James S. *Union Democracy: The Internal Politics of the International Typographical Union*. Glencoe, Ill.: Free Press, 1956.

"Little Room at the Top for Labor's Women." *Business Week*, May 28, 1966, 62–64.

Livernash, E. Robert. "The Relations of Power to the Structure and Process of Collective Bargaining." *Journal of Law and Economics* 6 (Oct. 1961): 10–40.

————. "New Developments in Bargaining Structure." In *Trade Union Government and Collective Bargaining: Some Critical Issues*, edited by Joel Seidman, 242–253. New York: Praeger, 1970.

Loewenberg, J. Joseph. "Effects of Change on Employee Relations in the Telephone Industry." Ph.D. diss., Harvard University, 1962.

Maddox, Brenda, "Women and the Switchboard." In *The Social Impact of the Telephone*, edited by Ithiel de Sola Pool, 262–280. Cambridge: MIT Press, 1977.

Mason, Lucy Randolph. *To Win These Rights: A Personal Story of the CIO in the South*. New York: Harper and Brothers, 1952.

Mayer, Henry, and Weiner, Abraham. "The New Jersey Telephone Company Case." *Industrial and Labor Relations Review* 1 (Apr. 1948): 492–499.

Michigan Federation News. Apr.–May 1946. Lansing, Federation of Telephone Employees of Michigan.

Millis, Harry A., and Montgomery, Royal E. *Organized Labor*. New York: McGraw-Hill, 1945.

Montgomery, David. *Workers' Control in America: Studies in the History of Work, Technology, and Labor Struggle*. Cambridge: Cambridge University Press, 1979.

Mulcaire, Michael A. *The International Brotherhood of Electrical Workers: A Study in Trade Union Structure and Functions*. Washington, D.C.: Catholic University of America, 1923.

Myers, Frederic. *Economics of Labor Relations*. Chicago: Richard D. Irwin, 1951.

National Federation of Telephone Workers. *Official Proceedings of the Constitutional Convention and Fourth National Assembly*. New York, June 5–9, 1939.

———. *Official Proceedings of the Fifth National Assembly*. Salt Lake City, Utah, June 17–21, 1940.

———. *Official Proceedings of the Seventh National Assembly*. Baltimore, June 8–13, 1942.

———. *Official Proceedings of the Eighth National Assembly*. Cincinnati, Feb. 1–6, 1943.

———. *Official Proceedings of the Ninth National Assembly*. Cleveland, June 7–12, 1943.

———. *Official Proceedings of the Tenth National Assembly*. Denver, June 12–17, 1944.

———. *Official Proceedings of the Eleventh National Assembly*. Chicago, June 11–16, 1945.

———. *Report of the Twelfth National Assembly*. Galveston, June 3–7, 1946.

———. *Summarized Report of the Thirteenth National Assembly*. Denver, Nov. 4–16, 1946.

National Industrial Conference Board. *Wages in the United States in 1931*. New York, 1932.

———. *Effects of the Depression on Industrial Relations Programs*. New York, 1934.

———. *Individual Bargaining in Public Utilities and Railroads*. New York, 1934.

New York. Department of Labor. Bureau of Women in Industry. *Report Submitted Relative to the Telephone Industry in New York State*. Albany: J. B. Lyon, 1920.

New York Times. 1912–1948.

Newell, Barbara Warne. *Chicago and the Labor Movement: Metropolitan Unionism in the 1930s*. Urbana: University of Illinois Press, 1961.

O'Connor, Julia. "History of the Organized Telephone Operators' Move-ment." *Union Telephone Operator* 1, Jan.–Mar., May–July 1921, in six parts.

——. "Before and After Taking Unionism: A Cure." *Journal of Electrical Workers and Operators* 25 (Jan. 1926): 18–19.

——. "The Blight of Company Unionism." *American Federationist* 33 (May 1926): 544–549.

Pact News. Sept. 1938, Mar. 1940–June 1947. Omaha, Northwestern Union of Telephone Workers.

Page, Arthur W. *The Bell Telephone System*. New York: Harper and Broth-ers, 1941.

Park, Alvin Loren. "The National Telephone Strike, 1947." M.A. thesis, University of Illinois, 1948.

The Pen. July 1938. Chicago, Illinois Bell Telephone Employees' Association.

Perry, Louis B., and Perry, Richard S. *A History of the Los Angeles Labor Movement, 1911–1941*. Berkeley: University of California Press, 1963.

Pilgrim, A. [pseud.] "Pilgrim's Progress in a Telephone Exchange." In *America's Working Women*, edited by Rosalynn Baxandall, Linda Gordon, and Susan Reverby, 236–240. New York: Vintage, 1976.

Porter, H. B. "Technique of Holding Council or Committee Meetings: Male Manual Workers Predominating." *Personnel* 4 (Feb. 1928): 138–146.

Raskin, A. H. "Trends in Collective Bargaining." In *Proceedings of the Third Annual Conference on Labor, 1950*, 21–46. New York: New York Univer-sity, 1950.

"Repeaterman's Log." Aug. 1961–Nov. 1967. Monthly column, written by Albert Kanagy, appearing in the *Toll Reporter*. San Francisco, Order of Repeatermen and Toll Testboardmen, Local 1011, IBEW.

Riegel, John W. "Caldwell Telephone Company." *Harvard Business Reports* 4 (1927): 309–314.

Sangster, Joan. "The 1907 Bell Telephone Strike: Organizing Women Work-ers." *Labor/le travailleur* 3 (1978): 109–130.

Saposs, David J. "Organizational and Procedural Changes in Employee Rep-resentation Plans." *Journal of Political Economy* 44 (Dec. 1936): 803–811.

Schacht, John N. "Toward Industrial Unionism: Bell Telephone Workers and Company Unions, 1919–1937." *Labor History* 16 (Winter 1975): 5-36.

Schatz, Ronald W. *The Electrical Workers: A History of Labor at General Electric and Westinghouse, 1923–60*. Urbana: University of Illinois Press, 1983.

Segal, Melvin J. "Industrial Relations in Communications." In *Labor in Post-*

war America, edited by Colston E. Warne, Dorothy W. Douglas, Everett C. Hawkins, Lois MacDonald, Emmanual Stein, and Katherine Lumpkin, 429–448. New York: Remsen Press, 1947.

Seidman, Joel. *American Labor from Defense to Reconversion*. Chicago: University of Chicago Press, 1953.

———. "Democracy in Labor Unions." *Journal of Political Economy* 61 (June 1953): 220–231.

Seidman, Joel; London, Jack; Karsh, Bernard; and Tagliacozzo, Daisy L. *The Worker Views His Union*. Chicago: University of Chicago Press, 1958.

Selznick, Philip. "An Approach to the Theory of Bureaucracy." *American Sociological Review* 8 (Feb. 1943): 51–54.

Shapiro, Harold Arthur. "The Workers of San Antonio, Texas, 1900–1940." Ph.D. diss., University of Texas, 1952.

Sheed, Wilfrid. "What Ever Happened to the Labor Movement?" *Atlantic*, July 1973, 42–69.

Shellabarger, Eloise. "'Hurry, Girls, Hurry!'" *Survey*, June 12, 1920, 367–368.

Shister, Joseph. "The Locus of Union Control in Collective Bargaining." *Quarterly Journal of Economics* 60 (Aug. 1946): 520–522.

Shostak, Arthur B. *America's Forgotten Labor Organizations: A Survey of the Role of the Single-Firm Independent Union in American Industry*. Research Report Series, no. 103. Princeton: Industrial Relations Section, Princeton University, 1962.

Simpson, Edith. "Trade Union Organization among the Telephone Operators in the United States." *Union Telephone Operator* 1, Oct. 1921–Nov. 1921, in two parts.

Smith, Mapheus. "An Empirical Scale of Prestige Status of Occupations." *American Sociological Review* 8 (Apr. 1943): 185–192.

Smith, Mary Phlegar. "Restrictions Affecting the Rights of Married Women to Work." *Annals of the American Academy of Political and Social Science* 143 (May 1929): 255–264.

Stimson, Grace Heilman. *Rise of the Labor Movement in Los Angeles*. Berkeley: University of California Press, 1955.

Strom, Sharon Hartman. "Challenging 'Woman's Place': Feminism, the Left, and Industrial Unionism in the 1930s." *Feminist Studies* 9 (Summer 1983): 359–386.

Tax, Meredith. *The Rising of the Women: Feminist Solidarity and Class Conflict, 1880–1917*. New York: Monthly Review Press, 1980.

"Telephone Operators: Bloomington, Ill. Labor Agreement," *Monthly Labor Review* 22 (Feb. 1926): 104–106.

Tel-U. Oct. 1941–Mar. 1946. Dallas and St. Louis, Southwestern Telephone Workers Union.

Tentler, Leslie Woodcock. *Wage-Earning Women: Industrial Work and Family Life in the United States, 1900–1930.* New York: Oxford University Press, 1979.

Torrence, William David. "A Case Study of Industrial Relations: The Lincoln Telephone and Telegraph Company and the Communications Workers of America Local 7470." Ph.D. diss., University of Nebraska, 1962.

Troy, Leo. "The Course of Company and Local Independent Unions." Ph.D. diss., Columbia University, 1958.

———. "Local Independent and National Unions: Competitive Labor Organizations." *Journal of Political Economy* 68 (Oct. 1960): 487–508.

Twentieth Century Fund Labor Committee, ed. *How Collective Bargaining Works: A Survey of Experience in Leading American Industries.* New York: Twentieth Century Fund, 1942.

Ulman, Lloyd. *The Rise of the National Union.* Cambridge: Harvard University Press, 1955.

———. *The Government of the Steel Workers' Union.* New York: John Wiley and Sons. 1962.

Ulriksson, Vidkun. *The Telegraphers: Their Craft and Their Unions.* Washington, D.C.: Public Affairs Press, 1953.

Union Telephone Operator. Jan. 1921–June 1922. Boston, International Brotherhood of Electrical Workers, Telephone Operators' Department. Signed articles in this journal are listed individually under authors' names.

U.S. Census Bureau. *Fourteenth Census of the United States, Taken in the Year 1920, Population.* Vol. 4, *Occupations.* Washington, D.C.: GPO, 1923.

———. *Women in Gainful Occupations, 1870–1920,* by Joseph A. Hill. Washington, D.C.: GPO, 1929.

———. *Fifteenth Census of the United States: 1930, Population.* Vol. 5, *General Report on Occupations.* Washington, D.C.: GPO, 1933.

———. *Sixteenth Census of the United States: 1940, Population.* Vol. 3, *The Labor Force, Pt. 1 U.S. Summary.* Washington, D.C.: GPO, 1943.

———. *Sixteenth Census of the United States: 1940, Population. The Labor Force (Sample Statistics), Industrial Characteristics.* Washington, D.C.: GPO, 1943.

———. *Sixteenth Census of the United States: 1940, Population. The Labor Force (Sample Statistics), Occupational Characteristics.* Washington, D.C.: GPO, 1943.

———. *Sixteenth Census of the United States: 1940, Population. The Labor Force (Sample Statistics), Usual Occupations.* Washington, D.C.: GPO, 1943.

———. *Sixteenth Census of the United States: 1940, Population. The Labor*

Force (Sample Statistics), Wage or Other Income in 1939. Washington, D.C.: GPO, 1943.

———. *Statistical Abstract of the United States.* Washington, D.C.: GPO, 1980.

U. S. Congress. House. *A Report of the Federal Communications Commission on the Investigation of the Telephone Industry in the United States, As Unanimously Adopted by the Commission.* 76th Cong., 1st sess., 1939. H. Doc. 340.

———. Senate. Committee on Education and Labor. *Investigation of Telephone Companies.* 61st Cong., 2d sess., 1910. S. Doc. 380.

———. *Final Report and Testimony Submitted to Congress by the Committee on Industrial Relations.* 64th Cong., 1st sess., 1916. S. Doc. 415.

———. *Violations of the Right of Free Speech and Assembly and Interference with the Right of Labor to Organize and Bargain Collectively: Hearings before the LaFollette Subcommittee of the Committee on Education and Labor.* 74th Cong., 1st sess., 1939.

———. Committee on Labor and Public Welfare. *Labor-Management Relations in the Bell Telephone System: Hearings before the Subcommittee on Labor-Management Relations of the Committee on Labor and Public Welfare.* 81st Cong., 2 sess., 1950.

———. *Labor-Management Relations in the Bell Telephone System.* 82d Cong., 1st sess., 1951. S. Rept. 139.

U.S. Department of Labor. Bureau of Labor Statistics. *Characteristics of Company Unions.* Bulletin no. 634. Washington, D.C.: GPO, 1938.

———. Women's Bureau. *The Change from Manual to Dial Operation in the Telephone Industry.* Bulletin no. 110. Washington, D.C.: GPO, 1933.

———. *Women's Hours and Wages in the District of Columbia in 1937.* Bulletin no. 153. Washington, D.C.: GPO, 1937.

———. *Typical Women's Jobs in the Telephone Industry.* Bulletin no. 207-A. Washington, D.C.: GPO, 1946.

———. *The Woman Telephone Worker.* Bulletin no. 207. Washington, D.C.: GPO, 1946.

U.S. Federal Communications Commission. *Proposed Report, Telephone Investigation, Pursuant to Public Resolution No. 8, 74th Congress.* Washington, D.C.: GPO, 1938.

———. *Statistics of the Communications Industry in the United States, 1939–1947.* Washington, D.C.: GPO, 1941–1949.

U.S. National Labor Relations Board. *Decisions and Reports.* Vols. 12, 30, 35, 57, 72, 76. Washington, D.C.: GPO, 1939–1948.

U.S. National War Labor Board. *War Labor Reports: Wage and Salary Stabilization.* Vol. 27. Washington, D.C.: Bureau of National Affairs, 1946.

————. *The Termination Report of the National War Labor Board*. Vol. 1. Washington, D.C.: GPO, 1949.

U.S. Works Progress Administration. *Production, Employment, and Productivity in 59 Manufacturing Industries, with an Appendix on the Electric Light and Power and Telephone Industries*, by Harry Magdoff, Irving H. Siegel, and Milton B. Davis. Studies of the Labor Supply, Productivity, and Production, Report no. S-1. Philadelphia: Works Progress Administration, 1938.

Van Tine, Warren A. *The Making of the Labor Bureaucrat: Union Leadership in the United States, 1876–1920*. Amherst: University of Massachusetts Press, 1973.

Vincent, M. J. "Labor Under Review, 1947." *Sociology and Social Research* 32 (May–June 1948): 856–868.

von Auw, Alvin. *Heritage and Destiny: Reflections on the Bell System in Transition*. New York: Praeger, 1983.

Walsh, J. Leigh. *Connecticut Pioneers in Telephony: The Origins and Growth of the Telephone Industry in Connecticut*. New Haven: Morris F. Tyler Chapter, Telephone Pioneers of America, 1950.

Wandersee, Winifred. *Women's Work and Family Values, 1920–1940*. Cambridge: Harvard University Press, 1981.

Waterson, K. W. "Talk of K. W. Waterson." In *Proceedings of the Bell System Educational Conference, 1926*, 54–65. New York: American Telephone and Telegraph, 1926.

Webb, Sidney, and Webb, Beatrice. *Industrial Democracy*. 2d ed. New York: Longmans, 1920.

Weber, Arnold. "Union-Management Power Relations in the Chemical Industry: The Economic Setting." *Labor Law Journal* 9 (Sept. 1958): 664–668.

————. "Competitive Unionism in the Chemical Industry." *Industrial and Labor Relations Review* 13 (Oct. 1959): 16–37.

————, ed. *The Structure of Collective Bargaining*. New York: Free Press of Glencoe, 1961.

Weir, Stan. "American Labor on the Defensive: A 1940s Odyssey." *Radical America* 9 (July–Aug. 1975), 163–185.

Wertheimer, Barbara, and Nelson, Anne. "The American Woman at Work." *Personnel Management* 6 (Mar. 1974): 20–23, 40–41.

————. *Trade Union Women: A Study of their Participation in New York City Locals*. New York: Praeger, 1975.

Wiebe, Robert H. *The Search for Order, 1877–1920*. New York: Hill and Wang, 1967.

Wilensky, Harold C. "Class, Class Consciousness, and American Workers." In *Labor in a Changing America*, edited by William Haber, 12–44. New York: Basic Books, 1966.

Williams, James Earl. "Labor Relations in the Telephone Industry: A Comparison of the Private and Public Segments." Ph.D. diss., University of Wisconsin, 1961.

Williamson, Harold F.; Andreano, Ralph L.; Daum, Arnold R.; and Klose, Gilbert L. *The American Petroleum Industry.* Vol. 2, *The Age of Energy, 1899–1959.* Evanston: Northwestern University Press, 1963.

Withington, Anne. "When the Telephone Girls Organized." *Survey*, Aug. 16, 1913, 621–623.

———. "The Telephone Strike." *Survey*, Apr. 26, 1919, 146.

Wolf, William B. *Conversations with Chester I. Barnard.* ILR Paperback no. 12. Ithaca: New York State School of Industrial and Labor Relations, Cornell University, 1973.

Wolfson, Theresa. "Trade Union Activities of Women." *Annals of the American Academy of Political and Social Science* 143 (May 1929): 120–131.

Wolman, Leo. *Growth of American Trade Unions, 1880–1923.* New York: National Bureau of Economic Research, 1924.

"Women Workers: Gaining Power, Seeking More." *U.S. News and World Report*, Nov. 13, 1972, 105–106.

"Wrong Number?" *Time*, June 2, 1947, 22–25.

INDEX